Study Guide

AN INTRODUCTION TO
MACROECONOMICS

■ ■ ■

■ ■

ALSO AVAILABLE FROM McGRAW-HILL RYERSON:

ECONOMICS
Third Canadian Edition
by Blomqvist/Wonnacott/Wonnacott
ISBN: 0-07-549915-0

AN INTRODUCTION TO MACROECONOMICS
Third Canadian Edition
by Blomqvist/Wonnacott/Wonnacott
ISBN: 0-07-549160-5

AN INTRODUCTION TO MICROECONOMICS
Third Canadian Edition
by Blomqvist/Wonnacott/Wonnacott
ISBN: 0-07-549916-9

STUDY GUIDE to accompany
AN INTRODUCTION TO MICROECONOMICS
Third Canadian Edition
by Blomqvist/Wonnacott/Wonnacott
ISBN: 0-07-551007-3

INSTRUCTOR'S MANUAL to accompany **ECONOMICS**
Third Canadian Edition
by Blomqvist/Wonnacott/Wonnacott/Sephton
ISBN: 0-07-549918-5

TEST BANK to accompany **ECONOMICS**
Third Canadian Edition
by Blomqvist/Wonnacott/Wonnacott/Sephton
ISBN: 0-07-551028-6

■ ■ ■

Study Guide

AN INTRODUCTION TO
MACROECONOMICS
THIRD CANADIAN EDITION

■ ■

ÅKE BLOMQVIST
University of Western Ontario

PAUL WONNACOTT
University of Maryland

RONALD WONNACOTT
University of Western Ontario

McGRAW-HILL RYERSON LIMITED

Toronto Montreal New York Auckland Bogotá
Caracas Hamburg Lisbon London Madrid Mexico
Milan New Delhi Paris San Juan São Paulo Singapore
Sydney Tokyo

■ ■ ■

STUDY GUIDE
AN INTRODUCTION TO MACROECONOMICS
Third Canadian Edition

Copyright © McGraw-Hill Ryerson Limited, 1990, 1987, 1983. Copyright © 1990 John Wiley and Sons, Inc. Copyright © McGraw-Hill, Inc. 1986, 1982, 1979. All rights reserved. No part of this publication may be reproduced, stored in a retrieval system, or transmitted, in any form or by any means, electronic, mechanical, photocopying, recording, or otherwise, without prior written permission of McGraw-Hill Ryerson Limited.

ISBN: 0-07-551007-3

1 2 3 4 5 6 7 8 9 0 MP 9 8 7 6 5 4 3 2 1 0

Typesetting by Jay Tee Graphics Ltd.
Printed and bound in Canada

Care has been taken to trace ownership of copyright material in this text. The publishers will gladly take any information that will enable them to rectify any reference or credit in subsequent editions.

Canadian Cataloguing in Publication Data

Main entry under title:

Study guide to accompany An introduction to macroeconomics, third Canadian edition

Supplement to: Blomqvist, Åke G., date—   .
An introduction to macroeconomics. 3rd Canadian ed.
ISBN 0-07-551007-3

1. Macroeconomics. I. Blomqvist, Åke G., date—   .
II. Blomqvist, Åke G., date—   . An introduction to macroeconomics. 3rd Canadian ed.

HB172.5.B562 1990   339   C90-094054-9

Contents

■ ■

■ ■ ■ ■

Preface

■ ■

This study guide is intended to help the student who is taking an introductory economics course using the third Canadian edition of *An Introduction to Macroeconomics* by Blomqvist, Wonnacott, and Wonnacott. It makes no attempt to be self-contained: it can be used as a supplement to, not as a substitute for, the textbook.

Each chapter is designed for you to read and work through after reading the corresponding chapter in the textbook. Each study-guide chapter contains nine sections:

1. *Major purpose*. This section sets out very briefly the basic ideas that will be developed in the chapter.

2. *Learning objectives*. This section consists of a list of tasks that you should be able to accomplish after you have studied the chapter in the textbook and in the study guide. The purpose of this section is twofold. First, it should help to give you direction and purpose while studying the rest of the chapter. Second, it should serve as a checklist to test your comprehension after reading the chapter.

3. *Highlights of the chapter*. This section contains a summary of the important points of the chapter. Its purpose is mainly to reinforce the textbook by going over these main points from a somewhat different perspective and adding illustrative examples. To a student learning a subject for the first time, everything is likely to appear equally important. This section should help sort out the more important from the less by focusing more narrowly than the text and by drawing attention to the particularly important material.

4. *Important terms: Match the columns*. This section sets out the important concepts along with the definition of each. Your task is to match each term with its definition. One of the best ways of doing this is to write out your own definition first; this provides the most effective form of review.

5. *True-false questions*.

6. *Multiple-choice questions*.

7. *Exercises*.

These three sections are meant to help you learn by doing. Besides providing reinforcement through repetition, many of the questions and exercises are designed to guide you toward discovering ideas that will not be explicitly introduced until later in the textbook. Spend a few minutes going over the true-false and multiple-choice questions as a self-test, even if you believe you understand the textbook chapter well enough to proceed without using the study guide in any other way. Answers to questions in these sections are provided at the end of each chapter.

8. *Essay questions*. This section is designed to help you apply important concepts that have been developed in the text, as well as to stimulate your imagination. No answers have been provided for this section. Thus the questions may be used as material for classroom discussion.

9. *Crossword puzzles*. These appear intermittently throughout the study guide. Our hope is that you will find them entertaining, whether or not you are a crossword puzzle enthusiast. Each puzzle, of course, draws heavily on the terms introduced in the related chapter.

This third edition of the study guide, now in Macro and Micro volumes, has a number of new or extensively revised chapters, corresponding to the changes in the textbook. We have also rewritten the old chapters in several places, with a view to improving the clarity of exposition. Many of the old true-false and multiple-choice questions have been replaced or reworked. The inclusion of suggested answers to some of the review problems that appear in the textbook is another new feature of this edition. They were added in response to the suggestion by a number of our students that ready access to "model answers" would enhance the value of the problems as aids in learning.

Åke Blomqvist
Paul Wonnacott
Ron Wonnacott
London, Ontario, and
College Park, Maryland

Note to Students and Instructors

Economics, Third Canadian Edition, by Blomqvist, Wonnacott, and Wonnacott, exists in three forms: the combined volume (chapters 1-40), the macroeconomics volume (chapters 1-20), and the microeconomics volume (chapters 1-5 and 21-40).

This study guide relates to chapters 1-20 (the introductory and macroeconomics chapters) of *Economics*, Third Canadian Edition, and the macroeconomics volume of this textbook.

A study guide to accompany the microeconomics volume and the microeconomics chapters of *Economics*, Third Canadian Edition, is available as well.

Part One

....

Basic Economic Concepts

Chapter 1

■ ■

Economic Problems and Economic Goals

MAJOR PURPOSE

The major purpose of this chapter is to provide a broad overview of *economic developments* and *economic objectives* as a background for the more detailed topics of the following chapters. Five major economic objectives are discussed: *high employment*, a *stable average level of prices, efficiency, equity*, and *growth*. You should gain some understanding of the problems which have arisen in the Canadian economy, and why it is not always easy to solve these problems. In particular, it may be difficult to deal with problems when the government has a number of goals, some of which are *in conflict*. That is, solving one problem may make others more difficult to solve. For example, inflation generally gets worse as the unemployment rate falls.

LEARNING OBJECTIVES

After you have studied this chapter in the textbook and study guide, you should be able to
- List five major economic goals
- Describe, in broad terms, what has happened to Canadian unemployment, inflation, growth, and the distribution of income in recent decades
- Distinguish the views of Adam Smith and J.M. Keynes with respect to the proper role of the government
- Define terms such as inflation, deflation, recession, and efficiency
- Distinguish between *allocative efficiency* and *technological efficiency*
- Describe briefly how changes in relative prices may contribute to allocative efficiency
- Explain why it is harder to identify the problems created by inflation than those created by unemployment
- Explain the distinction between equity and equality
- Explain how some goals may be *complementary*, while others are *in conflict*

If you have studied the appendix to Chapter 1 in the textbook, you should also be able to
- Describe some of the ways in which people may be misled by graphs
- Explain the advantage of using a ratio (or logarithmic) scale
- Explain the difference between a nominal and a real measure

HIGHLIGHTS OF THE CHAPTER

Economics is one of the social sciences—it involves the systematic study of human behaviour. The aspects of behaviour which interest economists is how people earn a living and the problems which may make it difficult for them to do so. In the words of Alfred Marshall, economics is the study of people "in the ordinary business of life."

The objective of *economic theory* is to discover and explain the basic principles and laws that govern economic life. Economic theory helps us to understand questions such as: Why are some prices higher than others? Why does the average level of prices rise? Why are some people richer than others? What causes large-scale unemployment?

Economic policy addresses such questions as: How can the government reduce inflation? How can it reduce the unemployment rate? What steps can individuals take to increase their incomes or reduce the risks of unemployment? How does a business increase its profits?

Economic theory and economic policy go hand-in-hand. Just as a physician needs to know how the human body works in order to heal patients, so the economic policy maker needs to understand economic theory in order to prescribe economic policies that will be successful. Scientific studies of how things work are often inspired by a policy motive—to do something about problems. Thus, scientists strive to unlock the mysteries of the human cell in order to find out why cancer occurs and, ultimately, to be able to cure cancer. Similarly, studies of how the economy works are often motivated by the desire to solve economic problems such as recession and large-scale unemployment.

Perhaps the most hotly contested issue in all of economics is the question of how much the government should intervene in the economy. Many of those in government are motivated by the desire to promote the public welfare. But well-meaning policy makers do not always adopt policies that work in practice. Furthermore, the government may be used to benefit individuals or groups at the expense of the public as a whole.

In the late 1700s, Adam Smith attacked many governmental interventions in the economy as being contrary to the public interest. Even though tariffs benefitted the protected sectors of the economy, they inflicted higher costs on consumers and acted as a drag on efficiency. Smith conceived of the private economy as a self-regulating mechanism. By pursuing their own interests, individuals would unwittingly contribute to the common good. There was no need for extensive government interference to ensure that things would come out all right.

A century and a half later, J.M. Keynes was skeptical of Smith's message of laissez-faire. Things were not com-

ing out all right. The economy was in a deep depression, with many people out of work. It was the responsibility of the government, said Keynes, to do something about this tragic situation. He recommended government spending on roads and other public works as a way to provide jobs.

Full employment is one of the major economic objectives. Four others are also described in this chapter: a *stable average level of prices, efficiency,* an *equitable distribution of income,* and economic *growth.* Other goals might be added to this list, for example, economic freedom, economic security, protection of the environment, and a reduction in Canada's dependence on foreign influences.

The first two goals—full employment and stable prices—come under the heading of maintaining a stable *equilibrium* in the economy. There has been, in fact, considerable instability in the Canadian economy. The most notable disturbance occurred during the Great Depression of the 1930s, when output and employment dropped sharply and remained at very low levels for a full decade. During World War II, there was an effort to produce as many munitions as possible. Unemployment ceased to be a significant problem, but prices began to rise substantially. Since the end of World War II in 1945, we have avoided severe disturbances comparable to those from 1929 to 1945. However, there have been periodic recessions, with rising unemployment; the most severe one occurred as late as 1982. Inflation was severe during the late 1940s and the 1970s. During the decade of the 1970s, the average level of prices doubled.

Of the major economic problems, unemployment is perhaps the most obvious. When employment declines, we have less output to enjoy. We not only forgo the output which might have been produced, but we also must face the demoralization that comes with unemployment.

The problems with inflation are less obvious. When people buy goods, they obviously dislike higher and higher prices. But there are two sides to every transaction—the buyer's side, and the seller's. With widespread inflation, not only do the prices of what we buy increase, but wage rates also go up as do the prices of what we sell. It is not clear whether individuals are net gainers or net losers.

However, there are certain segments of the population that do lose. Those who have pensions set in money terms lose: As prices rise, their pensions buy less. (However, some pensions, including the Old Age Security and Canada Pension Plan benefits paid by the government, are increased to compensate for inflation.) Those who own government bonds or other interest-bearing securities lose. Through the years, they receive payments whose value becomes smaller and smaller as prices rise. On the other hand, people who have borrowed can benefit: They repay their loans in money whose value has declined.

Inflation generates a feeling that the economic system is unfair. There are arbitrary redistributions of income and wealth, such as the gains to debtors and losses to bond owners. Inflation can also make it more difficult to make wise and well-informed decisions. *Prices* provide an important source of information to the business executive and consumer. During periods of rapid inflation, when all prices are rising at a brisk pace, the message carried by prices may be obscured. It becomes more difficult to make good decisions.

If inflation accelerates to very high rates—such as 1,000% per year—it becomes known as *hyperinflation*. Money is losing its value so rapidly that people may refuse to accept it. Because money is practically useless, sellers may feel compelled to barter their products for other goods. Such barter transactions are very cumbersome and time-consuming.

Most inflations do not accelerate into hyperinflation. Hyperinflation is relatively rare, except during wartime or early postwar periods in countries that have been defeated in wars. There are, however, a few cases where countries have had very rapid rates of inflation even though they have not been defeated in a war—for example, during some periods in Brazil.

There are two important types of efficiency. *Technological efficiency* means getting the most output from a given set of inputs (labour, machinery, raw materials). *Allocative efficiency* occurs when the economy is producing the best combination of outputs, using the lowest-cost combination of inputs. Allocative efficiency means producing the goods and services that the Canadian consuming public wants most, or that can be sold in foreign countries in exchange for goods and services that are difficult to produce here. It is possible for an economic system to produce "white elephants" in a technologically efficient manner. But this system would not be producing what people want; it would not be allocatively efficient. Similarly, if everyone were a lawyer and no one a doctor, there would be allocative inefficiency—even if everyone were a superb lawyer.

Equity means *fairness*, and that raises the question of what fairness means. There can be obvious disagreements. Those with low incomes are likely to argue that a more equal distribution of income would be fairer. Those with higher incomes often argue that their high incomes are the result of hard work; it is fair for them to be paid more because they have worked harder.

Most people agree that the government should take steps to help those who are poverty-stricken, for example, by taxing the rich to provide services for the needy. The question arises, however, as to how far this process should be taken. Clearly, if the government confiscated all incomes above the average, and gave the revenues to low-income people, then it would severely interfere with the incentive to work hard. (This would also greatly increase the incentive to cheat on taxes!) Even less drastic steps to redistribute income can decrease incentives, and thus decrease the size of the national "pie." The size of the pie depends in part on how it is cut up.

Economic growth is often advocated for its own sake. In a growing economy, we enjoy more goods and services. Furthermore, growth may make it easier to meet other goals, such as reducing poverty. However, we should not simply assume that the more growth, the better. Growth comes at a cost. Most obviously, if we produce more machinery and equipment to help us grow, then we will give up the current consumer goods that might have been produced instead of the machinery and equipment. And, in recent years, we have become increasingly aware of the potentially devastating consequences of the pollution that industrial growth may cause, unless it is properly controlled.

Some goals—such as a high level of employment and an elimination of poverty—are *complementary*. Progress on the one contributes to progress on the other. If jobs are provided for people, they are less likely to be poor.

Other goals are *in conflict*. If people buy more goods and services, they will help to increase the number of jobs. But they will also make it easier for sellers to raise their prices. Thus, if the government takes steps to encourage spending, it may help ease one problem (unemployment) while making another worse (inflation). In such circumstances, good policies may be particularly difficult to develop.

IMPORTANT TERMS: MATCH THE COLUMNS

Match each term in the first column with the corresponding explanation in the second column.

_____	1. Laissez-faire	a.	Put forward the idea of the "hidden hand"
_____	2. Great Depression	b.	Pursuing one helps in attainment of other
_____	3. Labour force	c.	When large-scale unemployment existed
_____	4. Population	d.	A change in relative prices
_____	5. Recession	e.	A tax on an import
_____	6. Duty	f.	Pursuing one makes other more difficult to attain

_____	**7.**	J.M. Keynes
_____	**8.**	Adam Smith
_____	**9.**	Inflation
_____	**10.**	Deflation
_____	**11.**	Allocative efficiency
_____	**12.**	Technical efficiency
_____	**13.**	Complementary goals
_____	**14.**	Conflicting goals
_____	**15.**	This can help promote allocative efficiency

g. A decrease in the average level of prices

h. A broad decline in production, involving many sectors of the economy

i. Avoiding sloppy management and wasted motion

j. Total number of people in a country

k. Put forward the idea that government should spend for public works when necessary to get economy out of depression, and restore full employment

l. Sum of those employed and those unemployed

m. An increase in the average level of prices

n. Leave the economy alone

o. Producing the best combination of outputs, using the lowest-cost combination of inputs

TRUE-FALSE

T F **1.** Adam Smith argued that the government should build public works whenever needed to reduce the rate of inflation.

T F **2.** By definition, a depression occurs whenever the output of the nation falls.

T F **3.** During the Great Depression of the 1930s, the unemployment rate rose above 15% of the labour force.

T F **4.** Between 1965 and 1986, output per person in the 30 poorest countries in the world grew at an average annual rate of less than 1.25%, much slower than in most advanced countries.

T F **5.** Since 1970, recessions have been much less severe than those of the 1950s and 1960s.

T F **6.** A recession is a decline in total output, employment, and income, and is marked by a widespread contraction in *many* industries.

T F **7.** Changes in the average level of inflation make an important contribution, since they are the key to improvements in allocative efficiency.

T F **8.** Throughout the 1980s, the percentage of the population living in poverty declined slowly but consistently.

T F **9.** Over the past three decades, there has been a consistent trend in Canada: the rich have gotten richer, and the poor have gotten poorer.

T F **10.** Inflation is caused by a decline in purchases by consumers.

MULTIPLE CHOICE

1. Since 1900, output per capita in Canada
  a. has approximately doubled, while the length of the work week has declined
  b. has grown more than fivefold, while the length of the work week has declined
  c. has approximately doubled, while the length of the work week has remained stable
  d. has grown more than fivefold, while the length of the work week has remained stable
  e. has remained stable, while the length of the work week has declined sharply; all the gains have come in the form of more leisure

2. Between 1960 and 1986/87, which of the following countries grew most rapidly?
  a. France
  b. Canada
  c. Japan
  d. United States
  e. West Germany

3. By the phrase, "invisible hand," Adam Smith was expressing the idea that
  a. there are no economic conflicts among nations
  b. there would be no economic conflicts among nations if countries would eliminate tariffs
  c. there are no conflicts between what is good for an individual and what is good for society as a whole
  d. by pursuing their own individual interests, people frequently promote the interests of society

e. business executives have a natural interest in keeping prices down and preventing inflation

4. Suppose that the American government is considering increasing the tariffs on steel imported from Canada. Which organizations in the United States are *most likely* to *oppose* such an increase?

    a. steelworkers' union and auto workers' union

    b. General Motors and Caterpillar

    c. steelworkers' union and the U.S. Treasury

    d. U.S. Steel and the U.S. Treasury

    e. U.S. Steel and General Motors

5. In his *General Theory*, Keynes' principal concern was with the goal of

    a. stable prices

    b. low unemployment

    c. allocative efficiency

    d. technological efficiency

    e. an equitable distribution of income

6. Unemployment is likely to be highest during

    a. war

    b. peacetime prosperity

    c. rapid growth

    d. recession

    e. depression

7. Between 1929 and 1933 (the early part of the Great Depression) total output in Canada

    a. declined about 30%

    b. declined about 20%

    c. declined about 10%

    d. declined about 5%

    e. remained approximately stable; the Depression represented an interruption of growth, not an actual decline in output

8. Which of the following is counted as being unemployed?

    a. someone who has just retired at age 65

    b. a full-time student not looking for a job

    c. someone who has recently graduated from college and is looking for his or her first full-time job

    d. convicts in prisons

    e. all of the above

9. A moderate rate of inflation (of, say, 4% per annum)

    a. creates no problems in the economy

    b. hurts people living on fixed money incomes

    c. hurts people who have borrowed money

    d. occurs whenever money wages rise more rapidly than prices

    e. is likely to be caused by war

10. The key role in promoting allocative efficiency is played by changes in

    a. the average level of prices

    b. the rate of inflation

    c. the rate of growth

    d. relative prices

    e. the distribution of income

11. Economists distinguish changes in the *average* level of prices and changes in *relative* prices. Changes in the average level of prices are generally considered

    a. undesirable, while changes in relative prices can perform a useful function in promoting efficiency

    b. undesirable, but changes in relative prices are even more undesirable, since they hurt some people while helping others

    c. undesirable, but changes in relative prices are neither good nor bad; they just happen

    d. desirable, but the government should attempt to prevent changes in relative prices

    e. desirable, but changes in relative prices are even more desirable, and the government should take steps to increase changes in relative prices

12. Suppose that every factory worker were in the job best suited for him or her, working as productively as possible, but producing cars that nobody wanted to buy. This would be an example of

    a. technical inefficiency and allocative inefficiency

    b. technical efficiency and allocative inefficiency

    c. technical inefficiency and allocative efficiency

    d. technical efficiency and allocative efficiency

    e. technical efficiency and allocative efficiency, but slow growth

13. During the past two decades, the prices of computers have fallen, while the price of oil has risen. As a result, manufacturers and other businesses have used more computers, and have conserved on energy. This switch toward more computers and less energy consumption is an illustration of

    a. allocative efficiency

    b. technological efficiency

    c. the effects of inflation

    d. a less equal distribution of income

    e. a more equal distribution of income

14. Which is the best example of *technological* inefficiency?

    a. producing too many cars, and not enough housing

    b. slow growth

    c. inflation

    d. inequality of incomes

    e. sloppy management

15. *Equity* in the distribution of income means

    a. equality

    b. fairness

    c. more for everyone as a result of growth

    d. more for those who can't work

    e. more for those who work hard

16. Suppose that the incomes of all families are perfectly equal. Then what share of total income will the poorest 10% of the families get?
    a. 5%
    b. 10%
    c. approximately 15%
    d. 20%
    e. 25%

17. Which of the following pairs is the clearest example of conflicting goals?
    a. less unemployment and less inflation
    b. less unemployment and less poverty
    c. less unemployment and more growth
    d. less unemployment and more efficiency
    e. more efficiency and less poverty

18. If, during the coming six months, there is a boom in the purchases of machinery by businesses, then we would be most likely to observe
    a. an increase in the rate of inflation and a decline in the rate of unemployment
    b. a decrease in the rate of inflation and a decline in the rate of unemployment
    c. an increase in the rate of inflation and an increase in the rate of unemployment
    d. a decrease in the rate of inflation and an increase in the rate of unemployment
    e. a decrease in inflation, growth, and unemployment

19. Economists study
    a. inflation
    b. unemployment
    c. efficiency
    d. poverty
    e. all of the above

(Appendix)

20. A reason for using a logarithmic or ratio scale on the vertical axis of a chart is that this
    a. makes it easier to start measuring from zero
    b. allows readers to quickly see when the rate of increase was most rapid
    c. avoids the necessity of choosing an arbitrary beginning year
    d. shows when profits were at a maximum
    e. shows when profits were at a minimum

EXERCISE

In the following passage, choose the correct word or phrase from those given in the brackets.

Economic history is a story of both progress and problems. Some evidence of progress shows up in Figure 1.1 in the textbook. Here we see that output per person has increased by a little more than (150%, 200%, 300%) since 1926, and about (25%, 100%, 200%) since 1960. If we were to look at total output of the economy—rather than at output *per person*—we would find that total output has increased by (an even greater percentage than output per person, a somewhat smaller percentage).

The right-hand panel of Figure 1.1 shows another source of gain. Not only have we produced more, but we have done so with a shorter work week. The decline in the work week was approximately (20%, 40%, 60%) between 1926 and the mid-1980s. Notice also the very sharp drop between 1926 and 1935. This decrease was the result of (a much more rapidly improving economy which allowed more leisure, the Depression which reduced the demand for output, a loss of the work ethic).

Successes and problems also show up in Figure 1.3 in the textbook. The (upward trend in output, downward trend in unemployment, both) since 1950 show(s) how things have improved. However, from time to time there have been problems such as in 1981/82 when (the unemployment rate increased, output declined, both). This was only one of several instances since 1950 when the Canadian economy suffered from the problem of (recession, depression, inflation, poverty).

Figure 1.4 shows the average level of prices. A rise in this curve is an indication of inflation. The more rapid is inflation, the steeper is the curve. We see that inflation was particularly rapid between (1950 and 1960, 1960 and 1970, 1970 and 1980).

Finally, Figure 1.5 shows the percentage of the population living in poverty; a decline in the percentage is a sign of success. Observe that, at the beginning of the period shown, the incidence of poverty declined, from about (15%, 22%, 35%) in the mid-1960s to about (8%, 11%, 14%) in the mid-1980s.

ANSWERS

Important Terms: 1n, 2c, 3l, 4j, 5h, 6e, 7k, 8a, 9m, 10g, 11o, 12i, 13b, 14f, 15d
True-False: 1F, 2F, 3T, 4T, 5F, 6T, 7F, 8F, 9F, 10F
Multiple Choice: 1b, 2c, 3d, 4b, 5b, 6e, 7a, 8c, 9b, 10d, 11a, 12b, 13a, 14e, 15b, 16b, 17a, 18a, 19e, 20b
Exercise: 300%, 100%, an even greater percentage than output per person, 40%, the Depression which reduced the demand for output, upward trend in output, both, recession, 1970 and 1980, 35%, 11%.

ANSWERS TO SELECTED REVIEW QUESTIONS FROM THE TEXT

1-1. In the first instance, the butcher gets money in exchange for the meat. In turn, this money can be used to buy the things the butcher wants—clothing, housing, etc. The butcher and the baker find that, by specializing in the preparation of food, they can obtain more clothing and housing than they could make themselves in an equivalent time.

1-2. Unemployment is the major problem of a depression. After a collapse, as many as 10% or 25% of the labour force may be unable to find jobs. Furthermore, joblessness tends to be of much longer duration during a depression than in more normal times. Unemployment is particularly severe for young people. During hard times, those who have jobs try to keep them. It is the new entrants into the labour force who are hit particularly hard when job openings dry up.

1-4. As people buy more clothes, cars, etc., more jobs become available in textiles, clothing, automobiles, rubber, steel, etc. As people are more eager to buy, producers find it easier to raise prices. Thus, the increase in purchases that helps to ease unemployment will make inflation worse; high employment and price stability are conflicting goals.

1-5.(a) Presumably, the main reason that the length of the work week has declined is that as real incomes have increased, people have felt that they could afford more leisure. In Sweden, tax rates are very high. This means that the "price of leisure" (that is, the after-tax income you forgo by not working) is relatively low, which may explain why Swedes choose more leisure. The difference between Canada and the United States also may be explained by higher taxes here.

(b) No; if people value leisure, they may be happy to give up some growth in income in order to have more leisure.

APPENDIX

This appendix provides additional information and practice for those who have already studied the appendix to Chapter 1 in the textbook.

Graphs

During rainy spells, sales of lawn furniture decline. A simple version of the relationship between weather and the sales of lawn furniture is illustrated in Figure 1.1 below.

The two measures used in this graph—sales of furniture and rainfall—are examples of **variables**. A variable is something that can change, or vary, from time to time or from place to place. For example, the amount of rain in April is generally different from the amount in July.

The statement that the sales of lawn furniture decline during rainy weather means that there is a relationship between the two variables in Figure 1.1. In particular, it means that when rainfall increases, sales decline. This idea can be illustrated in the figure.

The two *axes*, marked with numbers, meet at the **origin** 0. The vertical axis shows the quantity of lawn furniture sold. The horizontal axis shows the amount of rainfall. The relationship between the two variables is depicted by the line marked with the letters *A* through *F*. For example, point *A* shows that when the rainfall is 1 cm per month (measured along the horizontal axis), there are $6,000 worth of sales of lawn furniture (measured up the vertical axis). Likewise, at point *B*, 2 cm of rainfall result in sales of $5,000. In this way, each time you read a point on the line you get one bit of information. These "bits" are shown in Table 1.1.

Table 1.1.

Point	*A*	*B*	*C*	*D*	*E*	*F*
Rainfall	1	2	3	4	5	6
Sales	6	5	4	3	2	1

Thus, the rule for reading the graph is as follows. If you want to find out how much furniture will be sold

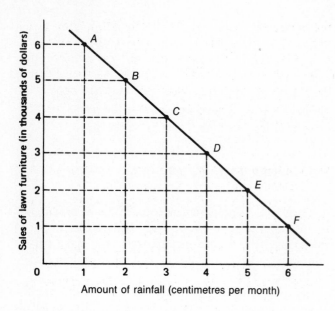

Figure 1.1

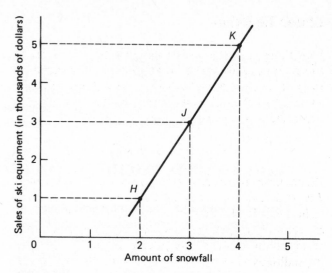

Figure 1.2

when there is some particular amount of rain (say, 3 cm), go along the horizontal axis to 3 units. Then go directly up to the line. This shows sales of $4,000 worth of furniture when the rainfall is 3 cm. Question 1 at the end of this appendix provides an exercise in reading graphs.

Slope

Figure 1.1 shows not only that rainfall and sales are related. It shows the *direction* of that relationship.

Specifically, when rainfall *increases*, sales *decrease*. In other words, sales are **negatively** or **inversely** related to rainfall. This negative relationship means that the line in Figure 1.1 slopes downward to the right. As you move to the right (as rainfall increases), the height of the line decreases (sales decrease). For example, by comparing points *A* and *B*, we see that when rainfall increases from 1 to 2 cm, sales decrease from $6,000 to $5,000.

A **positive** or **direct** relationship is illustrated in Figure 1.2; both variables change in the same direction. When snowfall increases, sales of skis increase, too. This means that as we move to the right (more snow), the line slopes upward (more sales of skis).

A graph such as Figure 1.2 shows not only the *direction* of the relationship between the two variables, it also shows the *strength*. For example, it shows that when snow increases by 1 cm (from 2 to 3 cm), 2000 more skis are sold. The *strength* of the relationship is shown by the **slope** of the line. The slope of the line is defined as the amount by which the height of the line changes when you go one more unit to the right on the horizontal axis. In Figure 1.2, the slope is 2; a 1 unit increase in snow causes a 2 unit increase in the sales of skis. Alternatively, the

slope of a line between two points (such as *H* and *K* in Figure 1.2) is defined as the *rise* (that is, the vertical change of 4 units) *divided by the run* (the horizontal change of 2 units). Again, we see that the slope of the line is 2 (that is, 4 divided by 2).

Observe that ski sales respond much more strongly to snow in Figure 1.2 than in Figure 1.3. In Figure 1.3, the much weaker response is illustrated by the relatively flat curve; when snowfall increases by 1 unit, ski sales increase only a half unit; the slope is only 1/2.

Back in Figure 1.1, an increase in one variable (rain) caused a decrease in the other variable (sales of lawn furniture). The line slopes downward; that is, the slope is negative. (For example, between points *A* and *C*, the rise is −2 while the run is 2; thus the slope is −1.) A negative slope means, therefore, that the two variables are negatively or inversely related.

In summary, the slope of the line shows two ideas—the direction and strength of the relationship between two variables. The *direction* of the relationship depends on whether the line slopes up or down—that is, whether the slope is positive or negative. The *strength* of the relationship depends on the steepness of the line. Questions 3 and 4 at the end of this appendix deal with the concept of slope.

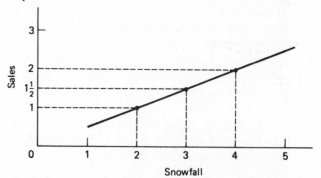

Figure 1.3

Linear Equations

Sometimes the relationship between two variables is shown not by a graph, but by an equation. For example, suppose that you are told that my expenditures on consumer goods (C) each month depends on my income (Y) according to the equation:

$$C = \$400 + 0.50Y$$

(Economists almost always use the letter Y for income. I is used to denote investment.)

In simple English, this equation says that I spend $400 plus half of my income that month. As my income varies from month to month, the equation tells you how my expenditures will vary. Whatever my income (Y) is, you can figure out how much I am likely to spend for consumer goods (C).

For example, choose some convenient value for my income, such as $1,000. Then substitute this into the equation to get $C = 400 + 0.5 \times 1,000 = 400 + 500 = 900$. This tells us that when my income is $1,000, my expenditures on consumer goods is $900. Now choose any other convenient value, such as $1,100. Substituting this value into the equation shows us that when my income is $1,100, my expenditures on consumer goods is $400 + 0.5 \times 1,100$ or $950. Each time you choose a value for Y and make this substitution, you get one bit of information. These two bits are shown in Table 1.2. As an exercise, fill in the rest of the table.

Table 1.2

Y	100	200	300	400	500	600	700	800	900	1,000	1,100
C										900	950

Figure 1.4 shows this relationship in a graph. The slope of the line is 0.5. This is because every time my income increases by $100 (shown as a move of one unit along the horizontal axis), I spend another $50 (shown as a rise of 0.5 of a unit). In contrast, the equation $C = 400 + 0.75Y$ represents the behaviour of individuals who spend $400 plus three-quarters of their income. In this case, the slope of the line would be 0.75, because every increase of $100 in income would cause an increase of $75 in consumption.

In general, any equation of the sort $C = a + bY$ represents a line with a slope equal to b. Such an equation is a **linear** equation. For example, the linear equation illustrated in Figure 1.4 has $a = 400$ and $b = 0.5$.

The number b (in this example, 0.5) is known as the **coefficient** of the variable Y. It indicates the slope of the line. The number a (400) shows how high the line is where it meets the vertical axis (point A). Thus, a is often called the **vertical intercept** of this equation. For example, the vertical intercept in Figure 1.4 is 400; this corresponds to the equation where $a = 400$.

At this time, you should do questions 5 and 6, which deal with linear equations.

Curves

So far we have drawn only straight lines. A straight line is easy to use because it has a *constant* slope. For example, in Figure 1.1, the slope of the line is the same between A and B as it is between any other two points on the line.

However, sometimes a relationship is described better by a curve, like the one in Figure 1.5 which illustrates how a student's final grade depends on how many hours he or she spends studying during the average week. A curve does not have a constant slope; as you move to the right on this curve, it gets flatter. For example, the first hour of studying causes an increase in the grade by 30 points—from 20 to 50. However, the second hour makes it rise by only 20 more (to 70), and the third hour causes an increase of only 5 more points. Each move to the right

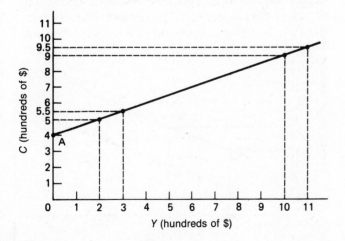

Figure 1.4

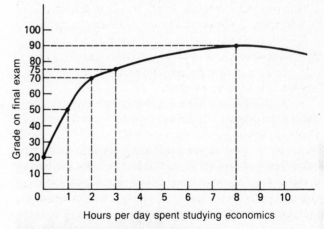

Figure 1.5

of 1 hour per week causes a smaller increase in the grade. In this example, it would obviously be impossible for the relationship to continue in a straight line in the way it began. The first hour caused an increase of 30 points. Four hours obviously couldn't cause an increase of 120 points, for the simple reason that the exam has a maximum grade of 100 points.

In this curve, as before, the slope is still identified as the amount by which the height of the curve changes as you go one more unit to the right along the horizontal axis. But, in this case, the slope changes as you go to the right. For the first hour, it is 30; for the second, 20; then 5; and so on.

The decreasing slope in Figure 1.5 indicates that as the student spends more and more time studying, each additional hour may raise the grade, *but not by as much as the previous hour*. The first hour raises the grade by 30 points, the next by only 20. This is an example of diminishing returns; the payoff (in terms of a higher grade) diminishes as a person studies more and more.

Notice that, according to Figure 1.5, the curve reaches its maximum. No matter how much time the student spends studying, he or she can't get more than 90. Indeed, after 8 hours, the student gets tired and stale. Any more time with the books will be counterproductive. The slope of the curve becomes negative; each additional hour results in a lower grade.

Other Graphs

Sometimes, in presenting a general argument, we don't bother to put numbers on the axes. For example, the linear relationship in Figure 1.6 shows no numbers (except for the 0 at the origin). Without numbers, we can't tell exactly how strong the relationship is between the variables X and Y. But the graph still provides important information—that the relationship is linear, with a constant direction and slope. In this diagram, we can put in letters as points of reference. Point E represents $0A$ units of X, and its height is measured as $0C$ units of Y.

When describing the movement from E to F along the line, it helps to look at triangle EFG. The change in X is the difference between distance $0B$ and $0A$, that is, distance AB. Likewise, the change in Y can be read from the vertical axis as CD, or from the triangle as distance GF.

The Ratio Scale

In the standard diagram (such as Figure 1.2) each vertical increase of one notch represents the same increase—in this example, an increase of 1000 skis. Equal distances along an axis represent equal changes in the variable.

But there is an important exception to this rule. Look at Figure 1.7. In this graph, going up one notch on the vertical axis doesn't always mean the same change in the

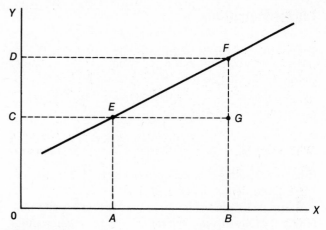

Figure 1.6

price level. The first notch takes you from 25 to 50—a change of 25. But, when you move up to the second notch, the price level goes from 50 to 100—a change this time of 50. The vertical axis measures the price level, not on the usual scale, but on the **ratio scale**, or **logarithmic scale**.

As you move up a ratio scale, equal distances represent equal *percentage* changes. Going up from 25 to the first notch, the price level goes up by 100% to 50. Going to the second notch, it again goes up by 100%—this time to 100. In this case, every notch higher represents a price level that is 100% higher.

In economics, a ratio scale is used most frequently along the vertical axis, with time shown on the horizontal axis (as in Figure 1.7). Such a diagram is used when we're interested in the percentage rate of growth of something—for example, the percentage rate of growth of population or the percentage increase in prices. When such a curve becomes steeper, the percentage rate of increase in population or prices is becoming greater. We can identify the period when the rate of growth was the most rapid. It is the period when the curve is the steepest.

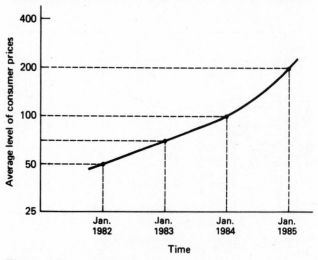

Figure 1.7

QUESTIONS

1. Point *A* in Figure 1.8 has a height of _____ and lies distance _____ to the right of the origin. Thus, it indicates that when there is a light rainfall of _____ centimetres during rush hour, _____ thousand workers will arrive to work on time. If rain is heavier, at 6 cm, only _____ thousand workers will be on time. With a very heavy rain of 10 cm, _____ thousand workers will be on time.

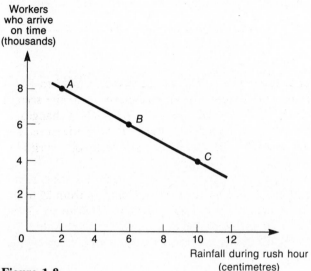

Figure 1.8

2. From Figure 1.2 fill in Table 1.3.

Table 1.3

Amount of snow	2	3	4
Sales of skis			

3. There are six different lines in Figure 1.9. In Table 1.4, fill in the slope of each line.

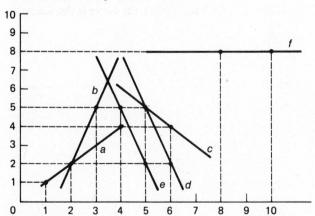

Figure 1.9

Table 1.4

Line	*a*	*b*	*c*	*d*	*e*	*f*
Slope						

4. Which of the lines in Figure 1.10 show a positive relationship between variables *X* and *Y*? _____. When *X* increases by 1 unit, which of these lines shows the greatest increase in *Y*? _____. When *X* increases by 1 unit, which of these lines shows the greatest decrease in Y? _____.

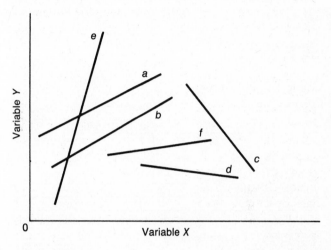

Figure 1.10

5. Consider two variables, *X* and *Y*, that are related according to the linear equation $Y = 8 - 2X$. From this equation, fill in Table 1.5.

Table 1.5

X	0	1	2	3	4
Y					

Draw the line representing this equation in Figure 1.11. The slope of this line is _____. The vertical intercept is _____.

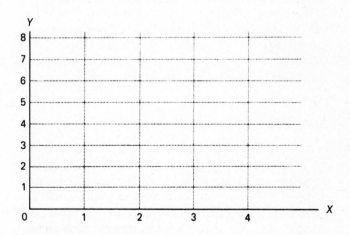

Figure 1.11

6. The following linear equations show how one variable, Y, depends on another variable, X.

(a) $Y = 90 + 10X$
(b) $Y = 50 + 15X$
(c) $Y = 80 - 5X$
(d) $Y = 3X$
(e) $Y = -10 + 5X$
(f) $Y = 50$

Line _____ has the largest vertical intercept and line _____ has the largest slope. When X increases by 1 unit, which line shows the largest increase in Y? _____. When $X = 0$, the highest line is _____.
Which equations show a positive relationship between X and Y? _____. Which a negative relationship? _____. What is the slope of (f)? _____. Which line has a vertical intercept of zero? _____. Which line passes through the origin? _____.

ANSWERS

Table 1.2 completed:

Y	100	200	300	400	500	600	700	800	900	1000	1100
C	450	500	550	600	650	700	750	800	850	900	950

1. 8, 2, 2, 8, 6, 4
2. Table 1.3 completed:

Amount of snow	2	3	4
Sales of skis	1	3	5

3. Table 1.4 completed:

Line	a	b	c	d	e	f
Slope	1	3	-1	-3	-3	0

4. (a, b, e, f), e, c
5. Table 1.5 completed:

X	0	1	2	3	4
Y	8	6	4	2	0

$-2, 8$
6. $a, b, b, a, (a, b, d, e), c, 0, d, d$

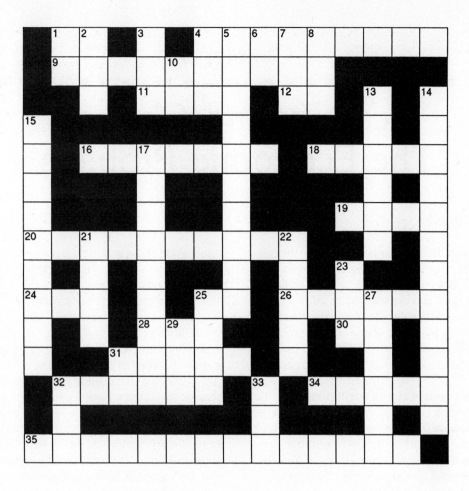

Across

1. university degree
4. His *Wealth of Nations* was an early classic (2 names).
9. getting the most from productive efforts
11. shedder of light
12. preposition
16, 18. keeping government involvement in economy to a minimum
19. assist (verb)
20. the _____ nations, also known as the Third World
24. industrious insect
25. above
26. fairness
28. charged particle
30. _____ garde! (French)
31. During hyperinflation, this becomes practically worthless.
32. advocated goverment spending to restore full employment
34. represents workers
35. Losing countries in war may suffer this.

Down

1. exist
2. toward the stern of a boat
3. be ill
4. purpose, or line up in your sights
5. the economic disease of the 1930s
6. indefinite article
7. 1101 in Roman numerals
8. artificial (abbrev.)
10. a professional business degree
13. important source of information to buyers and sellers
14. a major economic problem
15. international institution lending to developing nations (2 words)
17. rise in the average level of prices
21. document needed when looking for a job
22. large, powerful
23. owing
25. individuals
27. a deep violet-blue colour
29. number
31. first person possessive
32. under lock and _____
33. Its price skyrocketed in the 1970s.

Chapter 2

■ ■

Scarcity and Choice:
The Economic Problem

MAJOR PURPOSE

The major purpose of this chapter is to introduce the concept of *scarcity*. Because of limited resources, we cannot have all the goods and services that we want. Therefore, we must *make choices*, picking some items and forgoing others. This idea—that we face scarcity and therefore have to make choices—is at the centre of economics. A standard definition of economics is "the study of the allocation of scarce resources to satisfy alternative, competing human wants."

The ideas of scarcity and choice are illustrated by the *production possibilities curve*. This illustrates the idea of scarcity because we are limited to a point on (or within) the curve; we cannot go outside the curve with our present resources and technological capabilities. The curve also illustrates the need to *make choices*. When we pick one point on the production possibilities curve, we pass over all the other points and forgo the goods which we might have had if we had picked some other point.

This chapter applies the production possibilities curve to illustrate the choice between consumer goods now and consumer goods in the future. We can forgo some con-sumer goods now and use the resources to produce capital equipment instead. The additional capital will help us to produce even more consumer goods in the future. Mention is also made of the possibility that a country's productive capacity may grow—that is, its production possibilities curve may shift up and out—because it is importing *foreign* capital. However, when this happens, it must be kept in mind that the future *consumption* opportunities of the country's citizens will not be as great, because the foreign capital owners will be paid a return on the capital they have invested in the country.

Finally, this chapter provides an introduction to *economic theory*. Economic theory *must* be a *simplification* of the real world. If we strove for a complete theory which took into account all the complexities of our world, we would get bogged down in a swamp of detail. When we simplify, we should keep in mind a central question: Does our theory include the most important relationships in the economy, or *have we left out something of critical importance*?

LEARNING OBJECTIVES

After you have studied this chapter in the textbook and study guide, you should be able to
- Understand why the combination of limited resources and unlimited wants requires us to make choices
- Define the three major factors of production
- Explain the difference between real capital and financial capital, and explain why economists focus on real rather than financial capital when studying the productive capacity of the economy
- Explain the functions of the entrepreneur
- Explain the concept of opportunity cost and how it is related to the production possibilities curve (PPC)
- Explain why the PPC slopes downward to the right
- Explain why the PPC usually bows outward from the origin
- Explain a circumstance in which the PPC might be a straight line, instead of bowing outward
- Explain why production occurs *within* the PPC if there is large-scale unemployment

• Explain the difference between a high-growth and a low-growth policy, using a PPC with capital goods on one axis and consumer goods on the other (Figure 2-5 in the textbook)
• Explain the effects of an increase in the capital stock in Canada through a capital inflow from foreign countries
• Explain why it is impossible to develop a theory without making simplifying assumptions

HIGHLIGHTS OF THE CHAPTER

Scarcity is one of the most important concepts in economics. Scarcity requires us to *make choices*; we cannot have everything we want. Why? The answer is that our resources are limited, while our wants are not.

When we make choices, we pick some goods and services and forgo others. If we pick a college education, for example, we may have to put off buying a car for several years. The opportunity cost of our education is the car and other goods and services that we forgo to pay tuition and room and board. Similarly, for the society as a whole, opportunity cost is an important concept. For example, when we decide to produce more weapons, we forgo the consumer goods and services we might have produced instead. Individuals, corporations, and governments are constantly making choices among the options open to them.

The ideas of scarcity, of the need to make choices, and of opportunity cost are summarized by the production possibilities curve (PPC). The PPC shows the options from which a choice is made. The fact that we are limited by the PPC, and cannot pick a point outside it with our present resources and technology, illustrates the idea of scarcity. The slope of the PPC shows how much of one good we must forgo when we choose more of another. In other words, the slope shows the *opportunity cost* of choosing more of a specific good.

The PPC has two important properties. First, it slopes downward to the right. This means that if we decide to produce more of one good, we give up some of the other. The idea that there is an opportunity cost when we produce more of one good is illustrated by the downward slope of the PPC curve.

The second feature of the typical PPC curve is that it is bowed out—that is, it is *concave* to the origin. This is so because resources are *specialized*. If we decide to produce more and more wheat, we will use land which is less and less suited to the production of wheat, even though it was very good for producing wool. For each additional unit of wheat, we will have to give up more wool. Thus, the outward bend in the PPC illustrates the idea of *increasing opportunity cost*.

Under certain circumstances, however, the PPC need not bow outward. It is possible that two goods might require the same set of resources in their production. For example, radios and telephones might take the same combination of resources in their production—the same combination of copper, plastic, silicon, labour, etc.—in which case, the PPC would be a straight line. In this particular case, the *opportunity cost of radios would be constant* in terms of the telephones forgone. (The opportunity cost of both radios and telephones might nevertheless still increase, in terms of the food or clothing forgone. In other words, the PPC would be a straight line if we put radios and telephones on the two axes, but would bow out if we put radios on one axis and food on the other.)

It is worth emphasizing that a downward slope and an outward bow are two *different* features. A PPC can slope downward without bowing outward—as in the example of radios and telephones. A downward slope means that the opportunity cost is *positive*. An outward bow means that the opportunity cost *increases* as more of a good is produced.

One of the important choices facing the society is the choice between consumer goods and capital goods. If we produce only a little capital, we will be able to enjoy a large quantity of consumer goods now. But, with little investment, we will have slow growth. In other words, there is a *trade-off between a high current level of consumption and high growth*. This trade-off or choice is illustrated when we draw a PPC curve with consumer goods on one axis and capital goods on the other. For example, Figure 2.5 in the textbook illustrates the difference between a high-growth and a low-growth strategy. A high-growth strategy requires that a sizeable fraction of our resources be committed to investment in plant and equipment (capital goods). But this makes possible a rapid growth—that is, a rapid outward movement of the PPC.

When a nation is receiving a capital inflow from foreign countries, its stock of capital goods may expand rapidly even if the nation's citizens use most of their resources for present consumption. But there is an offsetting disadvantage: Part of the increased future production that is made possible by the nation's larger capital stock will have to be paid to the foreign investors or lenders who initially supplied the capital inflow, as a return on their investment.

This chapter provides a brief introduction to economic theory. When we develop economic theories, we must simplify. The world is much too complex to describe in all its detail. The objective of theory is to strip away the non-essential complications in order to see the important relationships within the economy. Theory should not be dismissed because it fails to account for everything, just as a road map should not be discarded as useless just because it doesn't show everything. But, because of simplifications, theory must be used carefully. Just as last week's weather map is useless for planning a trip in a car, so the theory which helps to explain one aspect of the economy may be inappropriate or useless for explaining others.

Finally, this chapter explains the distinction between *positive* and *normative* economics. Positive or descriptive economics is aimed at explaining what has been happening and why. Normative economics deals with policies; it deals with the way things *ought* to be.

IMPORTANT TERMS: MATCH THE COLUMNS

Match each term in the first column with the corresponding phrase in the second column.

_____	1. Economic resources	a. Outward bow of PPC
_____	2. Capital inflow	b. Choices open to society
_____	3. Financial capital	c. Specialized resources
_____	4. Real capital	d. Foreign-financed investment
_____	5. Increase in real capital	e. Stocks and bonds
_____	6. Entrepreneur	f. Straight-line PPC
_____	7. PPC	g. Organizer of production
_____	8. Opportunity cost	h. Basic inputs used in the production of goods and services
_____	9. Increasing opportunity cost	i. Investment
_____	10. Constant opportunity cost	j. Alternative forgone
_____	11. Cause of outward bow of PPC	k. Machinery, equipment, and buildings

TRUE-FALSE

T   F   1. Resources are said to be scarce because they are incapable of producing all the goods and services that people want; therefore, choices must be made.

T   F   2. Wants were "unlimited" during the early days of the study of economics in the eighteenth and nineteenth centuries. But they are no longer unlimited in the affluent countries of North America and Western Europe.

T   F   3. Suppose that a production possibilities curve meets the axes at 5 units of clothing and at 20 units of food. This illustrates that the society can have a total of 5 units of clothing plus 20 units of food, but no more.

T   F   4. The production possibilities curve bends outward because resources are not uniform in quality; some are better at producing one good than the other.

T   F   5. Just as it is possible to select a combination of goods inside the PPC, so it is possible to choose a combination of goods that lies outside the PPC.

T   F   6. An increase in the quantity of labour causes the production possibilities curve to move outward from the origin.

T   F   7. Suppose that two countries, A and B, were identical in 1979. Suppose that, between 1979 and 1989, the economy of A grew at 4% per annum, while B grew at 3% per annum. Then, from that fact, we may conclude that economy A was allocatively more efficient than B during the 1979-1989 period.

T   F   8. Positive economics is the study of how policy makers can achieve desirable (that is, "positive") social goals.

T   F   9. Less developed countries have a special problem. If they want to grow through creating more capital, they have to forgo some consumer goods or import capital. In the affluent countries in North America and Western Europe, no such choice is necessary.

T F   **10.** An inflow of American capital into Canada would help shift Canada's PPC outward from the origin.

T F   **11.** In most less developed countries, an increase in the population and in the quantity of labour will make it more difficult to raise income per person. In such a country, such a population increase will generally cause an inward movement of its PPC.

MULTIPLE CHOICE

1. Economists often speak of wants being "unlimited" because
  a. the cost of living has increased; it costs more to meet our basic needs now than it did twenty years ago
  b. more people live in the cities now than in an earlier age, and it is more expensive to live in cities than on the farm
  c. even though our incomes have risen, we still want "more"; we do not believe all our wants are satisfied
  d. resources such as oil have become scarcer because we have been using them up
  e. as people's incomes have risen, they have decided to take more leisure, and work fewer hours

2. By real capital, economists mean
  a. real estate, particularly land
  b. plant and equipment
  c. the real value of bonds, adjusted for inflation
  d. the real value of common stock, adjusted for inflation
  e. both c. and d.

3. The production possibilities curve has one major purpose: to illustrate the need to
  a. stop inflation
  b. cut taxes
  c. cut government spending
  d. make choices
  e. stop pollution

4. The textbook has a picture of a production possibilities curve (PPC), joining six points.
  a. all six points are equally desirable, since they all represent full employment
  b. all six points are equally desirable, since they all are consistent with zero inflation
  c. all six points are equally desirable, since they all provide for some growth
  d. all six points are possible, but the PPC curve doesn't give enough information to tell which point is best
  e. only one of the six points is presently achievable; the others can be achieved only if the economy grows

5. An outward bow in the production possibilities curve illustrates what concept?
  a. scarcity
  b. unlimited wants
  c. increasing opportunity cost
  d. unemployment
  e. inflation

6. The opportunity cost of a good is measured by
  a. the slope of the PPC
  b. how far the PPC is from the origin
  c. the slope of a line from the origin out to the PPC
  d. how far the economy is operating within the PPC
  e. how fast the PPC is shifting outward

7. Suppose the production possibilities curve is a straight line if goods X and Y are put on the axis. Then we know that
  a. X and Y are really the same good
  b. the problem of scarcity has been solved
  c. we can have all the X and Y we want without incurring an opportunity cost, even though the general problem of scarcity has not been solved
  d. the opportunity cost of X is zero, in terms of Y forgone
  e. the opportunity cost of X is constant, in terms of Y forgone

8. We speak of a production possibilities curve as a "frontier" because
  a. we can produce within it or on it, but not beyond it, with presently available resources and technology
  b. it reflects the concept of scarcity, and goods were particularly scarce for settlers on the western frontier in the nineteenth century
  c. it is no longer relevant, now that the frontier has been tamed and we have an affluent society
  d. unemployment problems provide the frontier for economic research
  e. differences among resources provide the frontier for economic research

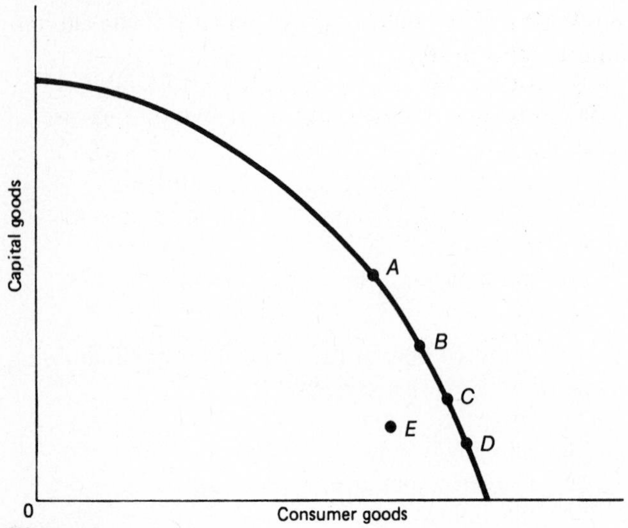

Figure 2.1

Table 2.1 Production Possibilities

Products	Options					
	A	B	C	D	E	F
Capital goods	0	1	2	3	4	5
Consumer goods	25	24	21	16	9	0

9. Suppose that the society has only one objective, to maximize growth. Then, the best choice among the five points shown on Figure 2.1 is
  a. A
  b. B
  c. C
  d. D
  e. E

10. In Figure 2.1, a growth of the economy can be illustrated by
  a. a move from point A to B
  b. a move from point B to A
  c. a move from point A to E
  d. a move from point D to E
  e. an outward shift of the production possibilities curve

11. In Figure 2.1, suppose that the economy is originally at point E. Then there will be
  a. rapid growth
  b. no capital formation
  c. more capital formation than at points A, B, or C
  d. a high rate of unemployment
  e. rapid inflation

12. The production possibilities curve generally bends outward because
  a. sensible people want to divide their purchases; they want to choose some food and some clothing
  b. there are economies of large-scale production
  c. most people have a comparative advantage in the production of at least one good
  d. there is much less unemployment now than during the Great Depression of the 1930s
  e. resources are not uniform in quality; some are better for producing one good than the other

13. In Table 2.1, the opportunity cost of the second unit of capital goods is how many units of consumer goods?
  a. 1
  b. 3
  c. 5
  d. 7
  e. 9

14. Given the options in Table 2.1, a total output of 5 units of capital goods and 25 units of consumer goods
  a. is unattainable at present
  b. represents a situation of large-scale unemployment
  c. can be achieved only if the economy achieves technological efficiency
  d. can be achieved only if the economy achieves allocative efficiency
  e. can be achieved only if the economy achieves both allocative and technological efficiency

15. Given the options in Table 2.1, a total output of 2 units of capital goods and 10 units of consumer goods
  a. is unattainable at present
  b. represents a situation of large-scale unemployment
  c. can be achieved only if the economy achieves technological efficiency
  d. can be achieved only if the economy achieves allocative efficiency
  e. can be achieved only if the economy achieves both allocative and technological efficiency

16. The choice of option C rather than B
  a. represents a mistake, since only 23 total units are produced (that is, 2 + 21) rather than 25 (that is, 1 + 24)
  b. represents a mistake, since consumers have fewer goods
  c. means that there will be more unemployment
  d. represents a choice of more growth
  e. represents a choice of less growth

17. The production possibilities curve shifts outward, away from the origin
  a. if the number of workers increases
  b. if the skill of workers increases
  c. if there is more capital
  d. if technology improves
  e. if any of the above happens

18. Oil now being pumped in a pipeline is an example of
   a. the land resource, because oil comes out of the ground
   b. real capital, because it has been produced in the past and will be used in the production of other goods
   c. financial capital, because it is valuable and is worth money
   d. financial capital, because it can be used as collateral for bank loans
   e. financial capital, because it was costly to pump out of the ground

19. Which of the following is an example of a capital inflow into Canada?
   a. a Canadian student spends $10,000 to study business administration at a U.S. university
   b. a Japanese construction firm buys $100,000 worth of timber from British Columbia
   c. a Finnish firm builds a plant in Quebec to produce cross-country skis
   d. an American couple spends $100 for a room and meals in Niagara Falls, Ontario
   e. a Canadian tourist brings back $100 worth of Mexican currency after a vacation in Acapulco

EXERCISES

1. Consider the following production possibilities table:

Table 2.2

		Options:						
	A	B	C	D	E	F	G	H
Consumer goods	0	1	2	3	4	5	6	7
Capital goods	23	22	20	17	13	9	5	0
Opportunity cost of consumer goods		1	2					

a. Complete the third line, showing the opportunity cost of each additional unit of consumer goods.
b. Draw the PPC on Figure 2.2.

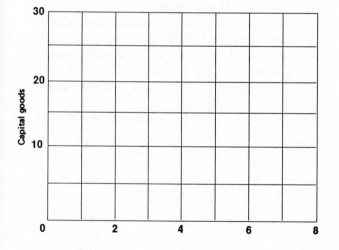

Figure 2.2

c. What is unusual about this curve?
d. In the range between points A and D, the PPC (bows outward, bows inward, is a straight line). This shows that opportunity cost is (increasing, decreasing, constant) in this range. However, between points D and G, the curve (bows outward, bows inward, is a straight line). This shows that opportunity cost is (increasing, decreasing, constant) in this range.

2. Consider a hypothetical economy with a labour force of 10 000 workers, each of whom can be put to work building either houses or roads. Each worker is available for 2000 hours per year. Thus, there are 20 million labour hours available during the year to produce houses and roads. Table 2.3 shows how many labour hours it takes to build various quantities of houses. For example, in order to build 18 000 houses, 15 million labour hours are needed. Likewise, Table 2.4 indicates how many labour hours are needed to build various amounts of roadway. In Figure 2.3, only one point, A, on the PPC has been plotted. It shows that if no houses are built, the 20 million labour hours can be used to produce 1000 kilometres of road. Using the data in Tables 2.3 and 2.4, plot four other points, and draw a PPC to connect them.

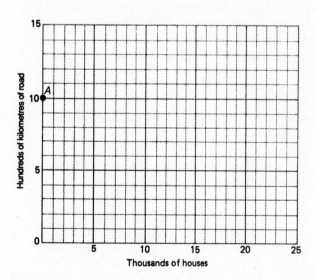

Figure 2.3

Table 2.3

Millions of labour hours	Thousands of houses
20	20
15	18
10	14
5	8
0	0

Table 2.4

Millions of labour hours	Hundreds of kilometres of road
20	10
15	9
10	7
5	4
0	0

ANSWERS

Important Terms: 1h, 2d, 3e, 4k, 5i, 6g, 7b, 8j, 9a, 10f, 11c
True-False: 1T, 2F, 3F, 4T, 5F, 6T, 7F, 8F, 9F, 10T, 11F
Multiple Choice: 1c, 2b, 3d, 4d, 5c, 6a, 7e, 8a, 9a, 10e, 11d, 12e, 13b, 14a, 15b, 16d, 17e, 18b, 19c
Exercises: **1a**. 3, 4, 4, 4, 5. **1c.** over part of its range, it is a straight line (between D and G). **1d.** bows outward, increasing, is a straight line, constant. **2.** Four other points are:

	B	C	D	E
Hundreds of kilometres	9	7	4	0
Thousands of houses	8	14	18	20

ANSWERS TO SELECTED REVIEW QUESTIONS FROM THE TEXT

2-1. The first definition covers the problem of unemployment, but the second does not. (If there is large-scale unemployment, production is not limited by the scarcity of productive factors.) The importance of the unemployment problem is one of the reasons Chapter 1 uses the broader definition of economics.

2-2. It may be true that Pocklington's material wants have been completely satisfied, but the vast majority of people consume less than they would if they had an unlimited budget. For society as a whole, scarce resources constrain behaviour even though some individuals may have great personal wealth. Although the wealth of very rich families is great, it is not capable of solving the economic problems of society as a whole.

2-3. No clearly correct answer; the best rate of growth is an interesting policy issue. In addressing this question, it is important to recognize that growth comes at a cost. When we direct more of our resources toward capital formation, we have less for current consumption (Figure 2-5 in text). Unless there are unemployed resources which can be directed toward capital formation, higher growth represents a choice between consumption today and consumption in the furture.

2-4. Question 2-3 falls within the category of normative economics. It addresses the question of the best rate of growth of the economy.

Chapter 3

■ ■

Specialization, Exchange, and Money

MAJOR PURPOSE

In this chapter, we study specialization, exchange, and money. People specialize and engage in exchange because there are *gains* from doing so. By specializing, people can achieve higher standards of living. There are *two major sources* of gain from specialization: (1) *comparative advantage,* and (2) *economies of scale.* These two phenomena are the forces that motivate specialization and exchange; that is, they are the *twin engines that drive commerce.*

Money, on the other hand, *is the oil* which makes the machinery of commerce run smoothly, with a minimum of friction. Without money, people would engage in cumbersome barter. But, if some money helps to make the system work smoothly, we should not conclude that more money would make it work even better. Just as too much oil can gum up an engine, so too much money can cause difficulty. Specifically, it causes inflation. The Bank of Canada (Canada's central bank), acts as the chief mechanic. Its task is to create the right amount of "oil" (money)—neither too much, nor too little. The operations of the Bank of Canada will be considered in detail in Chapter 12.

LEARNING OBJECTIVES

After you have studied this chapter in the textbook and study guide, you should be able to
- Explain why specialization and exchange go hand in hand
- Explain why barter is inferior to exchange with money
- Explain why people may nevertheless revert to barter in some circumstances
- Give an example of Gresham's law
- Explain the two major reasons that there can be gains from specialization and exchange
- Explain the difference between absolute advantage and comparative advantage
- Explain why a country may have an absolute advantage in a product without having a comparative advantage in that product
- Explain why a country cannot have a comparative advantage (or a comparative disadvantage) in every product
- Explain why economies of scale may lead to substantial gains from freer international trade, especially for small countries

HIGHLIGHTS OF THE CHAPTER

One reason for economic progress has been an increase in *specialization*. Individuals, cities, and countries are now more specialized than they were a hundred years ago. When production is specialized, people engage in exchange, selling the products they produce to buy the wide variety of goods and services that they want to consume. We live in a highly interdependent economy, in which each of us depends on the specialized production of others.

Specialization and exchange would be very cumbersome without money. It is easy to imagine the difficulties that would arise if we tried to do without money and engaged in barter exchange instead. Barter requires a *coincidence of wants*—people engaging in exchange must each be able to provide a good or service that the other wants. Furthermore, for barter to work, there must be some rough equivalence in the value of the two goods or services to be exchanged. To buy toothpaste, a farmer would scarcely offer a cow in exchange. However, with money, such problems of indivisibility do not arise. The farmer may sell the cow for $1,000 and spend just a bit of the money to buy toothpaste, using the rest for a wide variety of other purchases. Money provides people with *general purchasing power*; money can be used to buy any of the wide variety of goods and services on the market. Those wishing to make exchanges no longer have to search for unlikely coincidences (such as the ill-clad farmer looking for someone who not only has clothes to exchange, but who also wants to get beef in return).

Because it is so useful for those who wish to engage in exchange, money is used even in rudimentary societies with little or no government. The prisoner-of-war camp provides an example of such a simple society. However, governments have gotten deeply involved in the monetary system. Every country uses paper money printed by a central bank.

One reason for the government to be involved in the monetary system is that the government can provide a *uniform* currency. In Canada, for example, every $5 Bank of Canada note (five-dollar bill) is always worth exactly the same as every other five-dollar bill, or as five "loonies" (one-dollar coins). This uniformity of the money stock is very convenient. When selling something for $5, we have to find out only if the buyer has a $5 bill or the equivalent in other standard coins and bills. Except for the rare cases where counterfeiting is suspected, we do not need to ask the much more complicated question of whether the buyer's bills or coins are inferior to someone else's bills or coins.

(Canada has not always had a uniform currency. In the nineteenth century, privately owned banks issued currency. The value of this currency depended on the soundness of the bank that issued it. Thus, sellers did have to worry about the value of the notes or dollar bills they accepted. Similar problems have arisen throughout history. For example, when gold coins were in use, their value could depend on the amount of gold they contained. Before the development of modern methods of producing coins with hard edges, such coins were sometimes clipped. That is, people chipped off bits before spending them. As a result, not every coin was worth the same as every other coin of the same denomination. People had to examine the physical condition of the coins they were accepting.)

In addition to providing a uniform currency, the Bank of Canada has the responsibility of providing an appropriate *quantity* of money. If too many bills or coins are issued, there will be "too much money chasing too few goods." Inflation will result; the currency will decline in value. On the other hand, if the quantity of money is allowed to decline sharply, spending will decline. Sellers will have a very difficult time finding buyers. Sales will fall, unemployment will rise, and prices will be under downward pressure. The authorities do not always perform their monetary duties well. In some countries—for example, Brazil—prices are galloping ahead by more than 100% per year. This reduces the convenience of money. If prices are rising rapidly, sellers feel under pressure to spend their money as soon as possible, before its value declines significantly.

With the proper quantity of money, the monetary system can work very smoothly, making transactions very convenient. But this is all that money does—it makes exchange convenient. It is not the reason that exchange is desirable in the first place.

There are two reasons that specialization and exchange can yield benefits. The first is *comparative advantage*. The notion of comparative advantage is illustrated in the textbook by the example of the gardener and the lawyer. The lawyer has an absolute advantage in both the law and gardening; she can do both quicker than the gardener. It follows that the gardener has an absolute disadvantage in both the law and gardening—he is slower at both. However, the gardener has a comparative advantage in gardening, while the lawyer has a comparative advantage in the law. Comparative advantage provides the basis for mutually beneficial trade. Both the gardener and the lawyer can gain from specialization and exchange. (Details are provided in Box 3-2 in the text.)

Two points should be emphasized. (1) Absolute advantage is not necessary for gain; the gardener can gain by specializing in gardening, even though he is not the best gardener. (2) A person (or a nation) cannot have a comparative disadvantage in everything. In the simple case of two people and two activities (law and gardening), if one person has a comparative advantage in one activity, the other person must have the comparative advantage in the other activity.

Economies of scale provide the second major reason that there are gains from specialization and exchange. Economies of scale exist if an increase of x% in all inputs (labour, machinery, land, steel, etc.) leads to an increase of more than x% in output. Economies of scale are the major reason that big firms have an advantage in many industries, such as automobiles and mainframe computers. Economies of scale are the major reason that costs per unit of output often decline as more is produced. For example, a car company can produce 100 000 cars at a much lower cost per car than if it produces 1000 cars. Clearly, if a person tried to put together a car in the back yard or in a small shop, it would be very expensive. There are gains when car production is left to the specialists.

Comparative advantage and economies of scale also help explain international trade and specialization among *countries* in producing different goods. For example, land in Florida is not used to produce trees for wood-pulp even though Florida land can produce more wood-pulp per hectare per year than land in Northern Alberta. Instead, Florida produces oranges while wood-pulp is produced in Northern Alberta, even though Alberta (like the gardener in Box 3-2) has an absolute disadvantage in *both* wood-pulp and oranges.

Similarly, the desire to gain economies of scale was part of the explanation for Canada entering into an agreement with the United States to allow free trade in cars and car parts (the Auto Pact) in the 1960s. With this agreement, Canadian auto plants could gain scale economies by specializing and producing a narrow range of models for the whole North American market, rather than producing a wide range of models, each on a small scale, for the Canadian market alone. And the hope for greater efficiency through increased scale economies was an important reason for Canada's decision to enter into the wide-ranging Free Trade Agreement with the United States that came into effect in 1989.

IMPORTANT TERMS: MATCH THE COLUMNS

Match each term in the first column with the corresponding phrase in the second column.

_____	1. Barter	a.	Acting as medium of exchange
_____	2. Required by barter	b.	Bad money drives out good
_____	3. General purchasing power	c.	Reason the lawyer gains by practising law
_____	4. A function of money	d.	Exchange of one good or service for another
_____	5. Inflation	e.	Reason costs per unit fall as more is produced
_____	6. Cause of inflation	f.	Money
_____	7. Absolute advantage	g.	Adam Smith's pin factory
_____	8. Comparative advantage	h.	Good can be produced with fewest resources
_____	9. Economies of scale	i.	Coincidence of wants
_____	10. Example of economies of scale	j.	Fall in value of money
_____	11. Gresham's law	k.	Too much money chasing too few goods

TRUE-FALSE

T   F   1. One reason that barter is inconvenient is that many commodities cannot easily be divided into smaller parts.

T   F   2. Monetary systems develop only when there is a strong national government, since strong national governments are required to provide money with value.

T   F   3. Suppose that, in the prisoner-of-war camp with its "cigarette money," the value of cigarettes rises compared to the value of other items (such as beef, etc.). Such an increase is known as inflation.

T   F   4. Comparative advantage is the reason wheat is grown in rural Manitoba and not in downtown Vancouver.

T   F   5. If everyone had exactly the same talents and training, and exactly the same quantity of capital, then economies of scale would not exist.

T   F   6. In the absence of a government, money is valuable only if it is useful. Therefore, cigarette money would be used exclusively in transactions between smokers in the prisoner-of-war camp.

T   F   7. Economies of scale are the primary reason wood-pulp is produced in Northern Quebec rather than on the Niagara peninsula.

T   F   8. Even if everyone has the same abilities, specialization may be beneficial if there are economies of scale.

T   F   9. International trade is more important for a country such as the United States than for Canada because large-scale U.S. factories have a more urgent need for access to world markets.

T   F   10. If scale economies are important in many industries, then free international trade is likely to mean both cheaper products and a wider choice for consumers.

MULTIPLE CHOICE

1. One of the problems with barter is that it requires a "coincidence of wants." This means that
   a. everybody must want money
   b. everybody must want the same good
   c. at least two people must want the same good
   d. everybody must want my good, before I am able to exchange it
   e. for there to be an exchange between individuals A and B, individual A must want what B has, while B must want what A has

2. When a monetary system first replaces barter, it becomes possible for the first time to distinguish between
   a. a good and a service
   b. the buyer and the seller
   c. private enterpreneurs and the government
   d. owners of capital and workers
   e. all of the above

3. Money is said to represent "general purchasing power" because
   a. it can be used to buy any of the goods and services offered for sale
   b. the government guarantees its value
   c. the government is committed to accept money in payment of taxes
   d. Gresham's law no longer is valid
   e. Gresham's law applies to other goods, but not money

4. When we draw a diagram showing the circular flow of payments between households and businesses, the two major markets we show are
   a. goods and services
   b. capital and labour
   c. capital and land
   d. consumer goods and economic resources
   e. products made by private entrepreneurs, and those provided by the government

5. In the present-day Canadian economy, what would an economist consider to be the "medium of exchange"?

   a. supermarkets
   b. corner drug stores
   c. the Sear's catalogue
   d. real estate brokers
   e. 5-dollar bills

6. When the best-tasting cigarettes started to disappear from circulation in the prisoner-of-war camp, this was an example of
   a. economies of scale
   b. absolute advantage
   c. comparative advantage
   d. inflation
   e. Gresham's law

7. In the prisoner-of-war camp, in which cigarettes acted as money, suppose that the quantity of cigarettes coming into the camp remained constant, while the quantity of all other goods decreased. Then the most probable result would be
   a. a rise in the value of cigarettes, measured in terms of other items
   b. a fall in the prices of other goods, measured in terms of cigarettes
   c. inflation
   d. deflation
   e. bad money driving out good money

8. Suppose that a building supervisor can lay bricks more rapidly and better than a bricklayer. Then, considering only these two individuals, we may conclude that
   a. the bricklayer has an absolute advantage in bricklaying
   b. the supervisor has an absolute advantage in bricklaying
   c. the bricklayer has a comparative advantage in bricklaying
   d. the supervisor has a comparative advantage in bricklaying
   e. we can't tell which of the above is true without knowing how much bricks cost, compared to the wage for bricklayers

9. The theory of comparative advantage was put forward by
  a. Adam Smith
  b. John Maynard Keynes
  c. David Ricardo
  d. David Hume
  e. Karl Marx

10. Suppose that there are only two countries, A and B, and only two goods, food and clothing. If country A has a comparative advantage in the production of food, B is most likely to have a comparative advantage in
  a. food also
  b. clothing
  c. both food and clothing
  d. neither food nor clothing
  e. we don't have enough information to decide

11. Suppose 10 workers with 1 machine can produce 100 TV sets in a month, while 20 workers with 2 machines can produce 250 TV sets in a month. This is an example of
  a. technological efficiency
  b. allocative efficiency
  c. economies of scale
  d. comparative advantage
  e. absolute advantage

12. Suppose that (1) there are economies of scale in the production of each good, and (2) land and labour have specialized capabilities—for example, land and the climate give Brazil a comparative advantage in coffee. Then the gains from specialization will be
  a. larger than if either (1) or (2) had existed alone
  b. small, since (1) and (2) tend to offset each other
  c. negative, since the combination of (1) and (2) creates confusion
  d. about the same as with (1) alone, since (2) doesn't make much difference
  e. about the same as with (2) alone, since (1) doesn't make much difference

13. When tariffs among countries are reduced, this generally leads to gains from
  a. economies of scale
  b. wider use of money rather than barter
  c. comparative advantage
  d. **a.** and **b.**
  e. **a.** and **c.**

EXERCISES

1. This exercise illustrates the idea of comparative advantage. Assume the following. A doctor working on home repairs can fix a leaky faucet in 10 minutes. A plumber takes 15 minutes. Then the (doctor, plumber) has an absolute advantage in plumbing. The doctor's time is worth $80 per hour in the practice of medicine. The plumber is paid $20 per hour.

Suppose the doctor's house has six leaky faucets. If he fixes them himself, it will take _____ minutes. Thus, to fix the faucets, the doctor will use $ _____ worth of his time. If the plumber is hired to fix the faucets, he will take _____ minutes, which is (longer, shorter) than the doctor would take. The cost in this case is $ _____, which is (more, less) by $ _____ than if the doctor fixed the faucets himself. The (doctor, plumber) has a comparative advantage in plumbing.

2. Table 3.1 shows how many cars can be produced in a country with various amounts of inputs. Each unit of input represents a specific quantity of labour and capital. Table 3.2 provides similar information for TV sets. Table 3.1, by itself, illustrates the idea of (comparative advantage, absolute advantage, economies of scale, none of these). Table 3.2, by itself, illustrates the idea of (comparative advantage, absolute advantage, economies of scale, none of these).

Suppose that the economy has 5 units of inputs to be devoted to cars and TV sets. Plot the PPC for these 5 units of input in Figure 3.1. How is the shape of the PPC different from the PPCs in Chapter 2? _____. The opportunity cost of producing cars (increases, decreases, remains constant) as more are produced.

Table 3.1 Production of Cars

Number of cars (millions)	Units of input
1	1
3	2
6	3
12	4
20	5

Table 3.2 Production of TV Sets

Number of TV sets (millions)	Units of input
20	1
40	2
60	3
80	4
100	5

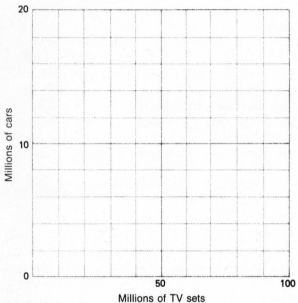

Figure 3.1

ESSAY QUESTIONS

1. The textbook explains why comparative advantage can mean that there are benefits from specialization and exchange. But it does not explain *why* specific people or nations might have a comparative advantage. How would you explain Saskatchewan's comparative advantage over New Brunswick in producing wheat? Why does Quebec have a comparative advantage over most American states in the production of wood-pulp and newsprint? Why does Taiwan have a comparative advantage in the production of transistor radios and TV sets?

2. Why do you think that most economists are usually in favour of reducing tariffs and other barriers to international trade? In the intense debate that preceded the signing of the 1989 Canada/United States Free Trade Agreement, many Canadians (including some economists) nevertheless opposed the removal of barriers to Canada-United States trade. What, do you think, were their reasons?

3. There are disadvantages associated with specialization as well as advantages. What are they?

ANSWERS

Important Terms: **1**d, **2**i, **3**f, **4**a, **5**j, **6**k, **7**h, **8**c, **9**e, **10**g, **11**b
True-False: **1**T, **2**F, **3**F, **4**T, **5**F, **6**F, **7**F, **8**T, **9**F, **10**T
Multiple Choice: **1**e, **2**b, **3**a, **4**d, **5**e, **6**e, **7**c, **8**b, **9**c, **10**b, **11**c, **12**a, **13**e
Exercises: **1.** doctor, 60, $80, 90, longer, $30, less, $50, plumber. **2.** economies of scale, none of these, it bows inward, decreases

ANSWERS TO SELECTED REVIEW QUESTIONS FROM THE TEXT

3-1. The simple answer to (a) and (b) is that we export those goods in whose production we have a comparative advantage, and import those goods for which our trading partners have a comparative advantage (that is, for which we have a comparative *dis*advantage).

In the case of an industry like cars (item (c)), economies of scale provide a reason for exporting some models and importing others, as discussed in the text.

3-3. One reason for greater specialization is the development of more specialized machinery. The advantage is more output. One possible disadvantage is the boredom that can come from producing only one narrow product.

3-4. Measuring "number of wills per week" on the vertical axis and "flowers planted per week" on the horizontal axis, the lawyer's PPC will be a straight line from 40 wills on the vertical axis to 800 flowers on the horizontal axis. It is different because it is a straight line.

Chapter 4

■ ■

Demand and Supply: The Market Mechanism

MAJOR PURPOSE

This chapter is one of the most important in the book. It introduces the concepts of *demand* and *supply*, which help us to understand what is happening in the market for a specific product. The demand curve illustrates how buyers respond to various possible prices: At lower prices, they buy more. On the other hand, sellers react negatively to low prices: They offer less for sale. This response of sellers is illustrated by the supply curve.

When drawing a demand or supply curve, we isolate the effect of *price alone* on the behaviour of buyers and sellers. Of course, many other things besides price can affect their behaviour. When we draw a demand or supply curve and look at the effect of price alone, we make the *ceteris paribus* assumption—that all these other things do not change. In cases where they do, in fact, change, we are no longer on a single demand or supply curve; the demand or supply curve *shifts*.

Other important concepts introduced in this chapter are the concepts of *equilibrium, surplus* and *shortage,* and *substitutes* and *complementary goods.*

LEARNING OBJECTIVES

After you have studied this chapter in the textbook and study guide, you should be able to
- Explain why the supply curve slopes upward to the right
- Explain why a price that begins away from equilibrium will move to equilibrium
- List and explain three things that can shift the demand curve and four that can shift the supply curve
- Give one example each of two goods that are (1) substitutes in use, (2) complements in use, (3) substitutes in production, and (4) complements in production. In each case, you should be able to explain why they fit into the category.
- Explain the distinction between product markets and markets for factors of production
- Explain how the factor markets can help answer the question, *For whom?*
- Explain how changes in factor markets can affect what happens in a product market, and vice versa
- Explain the main strengths and main shortcomings of the market mechanism as a way of answering the questions, *What?*, *How?*, and *For whom?*

HIGHLIGHTS OF THE CHAPTER

In every economy, some mechanism is needed to decide three major questions: *What* will be produced? *How* will it be produced? And *for whom* will it be produced? There are two major ways of answering these questions: (1) through the market—that is, through voluntary exchanges between buyers and sellers, and (2) through governmental decision making. (Other ways are sometimes used—for example, in a family or in a monastery. But we are not primarily interested in these alternatives.)

All nations have some reliance on markets and some reliance on governmental decision making. However, there are substantial differences among nations. In Canada and the United States, the market is the most important mechanism, although the government does play a significant role in modifying the outcome of the market. In the U.S.S.R., government plays a much more central role, although there is some reliance on markets.

The central feature of a market is *price*. Different prices for different goods provide *incentives* for producers to make some goods rather than others, and incentives for consumers to purchase cheap goods rather than expensive ones. Prices also provide *signals* and *information* to buyers and sellers. For example, the willingness of buyers to pay a high price acts as a signal to producers, showing that people are eager to obtain the product.

To study how buyers respond to different prices, we use a *demand curve* or *demand schedule*. This curve or schedule shows the quantity of a specific good that buyers would be willing and able to purchase at various different prices. The demand curve slopes downward to the right, illustrating that people are more eager to buy at lower prices. A major reason is that, at a lower price, people have an incentive to *switch* away from other products and buy the product whose price is lower instead.

On the other side of the market, the supply curve shows how much sellers would be willing to offer at various prices. It slopes upward to the right, because sellers will be increasingly eager to sell as the price rises. Again, the willingness to *switch* is an important reason for the slope. If the price of a good is higher, firms have an incentive to drop other products, and make more of this good instead.

What happens in the market depends on both demand and supply. To find the *equilibrium* price and quantity, we put the demand and supply curves together, to find where they intersect. At this price, the quantity offered by sellers is equal to the quantity which buyers want to purchase. There is no unfulfilled demand to pull prices up, nor any excess offers to pull prices down.

When the price is not at its equilibrium, there are pressures for it to change. If the price is below its equilibrium,

for example, there are eager buyers who are unable to find the good for sale. In other words, there is a *shortage*. Producers notice this and conclude that they can sell at a higher price. The price rises to its equilibrium level. On the other hand, if the price is initially above its equilibrium, there is a *surplus*. Eager sellers are unable to find buyers. They are willing to sell at a lower price. The price falls to its equilibrium.

When we draw a demand or supply curve, we are looking at the way in which buyers and sellers respond to price, and to price *alone*. In practice, of course, buyers and sellers are influenced by many other things than the price of the good—for example, buyers generally purchase more when their incomes rise, and sellers are less willing to sell when the costs of their inputs rise. But these other things are held constant when a single demand or supply curve is drawn. This is the important assumption of *ceteris paribus*, that other things do not change. If they do change, the demand or supply curve shifts. For example, an increase in income generally causes a rightward shift in the whole demand curve. However, in the case of inferior goods, the demand curve shifts left; when people can afford better alternatives, they choose them instead.

If the demand curve shifts to the right while the supply curve remains stable, then both price and quantity will increase. On the other hand, if the supply curve shifts to the right while the demand curve remains stable, then quantity will increase but price will fall. In brief, *a change in demand makes price and quantity change in the same direction, whereas a change in supply makes price and quantity move in opposite directions*. In practice, of course, many things can happen at once; often the demand and supply curves both shift. In this case, it becomes more difficult to predict what will happen.

Supply and demand theory is often used to study the market for a single good. However, there are strong connections among markets. When a price changes in one market, it can change conditions in other markets. For example, an increase in the price of gasoline in the 1970s caused a decline in the demand for large cars. This is an example of *complementary goods*—large cars and gasoline are used *together*. When the price of gasoline increases, the demand for large cars shifts left.

Whereas gasoline and cars are complements, some other products—such as bus tickets and train tickets—are *substitutes*. A person wanting to travel to the next city can go either by train or by bus. The higher is the train fare, the more people will use busses instead. Thus, a higher price of train tickets causes the demand for bus tickets to shift to the right.

Goods may also be substitutes or complements in

production. Substitutes in production are goods which use the same inputs; the inputs can be used to produce either the one good or the other. For example, land can be used to produce either wheat or corn. If there is a crop failure abroad and an increase in North American exports of wheat, the price of wheat will be bid up. Farmers will be encouraged to switch out of the production of corn and produce additional wheat instead. The supply curve for corn will shift to the left.

On the other hand, complements are produced together. For example, wheat and straw are produced together. If the price of wheat is bid up, more wheat will be produced. In the process, more straw will be produced as a by-product. The supply curve of straw will shift to the right.

The question of *what* will be produced is decided primarily in the product market. To throw light on the other two questions—*how*? and *for whom*?—we look first at the markets for inputs. For example, the market for labour helps to answer these two questions. If the demand for labour is high compared to its supply, then wage rates will be high. Thus, wage rates are much higher in Canada than in India because there are fewer workers for each unit of land and capital in Canada. As a result of the high wage, producers in Canada have an incentive to use only a little labour, and substitute capital instead. In an Indian factory, in contrast, many more things are done by hand because of the low wage rate. The wage rate not only helps to determine how things are produced, but it also helps to determine who gets the product. Because wage rates are high in Canada, a typical worker here can buy and consume many more products than the Indian worker.

Observe that high wage rates affect what the worker can buy; with high wages, workers are more likely to buy TV sets and homes. This means that wages—determined in the factor markets in the lower box in Figure 4-8 in the textbook—have an impact on the demand for TV sets, homes, and other products in the upper box. Thus, there are important connections among markets.

Finally, this chapter summarizes the strengths and weaknesses of the market as a mechanism for answering the three central questions—*What?, How?,* and *For whom?* The strong points of the market are that (1) it encourages producers to make what consumers want, (2) it provides people with an incentive to acquire useful skills, (3) it encourages consumers to conserve scarce goods, (4) it encourages producers to conserve scarce resources, (5) it provides a high degree of economic freedom, and (6) it provides buyers and sellers with information on market conditions, including local conditions.

The market mechanism is also subject to major criticisms: (1) some people may be left in desperate poverty, (2) markets don't work in the case of public goods such as defence and the police, (3) monopolies and oligopolies may have the power to keep production down and keep prices up, (4) the market does not provide a strong incentive for producers to limit pollution and other negative side effects, (5) a market economy may be unstable (although government policies will not necessarily increase stability), and (6) producers may simply be satisfying a want that they have created in the first place through advertising.

To evaluate the market, it is important to compare it with the alternatives that exist in fact, not with some ideal, unattainable system. The textbook outlines a few of the problems which can arise when the government sets prices—in particular, the problem of black markets and shortages. A number of countries that have interfered very heavily in economic activity—such as the Soviet Union—have run into severe problems, including shortages.

IMPORTANT TERMS: MATCH THE COLUMNS

Match each term in the first column with the corresponding phrase in the second column.

_____	1. Capitalism	**a.**	All the producers of a single good
_____	2. Monopoly	**b.**	If price of A rises, demand for B increases
_____	3. Oligopoly	**c.**	Surplus
_____	4. Perfect competition	**d.**	Free enterprise
_____	5. Industry	**e.**	Demand for this declines as income rises
_____	6. Firm	**f.**	Nothing else changes
_____	7. Excess supply	**g.**	Goods used together
_____	8. Excess demand	**h.**	Market with only one seller
_____	9. Inferior good	**i.**	Where every buyer and seller is a price taker
_____	10. Complementary goods	**j.**	Shortage
_____	11. Substitutes	**k.**	A single business organization, such as Canadian General Electric
_____	12. Ceteris paribus	**l.**	Market dominated by a few sellers

TRUE-FALSE

T   F   1. Perfect competition exists only when the government fixes the price, so that no single buyer or seller is able to influence the price of the good.

T   F   2. Perfect competition will not exist in a market if there is only one seller, or if there is only one buyer.

T   F   3. In a perfectly competitive industry, every buyer and seller takes the quantity as given, and is left with only a pricing decision.

T   F   4. Even if there are many buyers, imperfect competition can exist in a market.

T   F   5. Even if there are many sellers, imperfect competition can exist in a market.

T   F   6. In a capitalist economy, most of the capital equipment is owned by the government.

T   F   7. A surplus drives the price down; a shortage drives the price up.

T   F   8. If the price of wheat increases, the supply curve of straw will probably shift to the right.

T   F   9. The demand curve for Pepsi-Cola will probably shift to the right if the price of Coke rises.

T   F   10. If the price of paper increases, the supply curve of books will probably shift to the right.

T   F   11. If demand increases while supply decreases, the price will increase.

T   F   12. If the demand curve shifts to the right, the result will be an increase in the quantity sold and an increase in the market price.

T   F   13. If both the demand and supply curves for a product shift to the right, we can expect the quantity sold to increase, but we cannot be sure whether the price will rise or fall.

T   F   14. One essential characteristic of a free enterprise economy is that the government make it easier to enter businesses freely by subsidizing new businesses.

T   F   15. Factor markets are different from the markets for most goods, in that goods markets are generally perfectly competitive, while the markets for factors are usually monopolized.

MULTIPLE CHOICE

1. Economists sometimes speak of a "free" market. By "free," they mean
   a. prices are low
   b. people do not have to pay admission to the marketplace
   c. transactions take place with little or no government interference
   d. the government is not a buyer or seller in the market
   e. there is perfect competition in that market

2. The Canadian government uses four major ways to influence what will be produced, how, and for whom. It uses every one of the following except one. Which one does not belong on this list?
   a. spending
   b. taxes
   c. regulation
   d. comprehensive central planning
   e. public enterprises

3. What is the most important characteristic of perfect competition?
   a. each seller has at least one powerful competitor to worry about
   b. there is at least one powerful, efficient producer who acts to keep prices down

   c. every buyer can go to at least three or four sellers to see who has the lowest price
   d. every buyer and seller is a price taker; none has any power to set price
   e. there must be many buyers, and at least three or four sellers

4. A market with one seller and a few buyers is an example of
   a. monopoly
   b. oligopoly
   c. perfect competition
   d. technological inefficiency
   e. a black market

5. It is most accurate to speak of Abitibi Paper Ltd. as
   a. a plant
   b. a firm
   c. an industry
   d. a monopoly
   e. a perfect competitor

6. A surplus of turnips exists when
   a. turnip production is lower than last year
   b. turnip production is higher than last year
   c. turnip production exceeds the production of all other vegetables combined

  d. the quantity of turnips demanded exceeds the quantity supplied
  e. the quantity of turnips supplied exceeds the quantity demanded

7. Suppose that a surplus exists in a market. Then we may conclude that
  a. the price is below the equilibrium
  b. the price is above the equilibrium
  c. the government has imposed a price ceiling
  d. the quantity demanded has decreased
  e. the quantity supplied has increased

8. When we draw the demand curve for a product, we assume that
  a. there are many sellers
  b. there are only a few sellers
  c. all "supply shifters" are held constant
  d. all "demand shifters" are held constant
  e. both **c.** and **d.**

9. When incomes increase, the demand curve for an individual good
  a. usually shifts down
  b. always shifts down
  c. usually shifts to the right
  d. always shifts to the right
  e. doesn't move, since only price affects demand

10. Suppose that we know that an increase in the price of good A will cause a rightward shift in the demand curve for good B. Then we may conclude that
  a. producers of A and B use the same set of inputs
  b. consumers of A and B have the same levels of income
  c. consumers of A and B have different incomes
  d. A and B are complementary goods
  e. A and B are substitutes

11. Tennis rackets and tennis balls are
  a. substitutes
  b. complementary goods
  c. inferior goods
  d. independent goods
  e. monopolistic goods

12. Apples and textbooks are
  a. substitutes
  b. complementary goods
  c. inferior goods
  d. independent goods
  e. monopolistic goods

13. Which illustrate best the idea of substitutes in production?
  a. copper and aluminum
  b. wheat and barley
  c. wheat and bananas
  d. beef and leather
  e. cream and sugar

14. Peanuts and tobacco can be grown on similar land. Therefore, they are
  a. substitutes in production
  b. joint products
  c. inferior goods
  d. normal goods
  e. an oligopoly

15. Suppose that the demand for beef increases. This is most likely to cause
  a. a rightward shift in the supply curve for beef
  b. a leftward shift in the supply curve for beef
  c. a fall in the price of beef
  d. a fall in the price of leather
  e. an upward shift in the demand for leather

16. In a typical market
  a. an increase in demand, with no change in supply, will result in a fall in price
  b. an increase in demand, with no change in supply, will result in a decrease in quantity
  c. an increase in demand, with no change in supply, will result in an increase in both price and quantity
  d. an increase in supply, with no change in demand, will result in a decrease in quantity
  e. an increase in supply, with no change in demand, will result in an increase in price

17. Suppose that, between year 1 and year 2, the demand curve and the supply curve for wheat both shift to the right. From this information, we may conclude that, in year 2,
  a. the quantity of wheat sold will be larger, while the price will be higher
  b. the quantity of wheat sold will be larger, while the price will be lower
  c. the quantity of wheat sold will be larger, while we do not have enough information to tell if the price will be higher or lower
  d. the quantity of wheat sold will be smaller, while we do not have enough information to tell if the price will be higher or lower
  e. we do not have enough information to tell what will happen to either the price or the quantity

18. Incomes are determined primarily in the markets for
  a. goods
  b. services
  c. factors of production
  d. machinery
  e. parts

19. The advantages of the market mechanism (as contrasted to government controls) as a way of deciding What?, How?, and For whom? include
  a. prices provide incentives for producers to make what the public wants

b. prices provide incentives for producers to conserve scarce resources

c. prices provide incentives for consumers to conserve scarce goods

d. high wages in skilled occupations act as an incentive for workers to undertake training

e. all of the above

20. A black market is most likely to exist when
   a. the government controls the price of a good

b. the supply of a good is controlled by a monopolist

c. the supply of a good is controlled by two or three producers

d. the government imposes an excise tax on a good

e. the government urges producers to produce more to promote the general welfare of the public

EXERCISES

1. Using the demand schedule in the first two columns of the table below, plot the demand and supply curves in Figure 4.1. Label the axes and mark in appropriate numbers on each axis. Then fill in the last column of the table.
   a. The equilibrium quantity is _____.
   b. The equilibrium price is _____.
   c. At the equilibrium price, what is the surplus or shortage shown in the last column? _____. Does this confirm that this price is an equilibrium?

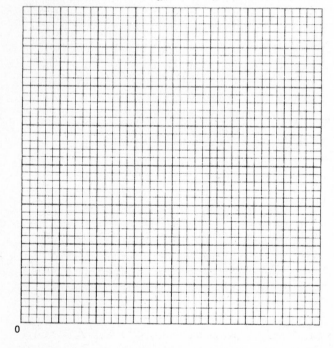

0

Figure 4.1

d. Now suppose that the government sets a price of 60 cents. At this price, there will be a (surplus, shortage) of _____.

2. Figure 4.2 illustrates some of the issues that arise when the government undertakes price supports (for example, in agriculture). **D** shows the demand curve, and **S₁** the supply curve. Initially, the equilibrium quantity is _____ million bushels, and the price is _____. Now suppose that the government passes a rule that says that wheat cannot be sold at a price less than P_3. The result of this law will be a (surplus, shortage) amounting to _____ million bushels.

If all the government does is set a high price, not all wheat farmers will be better off. Those who are better off will be those who (cut back production, sell their wheat at the high price). On the other hand, some will be worse off, specifically those who (are unable to sell their wheat at the high price, sell their wheat at a low price). To ensure that wheat farmers are better off, the government can (buy the surplus wheat, reduce the price to P_1).

Now, suppose that the government undertakes irrigation projects to help agriculture in dry areas. This will cause an increase in supply from **S₁** to **S₂**, and the (surplus, shortage) of wheat will (increase, decrease) to _____ million bushels. The government will find the costs of its price support program (increasing, decreasing). If it now eliminates the price support, the free market price will settle at _____.

Price of Hamburgers	Quantity Demanded (thousands per week)	Quantity Supplied (thousands per week)	Surplus (+) or Shortage (−)
$1.40	200	700	
$1.20	240	600	
$1.00	300	500	
$0.80	400	400	
$0.60	600	300	
$0.50	800	250	

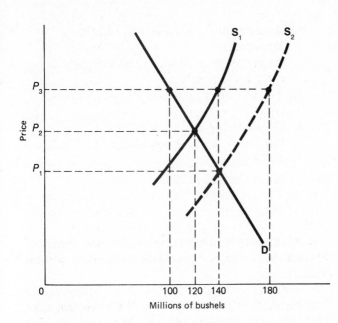

Figure 4.2

3. Suppose that supply is given by the equation:

$$Q = -30 + 4P$$

This supply is plotted in Figure 4.3 in the following way. First, choose some convenient value for P, such as 10. Put this value into the equation to get $Q = -30 + 40 = 10$. This means that when $P = 10$, $Q = 10$, so that point A is on the supply "curve." Then, choose another value of P, say, 15. Substituting this into the equation, we find that the corresponding $Q = $ _____. This is plotted as point B. The supply relationship is a straight line; there are no squared terms or other reasons for supply to bend. Thus, with the two points A and B, we can draw the straight-line supply S_1.

a. Suppose that demand is also a straight line:

$$Q = 20 - P$$

Then, if $P = 15$, $Q = $ _____, and if $P = 5$, $Q = $ _____. Plot demand in Figure 4.3 and label it D_1. On this figure, we see that the equilibrium price is _____ and the equilibrium quantity _____. Confirm these figures by solving the two equations algebraically, to find P and Q.

b. Suppose now that income increases and demand consequently increases, with 15 more units being demanded at each price. Thus, the new demand is

$$Q = 35 - P$$

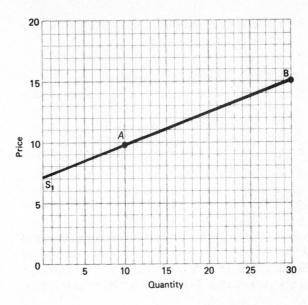

Figure 4.3

To plot this new demand, we find two points. For example, if $P = 15$, $Q = $ _____, and if $P = 5$, $Q = $ _____. Plot the new equilibrium demand, labelling it D_2. At the new equilibrium, $P = $ _____ and $Q = $ _____. Again, confirm these numbers by solving the demand and supply equations. The price has (increased, decreased), and the quantity has (increased, decreased) as a result of this increase in demand.

c. Now, suppose we are back with the original demand, D_1, but that supply is now:

$$Q = -10 + 2P$$

If $P = 10$, $Q = $ _____, and if $P = 15$, $Q = $ _____. Plot this new supply and label it S_2. With supply S_2 and demand D_1, the equilibrium price is _____, while quantity is _____. Again, confirm these numbers by solving the demand and supply equations.

d. Finally, suppose that demand shifts from D_1 to D_2, while supply remains at S_2. At the new equilibrium $P = $ _____ and $Q = $ _____. When the demand curve shifted this time, why is it that the price rose more, and the quantity less, than in part **b**?

Answer: _____.

ESSAY QUESTIONS

1. A demand or supply curve applies to a specific time and a specific location. For example, the market for maple syrup in London, Ontario, is not the same thing as the market for maple syrup in Winnipeg, Manitoba. Would you expect the price of maple syrup in these two cities to be similar? Precisely the same? Explain.

2. Suppose that, as a result of an increase in the number of pancake eaters in Winnipeg, there were an increase in the demand for maple syrup in that city. If you were an all-powerful social planner, you would probably want to persuade people in London to give up some of their maple syrup in order to provide for the higher demand in Winnipeg. What sort of rationing scheme might you devise to accomplish this goal? How would you know how much to allocate to each family? How large a staff do you think you would need?

Suppose, alternatively, that you allowed market forces to work freely. What would happen to the price of maple syrup in London, Ontario? What would happen to the quantity? How would the changing conditions in Lon-

don affect the supply curve for maple syrup in Winnipeg? What would happen to the price of maple syrup in Winnipeg? To the quantity? Draw demand and supply curves for London and Winnipeg to illustrate what is happening. Would your intentions as a social planner be carried out by the market instead? Which policy—rationing or the market—works more efficiently? Are there any disadvantages to the more efficient system?

3. The prices printed on a restaurant menu apply whether the restaurant is crowded or half empty on any particular evening. If you ran a restaurant,

   a. would you charge higher prices on Friday and Saturday evenings, when the restaurant is crowded, than on other evenings?

   b. would you charge higher prices during the evening than for an identical meal at lunch? Why or why not? (Or, under what circumstances might you?)

   c. Does McDonald's behave in the way you have suggested? How do you explain that?

ANSWERS

Important Terms: 1d, 2h, 3l, 4i, 5a, 6k, 7c, 8j, 9e, 10g, 11b, 12f
True-False: 1F, 2T, 3F, 4T, 5T, 6F, 7T, 8T, 9T, 10F, 11T, 12T, 13T, 14F, 15F
Multiple Choice: 1c, 2d, 3d, 4a, 5b, 6e, 7b, 8d, 9c, 10e, 11b, 12d, 13b, 14a, 15d, 16c, 17c, 18c, 19e, 20a
Exercises: **1a.** 400, **b.** \$0.80, **c.** zero, yes, **d.** shortage, 300
2. 120, P_2, surplus, 40, sell their wheat at the high price, are unable to sell their wheat at the high price, buy the surplus wheat, surplus, increase, 80, increasing, P_1
3. 30, **a.** 5, 15, 10, 10, **b.** 20, 30, 13, 22, increased, increased, **c.** 10, 20, 10, 10, **d.** 15, 20, because S_2 is steeper than S_1.

ANSWERS TO SELECTED REVIEW QUESTIONS FROM THE TEXT

4-1. When there is a freeze on the coffee plantations, the supply of coffee shifts to the left, causing the price to rise. Because tea and coffee are substitutes, the rise in the price of coffee causes a rightward shift in the demand for tea. This causes an increase in the price of tea. The effects are the same as those shown in Figure 4-7.

4-2. Some other relevant questions in deciding careers are these: Is a job interesting? Does it provide satisfaction? Are the surroundings pleasant? Does the job offer prestige? Do you get to meet interesting people? Are you likely to get along with your colleagues? Is the job safe?

4-3. (a) The supply will shift to the left. The demand will also shift to the left, to the extent that social pressures mean less drinking.

(b) The demand for and supply of funds will likewise shift left. Profitability may go up or down, depending on whether the demand or supply shifts more.

4-4. The supply will shift left or upward. Suppliers will not be willing to offer the item unless they are compensated for the risk of prison. The demand is likely to shift to the left, too, although we cannot be certain. (The thrill of doing something mildly illegal may appeal to some users.) The quantity will therefore probably fall, and the price will probably rise. The money incomes of sellers will probably increase (although their risk-adjusted returns will probably fall, unless there is a perverse outward shift of the demand curve).

Chapter 5

■ ■
The Economic Role of the Government

MAJOR PURPOSE

The major objective of this chapter is to explain how the government affects the economy. It does so in four ways: spending, taxation, regulation, and the operation of public enterprises.

There are a number of reasons for government intervention in the economy. (1) The government provides *public goods*—that is, goods that cannot be provided by the private sector because everyone can enjoy them, regardless of who pays for them. An example is police protection; we all gain the benefits from an orderly society, whether we pay taxes or not. (2) The government can control or discourage externalities, such as pollution. Free markets don't work very well in the control of polluting industries, since they provide no incentive to keep pollution down. (3) The government provides merit goods—such as education--that it considers particularly important for the society. (4) The government provides programs to help the poor. (5) Another important objective of the government is to promote stability. Badly designed policies may lead to rapid inflations and deep depressions. An important objective—to be considered in Parts 2 to 5, is to avoid such destabilizing actions.

LEARNING OBJECTIVES

After you have studied this chapter in the textbook and study guide, you should be able to
- Describe the four ways in which the government affects the economy
- Describe the major programs of the three levels of government
- Explain the difference between government spending for goods and services, and transfer payments
- Explain the difference between a progressive and a regressive tax, and give an example of each
- Describe the five major reasons for government intervention in the economy
- Explain the role and significance of Crown corporations in the Canadian economy
- Explain the objectives that should be kept in mind when designing a tax system
- Explain the difference between the *benefit principle* and the *ability to pay principle*
- Explain why the Canadian tax system is less progressive than we might guess by looking at the income tax schedule
- Describe the major elements of Canada's federal tax reform that was begun in the late 1980s

HIGHLIGHTS OF THE CHAPTER

The government affects the economy in four major ways: (1) spending, (2) taxation, (3) regulation, and (4) public enterprises.

Spending

In dollar terms, government spending has risen very rapidly in Canada, from about $4 billion per year in 1950 to $267 billion by 1988. However, if we look at the size of the government relative to the economy, we get a much less spectacular picture. For example, government *purchases of goods and services* have increased relatively slowly as a percentage of GDP since the mid-1940s, and the percentage remains well below what it was during World War II. Nevertheless, if transfer payments to individuals are included, government spending has risen substantially as a percentage of GDP in recent decades; in the mid-1980s this percentage surpassed its wartime peak. Thus, most of the increase in the relative size of government reflects the increase in transfer payments such as Old Age Security and Unemployment Insurance benefits, family allowances, and so on.

A large part of government spending at the federal level consists of revenue transfers to *provincial* governments, both as general equalization payments (to provinces with a relatively small tax base), and as conditional transfers for specific programs, such as health care and post-secondary education. Provincial governments, in turn, transfer substantial amounts to local governments.

Taxes

The primary purpose of taxes is to raise the revenue to finance government spending. The personal income tax is the largest revenue raiser, by a large margin, for the federal and provincial governments. Other important sources are the corporate income tax, sales taxes, and local government property taxes. At the federal level, unemployment insurance contributions and mandatory contributions to the Canada/Quebec Pension Plans represent another important revenue source.

On most income—up to a maximum of about $30,000 per year in 1988—a "tax" such as the worker's portion of the unemployment insurance contribution is *proportional*: It is calculated as a fixed percentage of income. However, no contributions are collected on incomes over the maximum, which means that, in this range, the "tax" is *regressive*. That is, it is a smaller percentage of an income of, say, $60,000, than of an income of $30,000. Nevertheless, the impact (*incidence*) of the overall sys-

tem of unemployment insurance, mandatory government pension plans, and other transfer payments, is *progressive* because the net benefits to lower-income people are greater, as a percentage of their incomes, than the benefits to people with higher incomes.

Unlike the "tax" rates for the unemployment insurance contributions, the income tax rates are progressive: The tax rate on high incomes is generally larger than the tax rate on low incomes. However, the overall tax system is less progressive than the tax rates suggest, both because of the existence of regressive components such as unemployment insurance contributions, and because of "loopholes"—that is, special rules in the tax law that allow certain kinds of income to be taxed at a lower rate, or escape tax altogether. The term "loophole" implies that these rules are undesirable, and there is considerable debate over what is desirable and what is not. One item sometimes put on the list of loopholes—the fact that the government does not levy any tax on the implicit return on homeowners' equity—has strong political support and is rarely mentioned in the debate on tax reform.

Other than raising revenues, there are a number of other objectives that should be considered in designing a tax code.

1. One objective is *equity,* or fairness. As we suggested in Chapter 1, there is some controversy over just what is fair. Nevertheless, discussions of fairness usually begin with one of two approaches to taxation:

a. *Ability to pay.* According to this idea, taxes should be imposed according to income or wealth; people with high incomes should pay more because they are better able to do so. The progressive income tax is one application of this principle.

b. *Benefit principle.* According to this idea, taxes should depend on who benefits most from government programs. Those who benefit most should pay the most.

2. *Simplicity* is an important objective in the tax system. Discussions of tax reform in recent years have often centred around the criticism that the income tax has become hopelessly complicated.

3. *Neutrality.* As a starting point, most economists believe that the tax system should be designed to disturb market forces as little as possible. It should not capriciously introduce incentives for people to change their behaviour in order to avoid taxes.

4. *Meeting social objectives.* Nevertheless, in some cases it may be desirable to encourage people to change their behaviour. For example, in order to encourage people to give to charities, the government allows people to deduct their contributions to charities from their taxable income. Taxes may also be used to discourage businesses from polluting the air or water.

In the 1980s, efforts were made to improve the federal tax system in Canada through a number of reforms. While some of the specific measures were controversial, there was widespread support for the basic underlying principles of the reform program: that the tax base should be broadened by reducing the number of loopholes; that income tax rates should be reduced; and that there should be more emphasis on *tax credits* (specific dollar reductions in the amount of tax payable) than on *deductions* from taxable income, as a way of reducing the tax burden on various categories of individuals.

Regulation

More direct means are available for encouraging some behaviour, and discouraging other activities. For example, there are regulations limiting the amount of pollutants that factories are allowed to discharge into the air and water. In the early days of regulation about a hundred years ago, the government took steps to discourage monopolistic behaviour by the industrial cartels— "combines"—that were being organized at the time. Other regulations are aimed at protecting the safety of workers and discouraging discrimination.

Government regulations are generally aimed at reducing major problems. Nevertheless, regulation has been a source of controversy. There are two major problems with regulation: (1) regulatory agencies may require major reporting efforts from business, and sometimes generate expensive red tape of little value; and (2) regulatory agencies sometimes come under the control of the industry they are supposedly regulating. The government may become the means for an industry gaining oligopolistic or monopolistic power.

Public Enterprise

Another important way in which the government influences the economy is through *Crown corporations*, government-owned firms that derive much of their revenue from selling goods or services to the public. In the 1980s, it was estimated that Crown corporations were responsible for as much as 15% of all capital investment in Canada.

Federal and provincial governments establish Crown corporations for a variety of reasons: as an alternative to regulation in the case of a *natural monopoly*; as a way of ensuring the provision of certain services (such as transportation and communications) to communities that would be inadequately served by private firms; to stimulate investment in risky ventures involving new technol-

ogy. Sometimes Crown corporations are created when the government takes over a financially ailing firm as a way of protecting employment opportunities in particular communities.

A possible problem with Crown corporations has to do with lack of *accountability*. If the political control over the corporation's managers is weak, there may be inadequate control over costs and some corporations may end up running deficits far higher than can be justified by the special objectives they are supposed to serve. One possible way of overcoming this problem is *privatization*— that is, selling Crown corporations to private shareholders. In the 1980s, a number of instances of privatization occurred at both the provincial and federal levels.

Reasons For Government Activity

The government becomes involved in the economy for many reasons. Here are the five most important:

1. Governments often provide goods and services which the private sector would otherwise fail to provide or would provide only with difficulty and at a high cost. Roads are one example. If the roads within a city were run by private entrepreneurs, motorists would have to stop frequently to pay tolls. National defence is unlikely to be organized and paid for privately. There is a problem of *free riders*—people who let others pay because they will reap the benefits even if they don't contribute. If people benefit whether they pay or not, we have an example of a *public good*.

2. The government may intervene when *side effects* prevent people from making socially desirable decisions. For example, vaccinations protect not only the individuals who are vaccinated; they also protect the public from communicable diseases. Smallpox has been eradicated by the combined action of governments and international organizations. Benefits that go to people other than those who are vaccinated (or their doctors) are known as *external benefits*. There also can be *external costs,* such as the cost to people downwind from a polluting factory. Just as the government encourages activities with external benefits—such as vaccinations—so it may discourage those with external costs.

3. The government may provide *merit* goods or services, such as education, that it considers very desirable from a social viewpoint.

4. The government has programs to *help the poor*; for example, subsidized housing and welfare programs.

5. The government may increase or decrease its expenditures in order to *promote economic stability*. For example, during a period of high unemployment, it may undertake public projects in order to provide jobs.

IMPORTANT TERMS: MATCH THE COLUMNS

Match each term in the first column with the corresponding phrase in the second column.

_____	1. Transfer payment		**a.**	Tax paid divided by income
_____	2. Progressive tax		**b.**	Federal payments to provinces with a low tax base
_____	3. Proportional tax		**c.**	One that takes the same percentage of high and low incomes
_____	4. Average tax rate		**d.**	Sale of government-owned businesses
_____	5. Marginal tax rate		**e.**	One that takes a higher percentage of high incomes
_____	6. Deficit		**f.**	People get the benefit of this, regardless of who pays
_____	7. Equalization payments		**g.**	Expenditure by government, for which government receives no good or service in return
_____	8. Conditional transfers		**h.**	Specified reduction in amount of income tax payable
_____	9. Privatization		**i.**	Tax which leaves market forces undisturbed
_____	10. Externality		**j.**	Side effect of production or consumption
_____	11. Public good		**k.**	Specified reduction in taxable income
_____	12. Neutral tax		**l.**	Excess of expenditures over revenues
_____	13. Tax credit		**m.**	Percentage of additional income paid in tax
_____	14. Tax deduction		**n.**	Federal contributions to specific provincial programs

TRUE-FALSE

T F **1.** Payments to the unemployed are a form of transfer payment.

T F **2.** If we include all levels of government (federal, provincial, and local), then government spending on goods and services is more, as a fraction of GDP, than it was even at the height of World War II in 1943/44.

T F **3.** Since 1960, transfer expenditures by the federal government have risen, both as a fraction of total federal government expenditures and as a fraction of GDP.

T F **4.** Public enterprise in Canada is about the same size (in relation to the economy as a whole) as public enterprise in the United States.

T F **5.** A tax is progressive if high-income people pay a larger percentage of their income than low-income people.

T F **6.** Suppose that a province imposes a tax of 5% on all income. Because it "hits the poor as hard as the rich," such a tax is regressive.

T F **7.** Suppose that the government imposes a federal sales tax of 7%. Because high-income people buy more than low-income people, they will pay more sales tax. Therefore, such a tax is progressive.

T F **8.** According to the benefit principle of taxation, government expenditures should be undertaken whenever they benefit the public.

T F **9.** According to the ability to pay principle of taxation, only those who have enough income that they are able to save should be required to pay taxes.

T F **10.** The term "merit good" is used in describing a feature of the British economy. Specifically, a "merit good" is one which the upper class consumes more heavily than the lower classes.

T F **11.** Since poor people are more likely than rich people to live in rented housing, the non-taxation of the implicit return on homeowners' equity makes the Canadian tax system less progressive.

MULTIPLE CHOICE

1. Which of the following is the best example of government expenditure for goods or services?
  a. salaries of judges
  b. Old Age Security benefits paid to the elderly
  c. social assistance payments to poor people
  d. unemployment compensation
  e. the progressive income tax

2. Of the following categories of expenditure for the federal government, which two are the largest: "Debt charges" (interest on the public debt); "Protection of Persons and Property" (national defence, etc.); "Education"; "Social Services" (including transfers to individuals, etc.)?
  a. debt charges and protection of persons and property
  b. protection of persons and property and social services
  c. debt charges and education
  d. debt charges and social services
  e. education and social services

3. The two largest categories of expenditures for provincial and local governments combined are
  a. health care and interest
  b. health care and education
  c. education and social services
  d. health care and social services
  e. interest and social services

4. Over the past three decades, transfer payments by the federal government have been rising as a percentage of GDP. From this we may conclude that
  a. transfer payments have become too large
  b. transfer payments may or may not be too large now, but they were too small in 1960
  c. transfer payments are still too small, since they continue to rise
  d. transfer payments will sooner or later bankrupt the government
  e. we don't have enough information to come to any of the above conclusions

5. In 1988, each person over the age of 65 was allowed to subtract about $550 when computing the amount they had to pay in federal income tax. This illustrates
  a. that the federal income tax is progressive
  b. the benefit principle of taxation
  c. a tax deduction
  d. a transfer payment
  e. a tax credit

6. Of the following, which provides the largest source of revenue for the federal government?
  a. sales taxes
  b. corporate income taxes
  c. personal income taxes
  d. customs duties
  e. excise taxes on cigarettes and alcohol

Table 1   Income Tax Rates (hypothetical)

Income	Tax
$10,000	$1,000
$20,000	$3,000
$30,000	$5,000

7. For a person with an income of $20,000, the *average* tax rate in Table 1 is
  a. 10%
  b. 15%
  c. 20%
  d. 30%
  e. we don't have enough information to tell what the average tax rate is

8. For a person with an income of $20,000, the *marginal* tax rate in Table 1 is
  a. 10%
  b. 15%
  c. 20%
  d. 30%
  e. 50%

9. If a tax takes $1,000 from someone with an income of $10,000, and $2,000 from someone with an income of $50,000, that tax is
  a. neutral
  b. progressive
  c. regressive
  d. proportional
  e. marginal

10. If unemployment insurance contributions are considered as a tax, then it would be characterized as
  a. neutral
  b. marginal
  c. mildly progressive
  d. highly progressive
  e. regressive

11. Last year, the government's debt increased by the amount of last year's
  a. tax revenues − expenditures
  b. interest payments
  c. transfer payments
  d. surplus
  e. deficit

12. During the past decade, the federal government has
  a. run a surplus every year
  b. run a surplus most years, but not every one

c. had about the same number of surpluses as deficits

d. run a deficit most years, but not every one

e. run a deficit every year

13. Prior to 1977, the federal government reimbursed half the total spending of each provincial government for health care and post-secondary education. This was an example of

a. government provision of public goods

b. equalization payments

c. unconditional federal-provincial transfers

d. the federal government's laissez-faire approach to economic policy

e. conditional federal-provincial transfers

14. According to the "neutrality" principle of taxation

a. income taxes should be progressive

b. taxes should be imposed only on goods about which people are neutral (that is, neither very enthusiastic nor very negative)

c. taxes should be imposed on tobacco and alcoholic beverages

d. taxes should be designed to disturb market forces as little as possible

e. the government should rely on the corporate profits tax, not the personal income tax

15. A public good

a. creates no positive externalities

b. creates no negative externalities

c. cannot be produced by a private corporation

d. can be enjoyed by all, even those who do not pay for it

e. must be provided by the federal government if it is to be provided at all

16. Which of the following is the best example of a negative economic externality?

a. an increase in the international price of oil

b. an increase in the international price of grain

c. air pollution created by a steel mill

d. the rise in the price of steel when the government requires steel mills to reduce pollution

e. vaccinations

17. Which of the following is designed specifically to be non-neutral?

a. a proportional income tax

b. a general sales tax of 5%

c. a tax on polluting activities

d. all of the above

e. none of the above

18. The presence of externalities means that

a. a tax system that seems to be progressive will, in fact, be regressive

b. a tax system that seems to be regressive will, in fact, be progressive

c. the market system will generally not work as well as it would in the absence of externalities

d. the rich will generally get richer, and the poor poorer

e. the federal government will find it much more difficult to balance its budget

EXERCISES

1. The table below shows two different taxes—tax A and tax B. For each of these taxes, fill in the column showing the average tax rate at various incomes, and the marginal tax rate. Also note on the last line whether the tax is proportional, regressive, or progressive.

2. Suppose that a family has an income of $35,000 which includes $5000 in benefits from a pension plan.

Suppose the family is allowed to deduct that $5000 when calculating its taxable income. As a result, taxable income falls from $35,000 to $30,000. This would mean a reduction of $ _____ in tax payable under Tax A, and a reduction of $ _____ under Tax B. Thus, the higher is the marginal tax rate, the (greater, less) is the tax saving from a deduction.

Income	TAX A			TAX B		
		Average Rate	Marginal Rate		Average Rate	Marginal Rate
$10,000	$1,500	____ %		$1,500	____ %	
$20,000	3,000	____ %	____ %	3,500	____ %	____ %
$30,000	4,500	____ %	____ %	6,000	____ %	____ %
$40,000	6,000	____ %	____ %	9,000	____ %	____ %

Type of tax: _____ ; _____ .

ESSAY QUESTIONS

1. What would it be like to live in Canada if there were no federal or provincial government regulatory agencies? Describe what would happen if specific agencies, such as Environment Canada, Health and Welfare, the CTC, and the CRTC, were absent. What do you think the effects were when the government revamped, and sharply reduced the role of, the Foreign Investment Review Agency (FIRA) in 1986?

2. In most communities, the following services are provided by the local government:
   a. Police
   b. Elementary education
   c. Street cleaning
   d. Garbage collection

Could these be provided by private enterprise? Is there any advantage in having them provided by the government? Would there be any advantage in having them provided by the private sector?

3. What externalities are created by individuals who:
   a. drive on a highway
   b. mow the lawn
   c. smoke in a theatre

In each case, do you think that the government should do anything to encourage or discourage the activity? If so, what? and why? If not, why not?

ANSWERS

Important Terms: 1g, 2e, 3c, 4a, 5m, 6l, 7b, 8n, 9d, 10j, 11f, 12i, 13h, 14k
True-False: 1T, 2F, 3T, 4F, 5T, 6F, 7F, 8F, 9F, 10F, 11T
Multiple Choice: 1a, 2d, 3b, 4e, 5e, 6c, 7b, 8c, 9c, 10e, 11e, 12e, 13e, 14d, 15d, 16c, 17c, 18c
Exercises: **1.** Tax A. Average rates: 15%, 15%, 15%, 15%. Marginal rates: 15%, 15%, 15%. The tax is proportional. Tax B. Average rates: 15%, 17.5%, 20%, 22.5%. Marginal rates: 20%, 25%, 30%. The tax is progressive. **2.** $750, $1,500, greater.

ANSWER TO A SELECTED REVIEW QUESTION FROM THE TEXT

5-3. In the case of defence research, a major reason is the need for secrecy. In the case of agricultural research, it may be necessary for government to do it since individual farmers produce on too small a scale to justify the high cost of doing research just to increase production on their own farms. Moreover, agricultural research often involves technology that cannot be patented or sold under licensing agreements. Thus, a private firm could not cover the cost of its research by selling the rights to its inventions (the way inventors in other sectors sometimes are able to do).

Across

1. It's important to distinguish between these two tax rates (2 words).
8. prefix meaning "two"
9. era
10. preposition
11. desirable characteristic for tax base
13. me (French)
15. what a completely flat tax would do to tax-rate schedule
18. At the end of April, you have to file your tax _____.
20. The United States imposed restrictions on this important Canadian export in 1986.
22. here (French)
23. second person pronoun
24. long time period
26. generally considered an undesirable kind of tax
27. keeps bridges and airplanes floating
30. thus (Latin)
31. When a dog is happy, its tail does this.
33. undertake
35. preposition
37. preposition meaning "belonging to"
39. The federal government had a $30 billion one in the mid-1980s. (2 words)
41. burns you up
42. goes with "either"
43. The federal and provincial governments have this kind of arrangement in health care and post-secondary education.

Down

1. one guide in designing taxes (3 words)
2. where grapes grow
3. what marginal tax rates do as your income increases
4. His theories shook the world.
5. before this time
6. end of the line
7. love (Latin)
12. what the economy was in the 1930s
13. when the crew takes over the ship (plural)
14. tells you who really pays a tax
16. worth
17. ineffectual, or incapable of movement
19. determines what characteristics you inherit from your parents
21. what people do at a bank
25. government payments without quid pro quo
28. the great outdoors
29. can't get it (abbrev.) or it's irrelevant (abbrev.)
32. They were waiting for him in Beckett's absurdist play.
34. happen
36. poem of praise
38. famous upper-class school in Britain
39. prefix meaning "two"
40. sometimes inflated when you don't know your limitations

Part Two

■ ■

High Employment and a Stable Price Level

Chapter 6

■ ■

Measuring Domestic and National Product and Income

MAJOR PURPOSE

Macroeconomics is about the overall magnitudes in the economy—total output and the average level of prices. The main purpose of this chapter is to provide an introduction to macroeconomics by explaining how total output and the average level of prices are measured. In calculating total output—or GDP—we want to count everything that is produced once, but only once. This means that there is an important problem to be avoided—the problem of double counting. This problem can be avoided by counting only final products such as TV sets, and excluding intermediate products such as the wire and chips that went into the TV sets.

Another important objective of the chapter is to draw a distinction between nominal (or current-dollar) magnitudes and real (or constant-dollar) magnitudes. Through time, GDP measured in dollar terms goes up rapidly. This rapid increase is the combined result of two things: (1) there is an increase in the quantity of goods and services that we are producing, and (2) the prices at which these goods and services are sold are going up. The first of these is desirable; the second is not. To see what is happening in real terms, national income accountants[1] eliminate the effects of inflation by measuring the GDP of each year in the prices of a single base year, 1981.

LEARNING OBJECTIVES

After you have studied this chapter in the textbook and study guide, you should be able to
- State the relationship between gross investment, net investment, depreciation, and the change in the stock of capital
- State the difference between GDP and NDP, and between GDP and GNP
- State the difference between NDP and NNP, and between NNP and National Income, between National income and Personal income, and between Personal income and Disposable personal income. (See Fig. 6-3 in the textbook.)
- State the relationship between nominal GDP, real GDP, and the GDP deflator. That is, you should understand equation 6-6 in the text.
- Explain why the GDP deflator is not exactly the same as the consumer price index
- Explain why real GDP is a better measure of how we are doing than is nominal GDP
- Explain why real GDP, nevertheless, is not a very good way to measure how well we are doing
- Explain why it is so hard to calculate a more comprehensive measure of economic welfare
- Explain why the "underground economy" exists, why its size may have increased in recent years, and why this is of concern to economists

1. Although we follow current Canadian practice and use Gross *Domestic* Product as the basic measure of aggregate economic activity, we continue to use the terminology of *national* income accounting in referring to the collection of statistics on economic activity.

HIGHLIGHTS OF THE CHAPTER

This chapter explains how domestic and national product are measured, in both *real* and *nominal* terms. It also explains some of the limitations of GDP as a measure of economic welfare.

To calculate the total output of the nation, we must somehow add apples and oranges, steel and airplanes, haircuts and medical services. The only reasonable way to add up different goods and services is to add together the total amount of money spent on each of them. Thus, when we put together a measure of total product, we use *market prices* as a way of judging the comparative importance of each product. A car selling for $10,000 contributes as much to total product as do 20 000 bottles of Coca-Cola selling for 50¢ each.

When we measure GDP, we want to measure everything produced in the economy (except for illegal products). However, we have to be careful. If we took the value of all the cars produced in the economy, plus all the steel and all the tires, then we would be exaggerating our output. Why is that? The answer is: because much of the steel and many of the tires were used by car manufacturers to produce their cars. We didn't produce a car plus four tires, but the car onto which the four tires went.

To *avoid double counting* of tires, steel, and other intermediate products, government statisticians concentrate on *final products*. These are placed in four main categories: (1) consumer expenditures for goods and services, (2) investment, (3) government purchases of goods and services, and (4) net exports (that is, exports minus imports).

Investment is perhaps the trickiest of these four to understand precisely. The first important point is that we are dealing with the production of capital goods—buildings, machines, etc.—and not what financial analysts mean by investment. That is, we do not include financial investments—such as the purchase of common stock—in the investment category of GDP. The reason is straightforward. When individual A buys 100 shares of common stock from B, there is simply a transfer of ownership, not a direct increase in production. (Of course, the ability of firms to issue stock or bonds may help them to finance new factories, and these new factories are included in GDP.) Recall that this distinction between financial capital (such as stocks and bonds) and capital goods (such as factories) was made back in Chapter 2.

A second complication with investment is that it includes some intermediate products, such as steel, tires, or wheat. Specifically, it includes the increases in our inventories of such products. These inventory increases are something we have produced during the year. They are not included elsewhere—for example, they have not yet been used in the production of consumer goods. They have not yet been included when we count consumer goods. Therefore, they are counted here, in the investment category.

The final complication is that, when we count all the factories and machines produced during the year, we are in an important sense exaggerating what we have produced. The reason is that existing factories and machines have been wearing out and become obsolete during the year. What we should be measuring is not the total production of capital goods during the year, but only the *increase* in our capital stock. In other words, it would make sense to include only the increase in the stock of equipment, plant, residential buildings, and public infrastructure, just as we include only the increase in the stocks of inventories.

This leads to the distinction between net investment and gross investment. Gross investment (I_g) is total output of plant, equipment, residential buildings, infrastructure such as roads and bridges built by the government, and increases in inventories. Net investment (I_n) is just the increase in our stock of plant, equipment, residential buildings, infrastructure, and inventories. The difference between the two is depreciation (Figure 6-2). GDP includes gross investment; NDP includes net investment. Accordingly, the difference between GDP and NDP is also depreciation (Figure 6-3). (In Canadian national income accounting, depreciation is often referred to as a Capital Consumption Allowance, or CCA.)

Since the mid-1980s, Canadian government statisticians emphasize GDP as the principal yardstick for measuring the economy's performance. In earlier national accounts statistics, the concept of Gross *National* Product (GNP) was more commonly used. The difference between the two (as well as between other "domestic" and "national" concepts, such as NDP and NNP) is that GDP measures the total value of production *inside Canada's boundaries* during the year. GNP, on the other hand, measures the total value of the goods and services produced by *factors of production owned by Canadian nationals*. Thus, to get from GDP to GNP, we should subtract the value of Canadian products attributable to foreign-owned factors of production in Canada, and add the value of output attributable to Canadian-owned factors of production that are employed in other countries. In practice, Statistics Canada uses a simplified approach: It gets GNP from GDP by subtracting the earnings of foreign-owned capital in Canada, net of the earnings of Canadian-owned capital abroad.

Other important magnitudes—national income, personal income, and disposable personal income—are also shown in Figure 6-3. While you should not try to memorize the numbers on that figure, you should know the differences between the five major measures. You should also have a general idea of the magnitudes. For example, you should know that personal saving is about 10% of disposable income; it is not 20% or 30%.

We have seen that market prices provide a feasible way to add various products. But, when we use market prices, a complication arises. Today, a person can use $100 to buy food, or clothing, or other things. The relative prices of food, clothing, or other things represents the relative amounts that people pay for the various goods; it is a way of measuring their relative value. But a person can't shop now out of an Eaton's catalogue of 1970. A car bought for $10,000 now is not worth four times as much as the car that sold for $2,500 in 1965. Money has lost some of its value as a result of inflation.

This raises an important problem. We want to use GDP figures as one measure of how well the economy is performing, of how healthy the economy is now as compared to the way it was 5 or 10 years ago. If we simply used GDP measured at current prices, we would not know what to do with the comparison. Does a higher GDP today reflect success? Are we producing more? Or does it simply reflect our failure to prevent inflation? In practice, it is likely to reflect both.

In order to separate the undesirable increase in prices from the desirable increase in output, national income accountants calculate *constant-dollar* GDP. That is, they

calculate what GDP would have been if prices had remained what they were in a single base year. Such constant-dollar or real GDP figures represent what has been happening to output over time.

Although real GDP is an important measure of the performance of the economy, it has major defects which mean that we should not concentrate single-mindedly on increasing real GDP. A lot of important things don't appear in GDP—the quality of the physical environment, the stability of the political system, or the degree of social harmony, to name but a few. Because of limits of GDP as a measure of welfare, some economists have considered the possibility of a broader measure, to include important features of our economic performance that are left out of GDP. This attempt has not been very successful. The problems are apparently insoluble. In particular, it is not clear how leisure should be counted. Suppose we found that, over some period, real output per person had risen by 90%, while per capita leisure had risen by 20%. It is not clear what this means, in terms of an overall measure. Were we more than 90% better off, since we had 90% more goods and more leisure too? Or was the improvement only some average of the 90% and the 20%? The answer is not obvious. The most promising approach, therefore, is not to search for some comprehensive single measure of welfare, but to look at a number of measures simultaneously—for example, not only real NDP, NNP, or real national income, but also literacy, life expectancy, infant mortality, and so on.

IMPORTANT TERMS: MATCH THE COLUMNS

Match each term in the first column with the corresponding phrase in the second column.

_____ 1. GDP
_____ 2. NDP
_____ 3. National income
_____ 4. Disposable income
_____ 5. Depreciation
_____ 6. Real investment
_____ 7. Financial investment
_____ 8. Intermediate product
_____ 9. Value added
_____ 10. Deflate
_____ 11. Underground economy
_____ 12. GNP

a. Personal income − [income taxes and other personal taxes]
b. Good intended for resale or further processing
c. Production of plant, equipment, and housing, and changes in inventories
d. NDP + depreciation
e. Remove the effects of inflation from a time series
f. GDP − earnings of foreign investment in Canada, net of Canadian investment earnings in foreign countries
g. NNP − sales taxes
h. Unreported income
i. GDP − NDP
j. $C + G + I_n + X - M$
k. Acquisition of bonds and corporate stocks
l. Sales − cost of intermediate products bought from outside suppliers

TRUE-FALSE

T F **1.** The easiest way to calculate GDP is to add the sales of all corporations.

T F **2.** Gross private domestic investment includes all the money spent on Canada's stock exchanges during the year, but it excludes money spent by Canadians on foreign stock exchanges.

T F **3.** It is possible for inventory investment to be negative during a year.

T F **4.** It is possible for gross investment to be negative during a year.

T F **5.** GDP can be determined by adding sales taxes to NDP.

T F **6.** It is possible for net exports to be negative during a year.

T F **7.** Suppose that there are no sales taxes in an economy. Then personal income will be the same as national income.

T F **8.** If real GDP has gone up and the price index has gone up, then we can be sure that nominal GDP has gone up.

T F **9.** If the earnings of Canadian capital invested in foreign countries were greater than the earnings of foreign capital in Canada, then Canada's GNP would be greater than her GDP.

MULTIPLE CHOICE

1. Which of the following is the best example of an intermediate product?

   a. a road
   b. steel
   c. bread
   d. a TV set
   e. an automobile

2. In the GDP accounts, which of the following is included as a final product?

   a. a plane bought by the government
   b. government expenditures to resurface roads
   c. purchases of washing machines by households
   d. purchases of washing machines by laundromats
   e. all of the above

3. Suppose that a firm sells its output for $40,000. It pays $22,000 in wages and salaries, $10,000 for materials bought from other firms, $3,000 for interest on its bonds, and it has profits of $5,000. Then, its value added is

   a. $18,000
   b. $22,000
   c. $30,000
   d. $35,000
   e. $37,000

4. In the GDP accounts, increases in inventories are

   a. excluded, since they are made up mostly of intermediate goods
   b. included as part of the consumption category, since they are made up mostly of consumer goods
   c. included as part of the government category, together with other miscellaneous items
   d. included as part of the investment category
   e. included as an item separate from C, I, and G

5. Suppose we know $C + I_g + G$. Then, to get GDP, we should

   a. add depreciation
   b. subtract depreciation
   c. add the increase in inventories
   d. add sales taxes
   e. add exports and subtract imports

6. Last year, the XYZ manufacturing corporation issued $10 million in new common stock, and used $8 million of the proceeds to build a new factory. The other $2 million was used to repay bank loans, and replenish XYZ's deposits at its banks. As a result, GDP went up by

   a. the $8 million spent for the factory
   b. the $10 million in new common stock
   c. $12 million
   d. $18 million
   e. $20 million

7. The GDP statistics show that gross investment in 1987 was $116 billion, while depreciation was $63 billion. We may conclude that

   a. net investment was $179 billion
   b. net investment was $53 billion
   c. net investment was -$53 billion
   d. net investment was negative, but we don't know how much
   e. inventory accumulation was negative

8. Some years ago, a U.S. government agency published a statistical report that, in 1932, gross domestic investment in the United States was $1.0 billion, while depreciation was $7.6 billion. What conclusion may we come to?

a. net investment was larger than gross investment
b. net investment was negative; the capital stock was smaller at the end of the year than at the beginning
c. most investment was in the form of inventory accumulation
d. imports were larger than exports
e. there is something wrong with the statistics; maybe the government got gross investment and depreciation mixed up

9. Suppose that gross investment has been 10% of GDP, but then it falls to zero during the current year. In the current year
a. depreciation is the same size as net investment
b. depreciation is the same size as gross investment
c. depreciation is also zero
d. net investment is also zero
e. net investment is negative

10. Consider the following incorrect definition: National income equals the sum of wages and salaries, rent and interest, proprietors' income, net exports, and corporation profits. To make this

statement correct, one item should be deleted. This item is
a. wages and salaries
b. rent and interest
c. proprietors' income
d. net exports
e. corporation profits

11. Most of the players on both Canadian and American teams in the National Hockey League are Canadian citizens. According to the definitions of the domestic and national product and income measures, this suggests that
a. hockey contributes more to U.S. GDP than to Canadian GDP
b. hockey contributes more to U.S. GDP than to U.S. GNP
c. hockey contributes more to Canadian GDP than to Canadian GNP
d. hockey contributes more to Canadian Personal Income than to Canadian GNP
e. none of the above; professional sports are not included in domestic and national product and income measures

The next six questions are based on the following table, which shows domestic product in a simple economy with only guns and butter.

	Production of guns	Price of guns	Production of consumer goods	Price of consumer goods
1982	200	$1,000	1,000	$500
1990	250	$2,000	2,000	$1,500

12. In this simple economy, current-dollar GDP in 1982 was
a. $700,000
b. $1,250,000
c. $1,900,000
d. $3,500,000
e. $4,200,000

13. In this simple economy, current-dollar GDP in 1990 is
a. $700,000
b. $1,250,000
c. $1,900,000
d. $3,500,000
e. $4,200,000

14. Suppose that 1982 is the base year in this simple economy. Real GDP in 1990 is
a. $700,000
b. $1,250,000
c. $1,900,000
d. $3,500,000
e. $4,200,000

15. Suppose that 1982 is the base year in this simple economy. In this economy, the GDP deflator in 1990 is
a. 162.5
b. 250
c. 271
d. 280
e. 300

16. In this economy, how much did the average level of prices rise between 1982 and 1990?
a. 150%
b. 171%
c. 180%
d. 200%
e. 280%

17. In this economy, how much did real GDP rise between 1982 and 1990?
a. 52%
b. 79%
c. 152%
d. 179%
e. 204%

18. This year's nominal GDP measures
  a. this year's output at base-year prices
  b. this year's output at this year's prices
  c. NDP less depreciation
  d. National income less depreciation
  e. NDP less sales taxes

19. Suppose that, since the base year, all prices have risen by 100%. This year's current-dollar GDP is $2,000 billion. Then, constant-dollar GDP is
  a. $4,000 billion
  b. $3,000 billion
  c. $2,000 billion
  d. $1,000 billion
  e. $500 billion

20. Suppose we divide current-dollar GDP for 1986 by constant-dollar GDP for 1986. Then the resulting figure is a measure of
  a. inflation during 1986
  b. real output during 1986
  c. nominal output during 1986
  d. the GDP price deflator for 1986
  e. depreciation

21. Last year, Sam Brown spent each Saturday from May to November building a new wing on his family home. In last year's GDP
  a. the full market value of the wing is included
  b. the lumber, windows, paint, and other materials he bought at the store were included, but the value of his labour was not
  c. the full market value of the wing was included, plus an additional 10% if Statistics Canada officials found that he actually enjoyed building the wing
  d. the wing was not included at all, since it was not a market transaction
  e. the wing was not included at all, since it probably is not as good as one built by a professional builder

EXERCISES

1. Suppose you have the following incomplete data:

C	$900
I_g	400
Wages and salaries	800
Interest and rent*	100
Corporate profits (after taxes)*	250
Personal taxes	350
Depreciation	50
G	450
Corporate income taxes*	150
Sales taxes	200
Transfer payments	200
Undistributed corporate profits*	150
Proprietors' income	400
Earnings of foreign capital in Canada	175
Returns on Canadian investments abroad	75

* Excludes amount relating to foreign-owned assets in Canada.

Compute the following:

NNP	_____
NI	_____
NDP	_____
GDP	_____
$X - M$	_____
Personal income	_____
Disposable personal income	_____
I_n	_____

2. Suppose a country produces two goods, a consumption good and an investment good. The first two rows of Table 6.1 give the current-dollar value of the total production of the two goods. Fill in the next row indicating nominal GDP each year. The next two rows indicate the market prices of the two goods each year. Fill in the next two rows giving the number of units of each good produced each year. Then fill in the final four rows, using 1982 as the base year.

Table 6.1

	1982	1985	1990
Current-dollar value of C production	200	450	600
Current-dollar value of I production	100	150	200
Nominal GDP			
Price of C	5	9	10
Price of I	20	25	40
Quantity of C production			
Quantity of I production			
Constant-dollar value of C production			
Constant-dollar value of I production			
Real GDP			
GDP deflator			

ESSAY QUESTIONS

1. In what ways does GDP overstate economic well-being? In what ways does it understate economic well-being?

2. Do the per-capita NDP figures of two countries give a measure of their relative economic welfare? Explain the major deficiencies of NDP as a way of comparing welfare in different countries.

3. "Transfer payments to the poor and the elderly are not included in the G segment of national product. But the assistance to the poor and elderly makes a very important contribution to economic welfare. Therefore, transfer payments should be added, to get a better measure of GDP." Do you agree or not? Explain why.

ANSWERS

Important Terms: **1**d, **2**j, **3**g, **4**a, **5**i, **6**c, **7**k, **8**b, **9**l, **10**e, **11**h, **12**f
True-False: **1**F, **2**F, **3**T, **4**F, **5**F, **6**T, **7**F, **8**T, **9**T
Multiple Choice: **1**b, **2**e, **3**c, **4**d, **5**e, **6**a, **7**b, **8**b, **9**e, **10**d, **11**b, **12**a, **13**d, **14**b, **15**d, **16**c, **17**b, **18**b, **19**d, **20**d, **21**b
Exercises:

1.

NNP	1,900
NI	1,700
NDP	2,000
GDP	2,050
$X - M$	300
Personal income	1,600
Disposable personal income	1,250
I_n	350

2. Table 6.1 completed:

	1982	1985	1990
Nominal GDP	300	600	800
Quantity of C production	40	50	60
Quantity of I production	5	6	5
Constant-dollar value of C production	200	250	300
Constant-dollar value of I production	100	120	100
Real GDP	300	370	400
GDP deflator	100	162	200

ANSWERS TO SELECTED REVIEW QUESTIONS FROM THE TEXT

6-1. (a) GDP $= C + I_g + G + X - M = 1000 + 300 + 200 + 10 = 1510$

(b) NDP $=$ GDP $-$ depreciation $= 1510 - 75 = 1435$

6-3. Expenditures by tourists abroad. Fares purchased by Canadian travellers from foreign airlines.

6-4. (a), (b), and (d). (c) is not included because it is a transfer payment.

6-5. (a) This is not included, since the car has not been produced this year.

(b) This is not included, because it does not represent production.

(c) This is included, as a component of consumption expenditures. The groceries are produced this year.

(d) It depends on the airline. If they flew on a Canadian airline, this is included. But purchases of tickets from a British airline are not included, nor are expenditures for hotels, etc. while in London. (More precisely, these items should be first included as consumption expenditures, and then subtracted as part of the imports of services, with the result that they make no net addition to GDP. They do, however, add to British GDP.)

6-8. (a) Wrong; most trucking services are intermediate products.

(b) Correct.

(c) Correct that investment would be higher; but wrong that living standards would change!

(d) Wrong; defence spending is just part of G.

(e) The logic is right, but the distinction is irrelevant since the "services of roads" are not included in GDP (though investment in road building is).

6-9. The approximation gets worse as the percentage changes get larger.

Chapter 7

■ ■

Fluctuations in Economic Activity: Unemployment and Inflation

MAJOR PURPOSE

This chapter describes the two major macroeconomic problems—*unemployment* and *inflation*. These two problems are closely related to *economic fluctuations*. During recessions, when output is declining, fewer workers are needed by business and the unemployment rate increases. During a rapid expansion, when spending by businesses and consumers is rising rapidly, inflation generally becomes more severe. Economic conditions were most unstable in Canada during the period between the two world wars. Between 1929 and 1933, output collapsed and the unemployment rate shot upward.

This chapter explains how the business cycle is divided into its four phases: *recession, trough, expansion*, and *peak*. It also describes how unemployment rises, while output and profits decline during recessions. Inflation generally declines during the later part of recessions and during early recoveries.

This chapter explains how the unemployment rate is calculated, and the various major types of unemployment. *Cyclical* unemployment is the result of fluctuations in overall economic activity. Reducing this type of unemployment is one of the major objectives of economic policy. *Frictional* unemployment results from the normal turnover of the labour force; some amount of frictional

unemployment is inevitable. *Structural* unemployment arises when the labour force does not have the type of skills needed for available jobs, or if workers live a long distance from available jobs. This type of unemployment is more severe than frictional unemployment. To escape structural unemployment, people must move or switch to different types of work.

The Canadian economy is quite flexible and changes rapidly. Even in the best of times, the unemployment rate does not get down to zero. It is not possible to identify any specific, unchanging unemployment rate as "full employment."

There is considerable disagreement on the issue of what impact the Canada/United States Free Trade Agreement (usually referred to as FTA) will have on unemployment in Canada. However, most economists believe that there will be some tendency for both frictional and structural unemployment to rise temporarily, as the economy adjusts to the FTA.

The most important characteristics of recessions are higher unemployment and declining output. The shortfall of output below the economy's potential is known as the *GDP gap*; it is a measure of output lost because of slack in the economy.

LEARNING OBJECTIVES

After you have studied this chapter in the textbook and study guide, you should be able to
- Describe the four phases of the business cycle
- Describe the major features of the Great Depression of the 1930s
- Explain the major features of recent business cycles—for example, what happens to profits, investment, and the purchase of consumer durables during recessions
- Explain how the unemployment rate is calculated
- Explain why the unemployment rate may understate the problem of unemployment during a recession
- Explain why the productivity of labour is adversely affected by recessions
- State what Okun's law is

- List the three major types of unemployment, and explain how they are different
- Explain potential GDP and the GDP gap

HIGHLIGHTS OF THE CHAPTER

The business cycle has four phases. During a *recession*, economic activity declines, and the unemployment rate increases. Economic activity reaches its low point at the *trough*. This is followed by the *expansion* phase, which ends at the upper turning point or *peak*.

The key to identifying a business cycle is to tell when a recession has occurred. While there is no universally accepted definition of a recession in Canada, most economists agree that the slowdown in the economy must be widespread and must last for at least six months (two quarters) before we should say that a recession has occurred; we should not classify every downward jiggle in the economy as a recession.

The most severe downturn in history occurred between 1929 and 1933 as the economies of Canada and the United States and many other countries collapsed into the Great Depression. In this chapter, the main events of the Great Depression are summarized. Although the depression may seem like ancient history, it remains a lesson in how badly things can go wrong. It thus provides a reason for studying macroeconomics. If things can go this badly when macroeconomic policy is mismanaged, it is important to have some idea of what macroeconomic policy is all about.

Between 1929 and 1933, the unemployment rate rose to almost 20%, real GDP fell by more than 30%, and the average level of prices declined by almost 20%. The production of capital equipment, buildings, and consumer durables fell particularly sharply. On the farm, the Depression caused a collapse of prices. On international markets, commodity prices also collapsed.

Recent recessions have been *much* milder than the downturn of 1929-33. Some have been very short and mild indeed—for example, the recession of early 1980. However, there has been no noticeable tendency for recessions to become progressively more mild over the past four decades. The most recent recession—that of 1981/82—was the worst in Canada since World War II.

The unemployment rate is calculated by Statistics Canada as a percentage of the labour force. The unemployed are people who are out of work who (a) are temporarily laid off but expect to be recalled, (b) are waiting to report to a new job, or (c) have been looking for work in the previous four weeks. If people without jobs do not meet one of these conditions, they are considered to be out of the labour force. The labour force is made up of those with jobs, plus those who are unemployed according to the above criteria.

During recessions, it becomes harder to find a job. As a result, those out of work may become discouraged and stop looking for work. In this case, they drop out of the officially measured labour force and out of the ranks of those who are counted as unemployed. Consequently, the unemployment rate may understate the unemployment problem during recessions. Nevertheless, the unemployment rate is one important indicator of what is happening during recessions.

During recessions, as sales of products fall, businesses lay off some employees. However, they are often reluctant to lay off highly skilled workers, since these workers may take jobs elsewhere and be unavailable when sales recover. Hence, employment does not fall as much as output. There is a decline in output per worker—that is, in the *productivity of labour*.

As the unemployment rate increases during recessions, so does the number of those who have been unemployed for a long period of time. Not only are more people unemployed, but the hardship faced by the average unemployed person also becomes more severe. Not all groups are affected equally by unemployment. The unemployment rate for teenagers is much higher than for adults, and unemployment in the Maritime provinces is consistently higher than in the rest of Canada.

No matter how prosperous the economy becomes, it is not possible to eliminate unemployment altogether. *Frictional* unemployment represents those who are temporarily unemployed because they are looking for a better job; *structural unemployment*, which is typically longer-lasting and more painful, results as changes in the economy make some skills obsolete, or lead to plant closings and job losses in some communities, even as new jobs are opening up elsewhere in the economy. Both types of unemployment are associated with the adjustments that continually take place in a dynamic, changing economy. In a changing economy, there is always some frictional and structural unemployment.

Opponents of the FTA are predicting that it will cause great hardship for Canadian workers as jobs will be lost in many industries under the pressure of intensified competition from more efficient U.S. producers. Those who favour the agreement, on the other hand, have pointed to the possibility that many new jobs will be created in Canadian industries, which will have improved access to the U.S. market under the agreement. While both sides may be right to some extent, and even if the number of new jobs created matches the number of jobs lost, the process of adjustment will, nevertheless, lead to some increase in frictional and structural unemployment, at least for some time.

Thus, if full employment is to be a meaningful goal, it cannot be defined as an unemployment rate of zero. There is some debate over the unemployment rate that should be considered full employment. During the 1960s, an unemployment rate of 3% was frequently looked on as representing full employment. Most economists have since put the figure higher—at 7% or even 8%—during the late 1970s and early 1980s. However, in the late 1980s, the figure identified as full employment has been reduced somewhat. Chapters 15 and 19 will investigate the idea of full employment in detail.

Potential GDP is estimated as the GDP path along which the economy would move if there were no business cycles and a high level of employment were maintained continuously. The shortfall of actual GDP below the estimated potential is the *GDP gap*. It provides an estimate of the output lost because of recessions.

IMPORTANT TERMS: MATCH THE COLUMNS

Match each term in the first column with the corresponding phrase in the second column.

_____	1.	Recession
_____	2.	Trough
_____	3.	Peak
_____	4.	Underemployed
_____	5.	Discouraged workers
_____	6.	Okun's law
_____	7.	Frictional unemployment
_____	8.	Structural unemployment
_____	9.	Cyclical unemployment
_____	10.	Potential GDP
_____	11.	GDP gap

a. To reduce this unemployment, people must move or acquire new skills

b. Downward movement of the economy, usually lasting two quarters or more

c. Those who have dropped out of the labour force because they were unable to find work

d. Potential output less actual output

e. Observation that unemployment rate moves less strongly than output during the business cycle

f. Turning point at the end of a recession

g. What output would be if the economy were at full employment

h. Unemployment associated with adjustments in a changing, dynamic economy

i. Discouraged workers plus those who are not kept busy because demand is low

j. Turning point as a recession is about to begin

k. Unemployment caused by recessions

TRUE-FALSE

T F 1. During the Great Depression, the prices of agricultural products fell much more than the prices of manufactured products.

T F 2. Recessions in the Canadian economy have become consistently less and less severe over the past three decades.

T F 3. Inflation responds to changes in business conditions. During rapid expansions of real output, the rate of inflation generally increases, and it generally decreases during recessions. However, inflation does not respond immediately; it responds with a lag.

T F 4. In percentage terms during the typical business cycle, investment fluctuates less than consumption but more than total GDP.

T F 5. During the business cycle, consumer spending for durable goods fluctuates more than consumer spending for nondurable goods.

T F 6. People temporarily laid off, but waiting to be recalled, are included among the unemployed.

T F 7. During a recession, as workers are laid off, the remaining workers can use the best equipment. Therefore, productivity of those remaining at work generally increases rapidly during a recession.

T F 8. According to Okun's law, recessions occur regularly, at intervals of between 5 and 7 years.

T F 9. In the long run, increased opportunities for international trade tend to increase average living standards of Canadians though, in the short run, they may cause an increase in unemployment.

MULTIPLE CHOICE

1. Between the peak of 1929 and the trough of the Great Depression in 1933, Canada's real GDP fell by approximately
   a. 30%
   b. 15%
   c. 10%
   d. 5%
   e. 2%

2. Which of the following is a turning point in the business cycle?
   a. expansion
   b. recovery
   c. peak
   d. recession
   e. depression

3. A simple, unofficial definition of recession has often been used by economists and journalists in both Canada and the United States. According to this definition, a recession occurs when there is a decline or stagnation in seasonally adjusted real GDP for at least
   a. one month
   b. two months
   c. three months
   d. two quarters
   e. four quarters

4. Between the peak of 1929 and the trough of the Great Depression in 1933, the prices of agricultural commodities
   a. rose about 15%, in spite of the decline in the prices of most other goods
   b. remained stable, in spite of the decline in the prices of most other goods
   c. remained stable, in spite of the increase in the prices of most other goods
   d. fell about 10%, or slightly less than the average of other prices
   e. fell much more than the average of other prices

5. During the typical recession
   a. profits, wages, and prices all fall sharply (normally by 10% or more)
   b. profits fall sharply, while wages and prices respond only slowly
   c. wages fall sharply, while prices and profits respond only slowly
   d. prices fall sharply, while wages and profits respond only slowly
   e. profits, wages, and prices all normally rise by 10% or more

6. During the typical recession
   a. government spending falls more than consumption

   b. government spending falls more than investment
   c. consumption falls more than investment
   d. investment falls more than consumption
   e. consumption and investment generally increase, but at a slow rate

7. During recent decades, one component of GDP has accounted for much of the downward movement during recessions. Recent recessions are, therefore, often referred to as
   a. export recessions
   b. import recessions
   c. inventory recessions
   d. government recessions
   e. consumption recessions

8. The labour force includes
   a. only those who are employed
   b. those who are employed, plus the unemployed
   c. the total population, less retirees
   d. the total population, less retirees and students
   e. the total population, less retirees, students, and government workers

9. Assume that the population is 20 million, the labour force is 10 million, and 9 million people are employed.
   Then, the unemployment rate is
   a. 4.5%
   b. 5%
   c. 9%
   d. 10%
   e. 55%

10. Which of the following groups is *not* counted as being unemployed?
   a. people who have left school and are still looking for their first job
   b. people who are re-entering the labour force, and are still looking for jobs
   c. people who are on temporary layoff, but are not looking for jobs because they expect to be recalled in the near future
   d. people who have been recently fired, and are looking for new jobs
   e. retired people

11. Suppose a person lost a factory job 6 months ago, spent 3 months in a fruitless search for work, and then stopped looking. In the collection of official statistics, such a person is considered
   a. still employed in the factory job
   b. structurally unemployed
   c. cyclically unemployed
   d. frictionally unemployed
   e. out of the labour force

12. Suppose a person quit a job in construction last month and has already lined up a job in a factory to begin next week. This person is
    a. counted as still being employed in construction
    b. counted as being employed in the factory job
    c. frictionally unemployed
    d. structurally unemployed
    e. cyclically unemployed

13. Who best fits into the category of the "underemployed"?
    a. university and college students
    b. high-school students
    c. government workers
    d. executives of major corporations
    e. people who can find only part-time work when they want full-time work

14. The productivity of labour is
    a. output divided by the number of hours of labour input
    b. the extra amount produced by skilled workers, as compared to unskilled workers
    c. the extra amount produced by people with college degrees, as compared to those without degrees
    d. the increase in the amount produced by the typical factory worker during the twentieth century
    e. the increase in the amount produced by the typical farm worker during the twentieth century

15. As a result of the FTA, there is likely to be
    a. more structural unemployment
    b. increased inflation, at least in the short run
    c. lower labour productivity, as workers in many industries are laid off
    d. more cyclical unemployment
    e. a. and c.

16. Okun's law refers to which of the following phenomena?
    a. employment fluctuates by a greater percentage than output during the business cycle
    b. output fluctuates by a greater percentage than employment during the business cycle
    c. investment fluctuates by a greater percentage than consumption during the business cycle
    d. inventories fluctuate by a greater percentage than gross investment during the business cycle
    e. investment fluctuates by a greater percentage than government spending during the business cycle

17. During a recession, the number of long-term unemployed (more than 14 weeks)
    a. rises, by a greater percent than the overall number of unemployed
    b. rises, but by a smaller percent than the overall number of unemployed
    c. is quite stable, since some of the unemployed get work as the labour force is reshuffled
    d. falls, since some of the unemployed get work as the labour force is reshuffled
    e. falls, since the government is most willing to help the unemployed during recessions

18. According to the official definition of unemployment, which of the following groups has the highest unemployment rate?
    a. men
    b. women
    c. teenagers
    d. university and college students, aged 20 and over
    e. retirees

19. A major objective of macroeconomic policy is to reduce
    a. cyclical unemployment
    b. frictional unemployment
    c. labour mobility
    d. product innovations
    e. all of the above

20. During the past three decades, the unemployment rate generally considered to represent "full employment"
    a. has been stable at 0%; at no other rate is there "full employment"
    b. has been stable, at about 3%
    c. has fallen, from about 10% to about 4%, as the economy recovered from the Great Depression
    d. has fallen, from about 8% to about 3%
    e. rose from 3 to 4% in the 1960s, to as high as 7 or 8% in the early 1980s

21. Suppose that the unemployment rate this month is 10%. Then we can conclude that
    a. the economy is still declining into a recession
    b. the economy is at the trough
    c. the economy has passed the trough, and is now in a recovery
    d. actual GDP is less than potential GDP
    e. potential GDP is less than actual GDP

EXERCISES

1. During recessions, output declines. So does employment (by even more than output, but by less than output). The relationship between changes and output and changes in unemployment is known as (Keynes' law, Okun's law). This relationship is reflected in a (rapid rise in productivity, fall in productivity) during the typical recession.

When a recession becomes very severe, it is called a (depression, stagnation). This occurred during the 1930s. At that time, prices fell, particularly those of (manufactured goods, agricultural commodities). Output declined very sharply, especially the output of (manufactured goods, agricultural commodities). There is a particularly sharp decline in the output of (consumer goods, capital goods). At that time, (cyclical, frictional, structural) unemployment was very high.

2. Figure 7.1 shows fluctuations in real output. Recessions occurred during the time periods _____ and

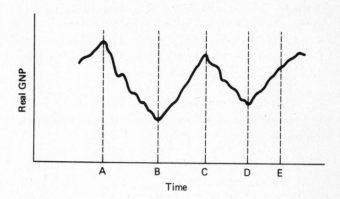

Figure 7.1

_____, and expansions during the periods _____ and _____. Peaks occurred at _____ and _____, while troughs occurred at _____ and _____.

ESSAY QUESTIONS

1. Explain why, during a recession:
a. production of consumer durable goods decreases more than production of consumer nondurables
b. production of capital goods decreases more than production of consumer nondurable goods
c. output generally declines more than employment
d. labour productivity generally declines

2. Explain the conceptual difference between structural and frictional unemployment. Explain also why it may be difficult in practice to distinguish whether specific unemployed individuals are part of "structural" or "frictional" unemployment. Might it also be difficult to tell if specific individuals are part of "frictional" or "cyclical" unemployment? Why or why not?

ANSWERS

Important Terms: **1**b, **2**f, **3**j, **4**i, **5**c, **6**e, **7**h, **8**a, **9**k, **10**g, **11**d
True-False: **1**T, **2**F, **3**T, **4**F, **5**T, **6**T, **7**F, **8**F, **9**T
Multiple Choice: **1**a, **2**c, **3**d, **4**e, **5**b, **6**d, **7**c, **8**b, **9**d, **10**e, **11**e, **12**c, **13**e, **14**a, **15**a, **16**b, **17**a, **18**c, **19**a, **20**e, **21**d
Exercises: **1.** but by less than output, Okun's law, fall in productivity, depression, agricultural commodities, manufactured goods, capital goods, cyclical. **2.** AB, CD, BC, DE, A, C, B, D.

ANSWERS TO SELECTED REVIEW QUESTIONS FROM THE TEXT

7-2. It takes time for inflation to work its way through the system. For example, when demand for goods increases, so does the demand for labour. But usually, wages do not respond quickly, since many workers are covered by contracts. However, as contracts are renegotiated, wages will increase, and higher wages are likely to be passed along in terms of higher prices. In addition, as demand rises in the early stages of a recovery, producers have excess capacity, and they can increase profits by producing more. Later, as they approach capacity, they take advantage of an increase in demand to raise prices.

7-4. Interest rates in the United States are likely to influence interest rates in Canada as well, and the level of interest rates here affects domestic investment in Canada. Moreover, investment in industries that produce for exports may also depend on export demand.

7-5. The following hypothetical data (all seasonally adjusted) illustrate the point:

Month	Monthly output (at annual rate)	Quarterly output (at annual rate)
October	985	
November	990	990
December	995	
January	1,000	
February	995	995
March	990	
April	988	
May	987	987
June	986	
July	985	
August	990	990
September	995	

Chapter 8

■ ■

Explaining Unemployment and Inflation: Aggregate Supply and Aggregate Demand

MAJOR PURPOSE

Chapter 7 provided an overview of macroeconomic problems—fluctuations in the overall level of production, periods of high unemployment, and the problem of inflation. The purpose of this chapter is to begin a study of why these macroeconomic problems arise. In explaining macroeconomic events, *aggregate supply* and *aggregate demand* are useful tools, just as supply and demand are useful in figuring out what is happening in the market for individual products such as hamburgers, shoes, or wheat.

The Great Depression of the 1930s was caused by a collapse in aggregate demand. The milder business cycles of recent decades have been caused primarily by more moderate fluctuations in aggregate demand. Thus, a more stable aggregate demand is the key to reducing fluctuations in output and employment.

LEARNING OBJECTIVES

After you have studied this chapter in the textbook and study guide, you should be able to
- Explain why we should not just assume that aggregate demand and supply curves look like demand and supply curves for an individual product
- Draw the aggregate demand curve of classical economists, and explain why it slopes downward to the right
- Explain why classical economists drew the aggregate supply function as a vertical line
- Explain why the simple version of the Keynesian aggregate supply curve is a reversed L, and what the explanation is for the horizontal section
- List the four major components of aggregate demand that Keynesians consider in detail to determine what is happening to aggregate demand as a whole
- Explain why classical economists believed that equilibrium would occur at full employment, while Keynesian economists believed that equilibrium might occur either at full employment or with large-scale unemployment
- Summarize how classical economists explained the Great Depression of the 1930s
- Summarize the three major propositions in Keynes' *General Theory,* including his major policy conclusion
- Summarize the major points of agreement between Keynesians and those in the classical tradition, and the major points of disagreement

HIGHLIGHTS OF THE CHAPTER

When studying the market for a specific good (such as apples or hamburgers), we use demand and supply curves. To study the overall behaviour of the economy as a whole—changes in total output and the average level of prices—we likewise use aggregate demand and aggregate supply curves.

There are major differences between demand and supply in an individual market, and wrong between aggregate demand and aggregate supply for the economy as a whole. The major difference is that when drawing a demand or supply curve for, say, hamburgers, we are looking at what happens when only the price of this one good changes. (Recall the *ceteris paribus* assumption—that everything else remains unchanged.) Thus, an increase in the price of hamburgers represents a change in *relative* prices; the price of hamburgers rises relative to the prices of other goods. Consumers and producers respond to the change in relative prices. Consumers *switch* away from hamburgers and buy hot dogs or other products instead. Such switching is the major reason that the quantity of hamburgers is smaller when the price is higher. Similarly, producers have an incentive to switch. When the price of hamburgers rises, producers have an incentive to make hamburgers instead of other products. Their willingness to switch from other products, and to produce hamburgers instead, is the principal reason why the supply curve slopes upward to the right.

On the other hand, when we look at *aggregate* demand and aggregate supply, we are looking at the responses of buyers and sellers when the *overall* level of prices rises. In simple terms, we are looking at what happens when *all* prices rise by, say, 10%. Since all prices are rising, there is no change in relative prices. Thus, there is no reason for either buyers or sellers to switch as a result. Switching does *not* provide a reason for the slope of the aggregate demand or aggregate supply curve.

Nevertheless, classical economists believed that the aggregate supply curve sloped downward to the right. The reason was that a fall in the average level of prices would increase the purchasing power of money. When prices fell, people would be able to buy more goods and services with the money in their pockets and their bank accounts. Therefore, they would buy more.

However, classical economists did not draw the aggregate supply curve sloping upward to the right. Instead, they believed that it was vertical, at the full-employment or potential quantity of output. If, starting at full employment, all prices—including the price of raw materials and labour—were to increase by, say, 10%, then producers would have no incentive to produce more. They would get 10% more for their products, it is true, but they would have to pay 10% more for their inputs.

Because they had the same incentive to produce, the total amount offered for sale would remain constant, regardless of the general level of prices.

Equilibrium occurred at the intersection of aggregate demand and aggregate supply. Because classical economists drew the aggregate supply curve as a vertical line at the full-employment output, they believed that there would be full employment whenever the economy was in equilibrium. This raised a question: How was the Depression to be explained? Within the classical framework, large-scale unemployment could be caused by disturbances that resulted in a temporary *disequilibrium*. During the early 1930s, the economy moved away from its full employment equilibrium as a result of the reduction in the money stock and a fall in aggregate demand. Classical economists believed that full employment could be restored by a decrease in wages and prices, which would lead to a new equilibrium at a lower overall price level, or by an increase in the money stock, which would bring aggregate demand back up.

Keynes saw the world differently. He believed that there could be a *long-lasting equilibrium* with high unemployment. The simplest way to illustrate this is with the reversed-L aggregate supply function. In the horizontal range, prices and wages are downwardly rigid. If aggregate demand is so low that it leaves the economy in this horizontal range, then an unemployment equilibrium can persist. The solution to the Depression, said Keynes, was to increase aggregate demand. The best way to get an increase would be through direct government action. The government had the responsibility, said Keynes, to increase its spending and thereby increase overall demand, leading the economy back toward full employment. (This major policy conclusion of Keynesian economics will be explained in detail in Chapter 10.)

The theoretical frameworks of both classical and Keynesian economics are still important, since they are both still used—in modified form—by present-day economists. In spite of the different approaches, there is a widespread agreement among economists on a number of central points:

1. A sharp decline in aggregate demand can cause large-scale unemployment, as it did during the Depression.
2. More moderate fluctuations in aggregate demand can cause milder business cycles and temporary periods of high unemployment.
3. If aggregate demand can be stabilized, the amplitude of business cycles can be reduced.
4. When the economy is already at full employment, any large increase in aggregate demand will cause inflation.

Nevertheless, differences remain, both in theoretical approach and in policy conclusions, between Keynesian economists and those in the classical tradition. Most important are the following differences:

1. Although most economists now believe that both monetary and fiscal policies are important, those in the classical tradition (monetarists) emphasize monetary policy, while those in the Keynesian tradition generally emphasize fiscal policies.

2. Keynesians believe that the government has the responsibility to *manage aggregate demand* by changing fiscal and monetary policies from time to time, in order to stabilize demand and minimize business fluctuations. Monetarists believe that active management is more likely to destabilize than to stabilize aggregate demand. They generally advocate a *policy rule*—the authorities should aim for a slow, steady increase in the stock of money. They believe that this will result in a slow, steady increase in aggregate demand and keep the economy at or close to full employment, without causing inflation.

IMPORTANT TERMS: MATCH THE COLUMNS

Match each term in the first column with the corresponding phrase in the second column.

_____	**1.** Purchasing power of money	**a.** Decline in aggregate demand
_____	**2.** Downward rigidity of prices	**b.** Money rule
_____	**3.** Long run	**c.** Vertical line
_____	**4.** Classical aggregate supply	**d.** Active demand management
_____	**5.** Keynesian aggregate supply	**e.** What a dollar will buy
_____	**6.** The classical equilibrium	**f.** Present-day classicist
_____	**7.** Cause of unemployment	**g.** Too much aggregate demand
_____	**8.** Cause of inflation	**h.** This occurs at full employment
_____	**9.** Monetarist	**i.** This accounts for the horizontal section of Keynesian aggregate supply function
_____	**10.** Monetarist policy	**j.** Reversed L
_____	**11.** Keynesian policy	**k.** In classical economics, the period when prices and wages adjust to their equilibrium levels

TRUE-FALSE

T **F** **1.** The aggregate demand curve slopes downward to the right because people switch away from services, and buy goods instead, when the average price of goods declines.

T F **2.** Even if relative prices remain stable, the aggregate demand curve can nevertheless slope downward to the right.

T F **3.** Classical economists explained the Great Depression as the result of a fall in the money stock, and downward stickiness of wages and prices.

T F **4.** According to classical economists, brief recessions represented periods of disequilibrium, but the economy could be in an unemployment equilibrium during a major depression.

T F **5.** According to classical economists, full employment could have been re-established during the 1930s, but this would have required that both of two conditions be met: (1) a large increase in the money stock, and (2) flexibility of wages and prices.

T F **6.** The major theoretical innovation in Keynes' General Theory was the proposition that the economy could reach an equilibrium with large-scale unemployment.

T F **7.** Sticky wages and prices are the reason for the horizontal section of the Keynesian aggregate supply curve.

T F **8.** One major shortcoming of Keynesian economics is that it assumes prices are permanently fixed. Inflation, therefore, cannot be explained within this theory.

T F **9.** Those who believe that there should be a policy rule are most likely to advocate a slow, steady increase in the money stock.

T F **10.** Monetarists advocate a slow, steady increase in the money stock because they believe that the economy will work best with a slow, steady inflation.

MULTIPLE CHOICE

1. When we draw a classical aggregate demand curve, what do we put on the vertical axis?
  a. total quantity of goods demanded
  b. total quantity of goods and services demanded
  c. full-employment output
  d. the quantity of money
  e. the average level of prices

2. There is an important reason that we cannot conclude that the aggregate demand curve must slope downward to the right, just because the demand for an individual product slopes downward to the right. The reason is
  a. there are no "other goods" for consumers to switch from
  b. relative prices rather than absolute prices are on the axis
  c. inflation-adjusted prices rather than relative prices are on the axis
  d. real prices rather than nominal prices are on the axis
  e. nominal prices rather than real prices are on the axis

3. According to the classical approach, people buy more goods and services when the price level falls (ceteris paribus) because
  a. they switch among products when prices fall
  b. the purchasing power of their money has increased
  c. the purchasing power of their money has decreased
  d. the economy is coming out of a recession
  e. potential GDP has increased because of past investment

4. When the price level doubles, then the purchasing power of the dollar
  a. also doubles
  b. increases, but only by 50%
  c. doesn't change much
  d. falls 50%
  e. falls 100%

5. Which of the following was put at the centre of aggregate demand analysis by classical economists?
  a. money
  b. government spending
  c. the government's tax revenues
  d. tax rates
  e. investment

6. According to classical economists, the aggregate supply curve was
  a. upward sloping, like the supply curve for wheat
  b. downward sloping, like the supply curve for wheat
  c. vertical, at potential GDP
  d. an L
  e. a reversed L

7. According to classical economists, when the economy was at equilibrium, then real GDP would be
  a. about 10% above the level in the most recent recession
  b. above potential GDP
  c. at potential GDP
  d. below potential GDP
  e. either **c.** or **d.**, but we can't tell which without information on aggregate demand

8. According to classical economists, the Great Depression represented
  a. a disequilibrium caused by a fall in the quantity of money
  b. a disequilibrium caused by a fall in exports
  c. a disequilibrium with the twin problems of high inflation and high unemployment
  d. an equilibrium with the twin problems of high inflation and high unemployment
  e. an equilibrium with large-scale unemployment and falling prices

9. According to classical economists, if the economy suffers from a high level of unemployment, full employment can be re-established by
  a. an increase in the productive capacity of the economy
  b. an increase in the price level
  c. a decrease in the price level
  d. an increase in the money stock
  e. either **c.** or **d.**, or a combination of the two

10. According to classical economists, the best thing the government could do to prevent recessions and depressions would be to
  a. cut government spending
  b. increase government spending
  c. provide a steady increase in the money stock
  d. promote investment
  e. promote imports

11. According to Keynes, the primary cause of large-scale unemployment is
  a. high prices
  b. low prices
  c. high exports
  d. low exports
  e. inadequate aggregate demand

12. According to Keynes, when the economy was at equilibrium, then real GDP would be

a. about 10% above the level in the most recent recession
b. above potential GDP
c. at potential GDP
d. below potential GDP
e. either **c.** or **d.**, but we can't tell which without information on aggregate demand

13. In its simplest form, the Keynesian aggregate supply function was
a. upward sloping, like the supply curve for wheat
b. downward sloping, like the supply curve for wheat
c. vertical, at potential GDP
d. an L
e. a reversed L

14. Consider the reversed L aggregate supply function of Keynesian economics. The effects of an increase in aggregate demand will differ, depending on where the economy begins. Specifically, an increase in aggregate demand will lead to
a. an increase in prices if the economy starts in the horizontal section, but an increase in output if it starts in the vertical section
b. an increase in prices if the economy starts in the vertical section, but an increase in output if it starts in the horizontal section
c. an increase in prices if the economy starts in the horizontal section, but a decrease in prices if it starts in the vertical section
d. an increase in prices if the economy starts in the vertical section, but a decrease in prices if it starts in the horizontal section
e. an increase in prices if the economy starts in the horizontal section, but a decrease in employment if it starts in the vertical section

15. The Keynesian and classical aggregate supply functions are similar in that they both
a. have a horizontal range
b. have an intermediate, upward-sloped range
c. are based on the assumption of downward price rigidity
d. are based on the assumption of price stickiness
e. lead to the conclusion that a large increase in aggregate demand will cause inflation if the economy is already at full employment

16. According to Keynes
a. a collapse in investment demand was the primary cause of the Depression, and an increase in investment demand provided the best hope of recovery
b. a collapse in government spending was the primary cause of the Depression, and an

increase in government spending provided the best hope of recovery
c. a collapse in investment demand was the primary cause of the Depression, but an increase in government spending provided the best hope of recovery
d. a collapse in government spending was the primary cause of the Depression, but an increase in investment demand provided the best hope of recovery
e. a collapse in government spending was the primary cause of the Depression, but an increase in saving provided the best hope of recovery

17. The principal cause of the Great Depression of the 1930s was
a. a collapse in aggregate demand
b. a collapse in aggregate supply
c. a collapse in prices
d. a collapse in government spending
e. the outbreak of the Second World War

18. Those in the classical and Keynesian traditions agree that
a. a decline in aggregate demand was the principal cause of the Great Depression
b. a decline in the money stock was the principal cause of the Great Depression
c. a decline in investment demand was the principal cause of the Great Depression
d. fluctuations in aggregate supply have been the major cause of fluctuations in output and employment in recent decades
e. the government has the responsibility to manage aggregate demand actively

19. Shifts in aggregate demand, rather than shifts in aggregate supply, seem to be the primary reason for fluctuations in output. We come to that conclusion because declines in output are usually associated with
a. rising inflation
b. declining inflation
c. more unemployment
d. less unemployment
e. increases in government spending

20. Some macroeconomists propose that the authorities adhere to a policy rule. The most common proposal of the proponents of a rule is for a moderate, steady increase in
a. the quantity of money
b. potential GDP
c. the average level of prices
d. tax rates
e. government tax revenues

EXERCISES

1. In Figure 8.1, AS_1 represents the part of the aggregate supply function above point A. A classical economist completing this function would draw the dashed section shown as (AS_a, AS_b). However, a Keynesian economist would be more likely to complete it with (AS_a, AS_b).

Suppose that AD_1 is the initial aggregate demand curve. Then the initial equilibrium will be at point _____, where the equilibrium quantity of output will be $0Q$ _____. According to (classical, Keynesian, both) economists, there will be full employment at this initial equilibrium.

Now suppose that aggregate demand collapses to AD_2. According to classical economists, the economy

will move in the short run to a point such as _____. However, this point does not represent a new equilibrium, since (the economy is not at full employment, prices are below P_1). If aggregate demand remains at AD_2, prices will (rise, fall), and the economy will move to a new equilibrium at point _____. At this new equilibrium, there will be (full employment, large-scale unemployment). In the face of a fall in aggregate demand from its initial AD_1 to AD_2, Keynesians see a different outcome. In the short run, the economy will move to point _____. If aggregate demand remains stable at AD_2, the long-run equilibrium will be at point _____, with output $0Q$ _____. With this output, there will be (full employment, large-scale unemployment).

2. On many matters, Keynesian economists and those in the classical tradition agree. However, there are still some disagreements. Mark each of the views below with a C if it is more likely to be held with those in the classical tradition, or with a K if it is more likely to be held by Keynesians:

_____ **a.** Money is by far the most important determinant of aggregate demand

_____ **b.** The government should manage aggregate demand to reduce cyclical swings in the economy

_____ **c.** Even when the unemployment rate is high, wages and prices will move down only slightly, if at all

_____ **d.** Following a rule, rather than periodically adjusting policies, is more likely to lead to a stable economy

_____ **e.** The best policy to follow is to increase the quantity of money at a slow, steady rate

_____ **f.** Large-scale unemployment represents a temporary disequilibrium.

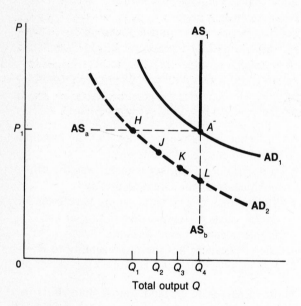

Figure 8.1

ESSAY QUESTIONS

1. Using diagrams, explain briefly how classical economists drew the aggregate demand and aggregate supply curve. What might cause a depression? How might the economy move out of a depression and to full employment?

2. Summarize the three main points in Keynes' General Theory. Which points, if any, might a classical economist agree with?

ANSWERS

Important Terms: 1e, 2i, 3k, 4c, 5j, 6h, 7a, 8g, 9f, 10b, 11d
True-False: 1F, 2T, 3T, 4F, 5F, 6T, 7T, 8F, 9T, 10F
Multiple Choice: 1e, 2a, 3b, 4d, 5a, 6c, 7c, 8a, 9e, 10c, 11e, 12e, 13e, 14b, 15e, 16c, 17a, 18a, 19b, 20a
Exercises: **1.** AS_b, AS_a, *A*, $0Q_4$, both, *J* or *K*, the economy is not at full employment, fall, *L*, full employment, *H, H,* $0Q_1$, large-scale unemployment.
2. a.C, **b.**K, **c.**K, **d.**C, **e.**C, **f.**C

ANSWERS TO SELECTED REVIEW QUESTIONS FROM THE TEXT

8-1. The demand curve for a specific good shows what happens to the quantity demanded when an individual price changes, with all other prices remaining the same. A decline in the price of the good represents a decline in this price relative to the prices of other goods. People respond by switching from other goods, and buy more of this good instead. When the aggregate demand curve is drawn, we are looking at changes in the average level of prices. Changes in relative prices may be minor or non-existent. Switching is therefore unimportant, and cannot explain the slope of the aggregate demand function.

8-4. The money supply might be increased, which would cause a rightward shift of the AD curve. In this way, full-employment equilibrium could be established without a decrease in prices and wages. Alternatively, we could wait until prices and wages had fallen enough to bring us back to equilibrium at the vertical AS curve and the original AD curve.

8-7. As Figure 8-6 shows, if the reason for output fluctuations were fluctuations in aggregate supply, then high levels of output (low unemployment) should typically be accompanied by falling prices (or at least by a reduced rate of price inflation), and low output (high unemployment) should be accompanied by high rates of price inflation. But this is not, in fact, the pattern that we see in the actual data on the economy's performance.

Across

1. Some recommend this to make the economy more stable. (2 words)
4. tree, and left over from fire
8. where you live
10. 3.14...
11. not (French)
12. builder
13. important economic objective (2 words)
17. metal
18. a fruit or a computer
19. before
20. _____ John's, Newfoundland
21. one of the three basic factors of production
22. In games of cards, it's either high or low.
23. To banks and pension funds, this is important.
25. where lawyers are called
26. He revolutionized economists' views on macroeconomics.
27. two directions (abbrev.)
28. peace (Russian)
29. long time period
31. According to Marx, capitalism would do this to the working class.
35, 38. According to classical economists, these constituted one reason why the Depression lasted so long.
39. Greek letter, used in English to refer to something very small.
40. third person singular (impersonal pronoun)
41. They pick the government.
43. what Queen Victoria did on her throne
45. the (Spanish)
46. According to Keynesians, this is the best type of policy.
48. catches the wind on a boat
49. Money has this type of power.

Down

1. encountered
2. nasty
3. major economic problem
4. the economy's performance during the Great Depression
6. Canadian character on TV
7. type of income
9. If there is too much of this, there will be inflation.
10. a football player
11. Lenin's economic program; also, Canadian government program regulating the oil and gas industry in the 1970s (abbrev.)
12. first person possessive
13. one of the two major policies for managing aggregate demand
14. big city in California (abbrev.)
15. Some advocate this for managing the economy.
16. providers of finance
22. rough or scratchy, and hard
23. exist
24. The intellectual ancestors of monetarism belonged to this school; also, type of music.
26. what the player in 10 down does
29. group of European countries (abbrev.)
30. keeps your fingers warm in winter
32. record that keeps going for a while (abbrev.)
33. _____, ye prisoners of starvation!
34. When you look for a job, you need this.
36. helpful when you are fixing something
37. French city
42. lower part of window
44. group of people organized for play or work
47. from or of (German); also group of health care workers (abbrev.)

Chapter 9

■ ■

Equilibrium with Unemployment: The Keynesian Approach

MAJOR PURPOSE

Chapter 8 presented the main outlines of Keynesian and classical economics. The purpose of this chapter is to explain the central proposition of Keynesian economics—*that the economy may reach an equilibrium with large-scale unemployment.* This happens when aggregate spending is too low to buy all the goods and services that could be produced by the economy at full employment. When aggregate spending is too low, businesses can't sell many of their products. Lacking sales, they cut back on production and lay off workers.

Aggregate demand is made up of four major components: personal consumption expenditures, investment demand, government purchases of goods and services, and net exports. In order to present the simplest explanation, this chapter deals with an economy with only consumption and investment—that is, the government and the foreign sectors are ignored in this chapter. (They are considered in Chapter 10.) Furthermore, investment

demand is not explained here; we simply assume that investment demand exists, and see what happens when it changes. (The reasons for a change in investment demand will be studied in Chapter 13 and in the appendix to Chapter 18.)

Thus, consumption is the only type of spending studied in detail in this chapter. The main determinant of consumption is disposable income: When people have more income, they generally spend more. This has important implications for what happens when *investment* demand increases. People are put to work producing factories and machines. Their incomes rise. Therefore, they consume more. Therefore, an increase in investment demand causes—or *induces*—an increase in consumption demand, too. As a result, an increase in investment demand has a *multiplier effect*—real domestic product goes up by a multiple of the increase in investment.

LEARNING OBJECTIVES

After you have studied this chapter in the textbook and study guide, you should be able to
- Explain the relationship between disposable income and consumer expenditures
- Explain what the MPC is, and why it is the same as the slope of the consumption function
- Explain why, when we put disposable income (or domestic product) on the horizontal axis, we can also measure disposable income (or domestic product) as the distance up to the 45° line
- Derive the saving function from the consumption function
- Explain the relationship between the MPC and the MPS
- Explain why equilibrium domestic product is found where the aggregate expenditure function cuts the 45° line
- Explain what will happen if domestic product is greater or less than this equilibrium quantity
- Explain the difference between a leakage and an injection, and give an illustration of each

- Express the equilibrium condition for domestic product in three different ways, and explain why these three different statements amount to the same thing
- Explain why there may be large-scale unemployment when the economy is in equilibrium
- Explain why an increase in investment has a multiplied effect on aggregate expenditures and domestic product
- Write the two equations for the multiplier in the simple economy with no taxes or international transactions

HIGHLIGHTS OF THE CHAPTER

This chapter introduces the basic framework of Keynesian theory. The major innovation of Keynes was the proposition that the economy could reach an equilibrium with large-scale unemployment. Domestic product would not automatically move to the full-employment level; it could stay much below that level if aggregate demand were low. This conclusion provided the reason for his policy conclusion: Since a policy of laissez-faire might result in large-scale unemployment, it was up to the government to adopt policies designed to bring aggregate demand up to the full-employment level. (This policy conclusion will be studied in Chapter 10.)

As we saw in Chapter 6, there are four components of aggregate demand: personal consumption expenditures, investment demand, government purchases of goods and services, and net exports. However, to make things simple, this chapter deals with an economy with only consumption and investment.

Consumption expenditures (C) depend on disposable income (DI). The relationship between C and DI is known as the *consumption function*. This function has three main characteristics:

1. As DI increases, so does consumption. This means that the consumption function *slopes upward.*

2. The change in C (ΔC) is less than the change in DI (ΔDI). The change in C, as a *fraction* of the change in DI, is known as the *marginal propensity to consume* (MPC). This fraction, $\Delta C/\Delta DI$, is also the *slope* of the consumption function. Because the MPC is less than one, the slope of the consumption function is likewise less than one.

3. At very low levels of DI, C is larger than DI. That is, people spend more than their incomes; they *dissave*. They do this by running down their assets or by borrowing.

These characteristics are illustrated in Figure 9-2 in the textbook.

In order to simplify the discussion, the consumption function is also given a fourth characteristic: It is drawn as a *straight line* in textbooks. This means that the MPC is constant. The evidence on consumer behaviour shown in Figure 9-1 suggests that the MPC need not, in fact, be constant. Thus, we should file away in the back of our minds that we have made a simplifying assumption that is not necessarily correct.

Saving may be identified by drawing a 45° line on the consumption function diagram. The 45° line is equidistant from the two axes; measuring up to the 45° line gives the same number as measuring horizontally to the line. Because we measure disposable income on the horizontal axis, we may also measure disposable income in an upward direction; it is the height of the 45° line. Saving is zero at the point where $C = DI$—that is, the point where the consumption function and the 45° line intersect.

In simple terms, saving equals $DI - C$. (It is standard procedure to use this simple relationship, and ignore the interest paid to consumers shown on Figure 6-3 in the textbook.) Thus, a saving function can be derived directly from the consumption function. Specifically, the height of the saving function (Figure 9-3) is the vertical distance between the consumption function and the 45° line (Figure 9-2). The saving function has three main characteristics:

1. As DI increases, so does saving. This means that the saving function *slopes upward.*

2. The change in S (ΔS) is less than the change in DI (ΔDI). The change in S, as a *fraction* of the change in DI, is the *marginal propensity to save* (MPS). This fraction, $\Delta S/\Delta DI$, is also the *slope* of the saving function. Because the MPS is less than one, the slope of the saving function is likewise less than one.

3. When people have very low incomes, S is negative. That is, people *dissave*.

Because each $1 of additional disposable income is either consumed or saved, MPC + MPS = 1.

To see a simple illustration of equilibrium, we look at a simple economy in which there is no depreciation, no government, and no international transactions; in particular, we assume there is no foreign capital in Canada or Canadian assets held abroad. In such an economy, GDP = NDP = NNP, and we can talk simply of domestic product which we denote by the symbol Y. Furthermore, in the absence of taxes and transfers, Y = NI = DI; therefore, we can redraw the consumption function with Y measured along the horizontal axis or up to the 45° line.

When we add investment demand (I^*) vertically to the consumption function, we get the *aggregate expenditure function*, which shows how aggregate spending depends on domestic product. Equilibrium occurs where AE = Y—that is, where the AE function cuts the 45° line. At this point, producers are able to sell what they produce. If domestic product were larger—say, at L in Figure 9-5 in the textbook—then production would be greater than aggregate expenditures. Unsold goods would pile up in *undesired inventory accumulation*. In order to reduce their undesired inventories, businesses would cut back on orders from suppliers and reduce their production. Output would fall back to its equilibrium at K. At equilibrium, aggregate expenditures may fall below the level needed for full employment. That is, equilibrium domestic product K may be to the left of full-employment point F, as shown in Figure 9-5. Figure 9-5 is one of the half-dozen most important diagrams in the book.

The circumstances under which there is equilibrium may be stated in three different ways, all of which amount to the same thing. Equilibrium occurs when:

1. AE = Y, as shown by the intersection of AE and the 45° line in Figure 9-5. At this point of intersection, there is a demand for all the goods and services produced. That is:

2. Undesired inventory accumulation equals zero, and I = I^*.

3. S = I^*, as shown in Figure 9-6 in the text.

If investment demand increases, the additional investment demand is added vertically to the AE function; the AE function shifts upward. As a result, domestic product increases. As it does so, incomes increase. People spend more. Thus, a $1 increase in investment demand leads not only to $1 more in the output of capital goods; it leads to more output of consumer goods and services, too. Overall output increases by a multiple of the $1 increase in investment. This is the important *multiplier* concept. Specifically, the multiplier is equal to $\Delta Y / \Delta I^*$. In the simple economy, this equals 1/MPS. Details on the multiplier are given in Figure 9-11 in the textbook.

IMPORTANT TERMS: MATCH THE COLUMNS

Match each term in the first column with the corresponding phrase in the second column.

_____	1. Marginal propensity to consume	**a.**	Saving
_____	2. Marginal propensity to save	**b.**	Y = AE
_____	3. Saving	**c.**	1/MPS
_____	4. Equilibrium domestic product	**d.**	I minus I^*
_____	5. Undesired inventory accumulation	**e.**	$\Delta C / \Delta DI$
_____	6. A leakage	**f.**	I^*
_____	7. An injection	**g.**	$DI - C$
_____	8. Multiplier	**h.**	1 minus MPC

TRUE-FALSE

T (F) **1.** If the MPC is constant, then the MPS is equal to the MPC.
T (F) **2.** The slope of the aggregate expenditures function is equal to the MPS.
(T) F **3.** The slope of the saving function = 1 − MPC.
T (F) **4.** If the consumption function is a straight line, then the MPC is greater than 1.
T (F) **5.** Businesses respond to undesired inventory accumulation by increasing their orders for goods.
(T) F **6.** If domestic product is above its equilibrium, then actual investment is greater than desired investment.
(T) F **7.** If undesired inventory accumulation is positive, then actual domestic product exceeds equilibrium domestic product.
T (F) **8.** Because all goods must be demanded if they are to be produced, the slope of the aggregate expenditures schedule equals 45°.
(T) F **9.** The higher is the MPC, the larger is the multiplier.

MULTIPLE CHOICE

1. In Keynesian theory, aggregate demand is studied as the sum of four components, including each of the items below *except one*. Which one?
  a. Personal consumption expenditures
  b. Personal saving
  c. Investment demand
  d. Government purchases of goods and services
  e. Net exports

2. Saving equals zero when
  a. $C + I^* =$ domestic product
  b. $C + I^* =$ aggregate expenditures
  c. Personal income = disposable income
  d. Consumption = disposable income
  e. MPC = 1

3. The slope of the consumption function is equal to
  a. the MPC
  b. the MPS
  c. the MPS + 1
  d. the multiplier
  e. 1/(the multiplier)

4. If the MPC is three-quarters, then an increase in disposable income will cause
  a. consumption to rise by three times the increase in disposable income
  b. consumption to rise by four times the increase in disposable income
  c. consumption to increase, while saving decreases
  d. consumption to decrease, while saving increases
  e. consumption and saving both to increase, with consumption increasing more than saving

5. Suppose that the consumption function is a straight line. Then
  a. consumption is a constant fraction of income
  b. saving is a constant fraction of income
  c. the MPC is constant
  d. the MPC becomes smaller as income becomes smaller
  e. the MPS becomes smaller as income becomes smaller

6. If the slope of the consumption function rises, then we may conclude that
  a. the slope of the saving function has fallen
  b. the marginal propensity to save has risen
  c. the marginal propensity to consume has fallen
  d. the multiplier has become smaller
  e. undesired inventory accumulation has become larger

7. The aggregate expenditure function shows how spending increases in real terms as
  a. prices fall
  b. prices increase
  c. real domestic product increases
  d. saving increases
  e. unemployment increases

8. Actual investment minus investment demand equals
  a. one
  b. zero
  c. inventory investment
  d. undesired inventory investment
  e. desired inventory investment

9. Suppose that, in a simple Keynesian system, domestic product exceeds its equilibrium quantity. Then
  a. aggregate expenditures exceed domestic product
  b. investment demand exceeds saving
  c. actual investment exceeds investment demand
  d. the multiplier equals 1
  e. MPC = MPS − 1

10. Domestic product is at its equilibrium when
  a. aggregate expenditures = $C + I^* + G$
  b. aggregate expenditures = domestic product
  c. saving = undesired inventory accumulation
  d. saving = desired inventory accumulation
  e. government spending = tax revenues

11. When undesired inventory accumulation equals zero, then
  a. $S = 0$
  b. $I = 0$
  c. $I^* = 0$
  d. government spending = tax revenues
  e. domestic product is at its equilibrium level

12. In *The General Theory,* Keynes argued that
  a. a market economy might reach equilibrium with large-scale unemployment
  b. large-scale unemployment is caused by inadequate aggregate demand
  c. the best way to cure large-scale unemployment is by increasing government spending
  d. all of the above
  e. none of the above

13. Suppose that saving is greater than investment demand. Then
  a. there must be full employment when the economy is in equilibrium
  b. there must be large-scale unemployment when the economy is in equilibrium
  c. domestic product is greater than the equilibrium
  d. domestic product is less than the equilibrium
  e. undesired inventory accumulation is negative

14. In the circular flow of spending
    a. investment is an injection, and saving a
       leakage
    b. saving is an injection, and investment a
       leakage
    c. saving and investment are both leakages, and
       consumption is an injection
    d. saving and investment are both injections,
       and consumption is a leakage
    e. consumption and saving are both leakages,
       and investment is an injection

15. The condition for equilibrium may be stated in
three different ways—in each of the following ways
except one. Which is the exception?
    a. aggregate expenditures = domestic product
    b. $I = I^*$
    c. $S = I^*$
    d. $S = I$

16. When investment demand increases, which of the
following functions shifts upward?
    a. aggregate supply
    b. aggregate expenditures
    c. consumption
    d. saving
    e. leakages

17. Consider a simple economy, with no government
or international trade, and with an MPC of 0.9.
According to the multiplier theory, if investment
demand increases by $10 billion, equilibrium domes-

tic product will rise by a multiple of the $10 billion.
Specifically, equilibrium domestic product will rise by
    a. $100 billion, made up of the original $10 bil-
       lion in investment plus an additional $90 bil-
       lion of investment stimulated by the initial
       investment
    b. $100 billion, made up of the $10 billion in
       investment plus $90 billion in consumption as
       consumers move along the consumption
       function
    c. $50 billion, made up of $10 billion in invest-
       ment plus $40 billion in consumption
    d. $50 billion, made up of the original $10 bil-
       lion in investment plus an additional $40 bil-
       lion of investment stimulated by the initial
       investment
    e. $50 billion, made up of $10 billion in invest-
       ment, $20 billion of consumption, and $20
       billion of government spending for goods and
       services

18. Consider a simple economy, with no government
and no international trade. Then, if the MPC = 0.9,
the multiplier is
    a. also 0.9
    b. 1
    c. 5
    d. 10
    e. 100

EXERCISES

1. Figure 9.1 shows a simple economy with only two
types of expenditure—consumption and investment. In
this economy, equilibrium occurs at point _____,
with domestic product of _____. At this domestic
product, consumption is distance _____, desired
investment is distance _____, actual investment is
distance _____, saving is distance _____, and
undesired inventory accumulation is _____. Now,
suppose that domestic product is equal to 0C. At this
domestic product, consumption is distance _____,
desired investment is distance _____, actual investment is distance _____, saving is distance
_____, and undesired inventory accumulation is dis-
tance _____.

In this diagram, we can also tell the size of the multiplier. If, from an initial point of equilibrium, investment
were to fall to zero, the equilibrium point would move
to _____. That is, when investment demand fell by
distance _____, domestic product would fall by distance _____. Thus, the size of the multiplier is distance AB divided by distance _____.

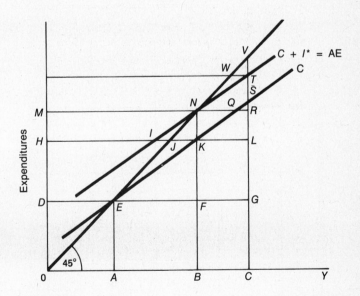

Figure 9.1

We can also tell the MPC in this diagram. Specifically,
it is distance _____ divided by distance EF.

2. Table 9.1 below represents the same type of simple economy studied in this chapter. Suppose that the MPC = 0.8. Fill in the second column, giving the consumption expenditures at each level of disposable income DI, which is the same as domestic product Y. Suppose that desired investment is 40. Now fill in the third column, giving aggregate expenditures at each level of disposable income. Now fill in the fourth and fifth columns, giving (respectively) the amount of saving and the amount of undesired inventory accumulation at each quantity of domestic product. Then fill in the sixth column, giving S minus desired investment. What is the equilibrium domestic product in this economy?

3. Suppose that the consumption function is $C = 25 + 0.75DI$. In other words, if $DI = 100$, then $C = 25 + 0.75 \times 100 = 100$. Plot the consumption function in Figure 9.2. Plot the corresponding saving function in Figure 9.3. Now suppose that desired investment is 25. Plot this investment in Figure 9.3, and plot the aggregate expenditures function and the 45° line in Figure 9.2. The MPC equals _____, the MPS equals _____,

the multiplier equals _____, and the equilibrium domestic product is _____. Now suppose that desired investment increases by 25; it is now 50. Plot the new aggregate expenditures function in Figure 9.2 and the new desired investment in Figure 9.3. The new equilibrium domestic product is _____. At the quantity of Y that used to be equilibrium, aggregate expenditures are now (more, less) than Y by quantity _____, saving is now (more, less) than desired investment by quantity _____, and undesired inventory accumulation equals _____.

4. Suppose that the MPC is 0.5 and that investment expenditures increase by 40 (that is, desired investment increases by 40). In the first column of Table 9.2, fill in the expenditures at each round, as in the table accompanying Figure 9-11 in the text. In the second column, fill in the cumulative total of expenditures (investment plus consumption) up to and including that round. The total expenditures in *all* the rounds, if the series is continued indefinitely, will be _____.

Table 9.1

(1) $DI\ (=Y)$	(2) C	(3) Aggregate expenditure	(4) Saving	(5) Undesired inventory investment	(6) S minus investment demand
0	20				
100					
200					
300					
400					
500					

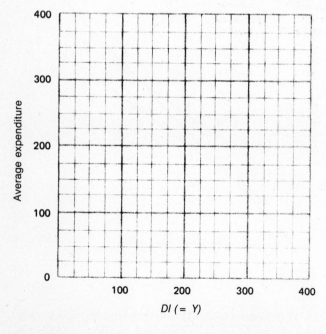

Figure 9.2

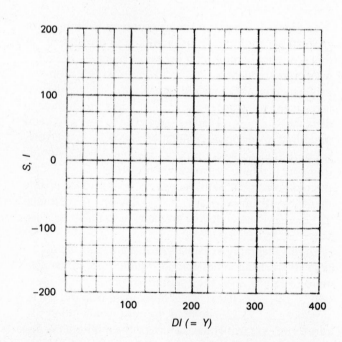

Figure 9.3

Table 9.2

		(1) Change in aggregate expenditure	(2) Cumulative total
First round	Investment of		
Second round	Consumption of		
Third round	Consumption of		
Fourth round	Consumption of		
Fifth round	Consumption of		
Sixth round	Consumption of		
Seventh round	Consumption of		

ESSAY QUESTIONS

1. In the textbook, disposable income is the main determinant of consumption expenditures. But consumption can depend on other things, too. What other variables do you think are important, and why? (Hints: Besides disposable income, what determines the expenditures of a retiree? Does it make sense for a student to consume more than his or her disposable income? Why?)

2. In the textbook, the level of investment is initially assumed to be constant, and then it is assumed to change without explanation. What do you think would be the important determinants of investment? Would investment demand depend on domestic product? *If so,* how would this change the way in which Figures 9-5 and 9-6 were drawn in the textbook? Would it make the economy more or less stable through time? *If not,* why do you think other determinants are more important than domestic product?

ANSWERS

Important Terms: **1**e, **2**h, **3**g, **4**b, **5**d, **6**a, **7**f, **8**c
True-False: **1**F, **2**F, **3**T, **4**F, **5**F, **6**T, **7**T, **8**F, **9**T
Multiple Choice: **1**b, **2**d, **3**a, **4**e, **5**c, **6**a, **7**c, **8**d, **9**c, **10**b, **11**e, **12**d, **13**c, **14**a, **15**d, **16**b, **17**b, **18**d
Exercises: **1.** N, 0B, BK, KN, KN, KN, zero. CS, ST, SV, SV, TV. E, KN, AB, KN. FK.
2. Table 9.1 completed:

DI (= Y)	C	Aggregate expenditure	Saving	Undesired inventory investment	S minus investment demand
0	20	60	− 20	− 60	− 60
100	100	140	0	− 40	− 40
200	180	220	20	− 20	− 20
300	260	300	40	0	0
400	340	380	60	20	20
500	420	460	80	40	40

Equilibrium domestic product is 300.

3. 0.75, 0.25, 4, 200, 300, more, 25, less, 25, − 25
4. Table 9.2 completed:

	(1)	(2)
First	40	40
Second	20	60
Third	10	70
Fourth	5	75
Fifth	2.5	77.5
Sixth	1.25	78.75
Seventh	0.625	79.375

The total expenditures in all rounds will be 80.

ANSWERS TO SELECTED REVIEW QUESTIONS FROM THE TEXT

9-4. With an MPC of 0.8, the multiplier is $[1/(1 - 0.8)] = 5$. with an MPC of 0.9, it is $[1/(1 - 0.9)] = 10$.

9-5. When MPS is 0.2, the multiplier is $[1/0.2] = 5$, so a $20 billion increase in investment raises equilibrium output by $100 billion. When MPS is 0.5, the multiplier is only $[1/0.5] = 2$, so the increase in output is only $40 billion.

9-6. Actual investment = desired investment plus undesired inventory accumulation. If follows that, if desired investment is greater than actual investment, undesired inventory accumulation is negative; that is, inventories are less than businesses want. More orders will be placed with producers as a way of building up inventories to desired levels, and production will consequently increase.

9-7.

DP	C	S	AE_1	AE_2
100	90	10	130	150
110	97.5	12.5	137.5	157.5
120	105	15	145	165
130	112.5	17.5	152.5	172.5
140	120	20	160	180
150	127.5	22.5	167.5	187.5
160	135	25	175	195
170	142.5	27.5	182.5	202.5
180	150	30	190	210

(b) 0.75; 0.25

(d) Equilibrium domestic product is outside the range of the table; by extending the table to higher values of DP, you will see that the equilibrium occurs at $220 billion.

(e) $300 billion

(f) 4

Part Three
The Management of Aggregate Demand

Chapter 10

■ ■

Aggregate Demand: The Effects of Fiscal Policy and Foreign Trade

MAJOR PURPOSE

The principal cause of recessions and depressions is the instability of aggregate expenditures. In the previous chapter, we looked at the way fluctuations in investment influence aggregate expenditures. In this chapter, we look at two additional influences on aggregate expenditures: foreign trade (exports and imports) and fiscal policy (government spending and taxes). One purpose of this chapter is to show how government spending and exports play a role analogous to investment as injections into the income stream, while taxes and imports, like savings, constitute leakages from the income stream.

Government spending and taxation can be used by economic policy makers as tools for deliberately influencing aggregate expenditures so as to stabilize the economy. The second major purpose of this chapter is to explain in detail how these two fiscal policy tools can be used.

Government spending for goods and services constitutes one of the components of aggregate expenditures, and an increase in such spending therefore increases aggregate expenditures directly. If, during a depression, the government builds new roads, people will be put to work building the roads and providing materials to construction companies. The initial increase in output and employment will be followed by a multiplier effect, as those engaged in roadbuilding activities find that their incomes are higher and, therefore, they buy more consumer goods.

A change in tax rates does not affect aggregate spending in the same way; taxes are not a component of aggregate expenditures. However, a cut in tax rates leaves the public with more disposable income and, therefore, encourages consumption spending.

Ideally, the government should cut taxes to fight recessions and raise taxes to fight inflation, thereby stabilizing the path of demand. In practice, however, the Canadian government has had only partial success in using its fiscal policy tools for this purpose.

LEARNING OBJECTIVES

After you have studied this chapter in the textbook and study guide, you should be able to
- Explain why a cut in tax rates causes an increase in aggregate expenditures
- Explain why a $100 change in government spending can have a more powerful effect on equilibrium domestic product than a $100 change in taxes
- Explain why taxes, nevertheless, have become the primary tool of fiscal policy
- Explain why an increase in tax rates causes the aggregate expenditure function to become flatter, thereby decreasing the size of the multiplier
- Explain how an increase in exports causes an increase in aggregate expenditures
- Explain how aggregate expenditures and the multiplier are influenced by the leakage into imports
- Give examples of automatic stabilizers, and explain how they act to stabilize the economy
- Describe how the full-employment budget is measured
- Explain what the full-employment budget is used for
- Explain why the government may destabilize the economy if it attempts to balance the budget every year
- Explain why a large and growing domestic debt can be a problem

HIGHLIGHTS OF THE CHAPTER

Government spending, like investment, is an injection into the income stream, and taxes, like saving, are a leakage. Similarly, exports, earnings generated when goods and services are sold to foreign countries, are an injection, and spending on imports is a leakage. As in Chapter 9, planned injections and leakages must be equal for domestic product to be at its equilibrium level. In other words, G plus X plus planned I, must equal T plus M plus S.

Canada's exports of goods and services, like investment spending, contribute directly to aggregate expenditures. Changes in exports have the same multiplied effect on domestic product and income as do changes in planned investment spending. Because foreign demand for our exports depends on economic conditions in foreign countries, this means that economic fluctuations in other countries sometimes cause fluctuations in the Canadian economy as well, via changes in our exports. Similarly, changes in foreign countries that affect the Canadian demand for imported goods (for example, a change in the prices of foreign goods) also have an effect on our domestic product because they affect the import leakage.

Like investment and exports, government spending contributes directly to aggregate expenditures; changes in government spending also have a multiplied effect on equilibrium domestic product. Changes in taxes also influence domestic product, but not to the same extent because they affect aggregate expenditures only indirectly.

Because government spending and taxation are controlled by the government, they can be used deliberately to stabilize the Canadian economy; that is, the government may use *fiscal policy* as a weapon to fight unemployment and inflation.

During a depression or severe recession, aggregate expenditures are below the full-employment output. If we look at the height of the aggregate expenditures function at the full-employment domestic product, we will find that it lies below the 45° line. The vertical distance between the two lines, measured at the full-employment domestic product, is the *recessionary gap*. This is the amount by which the aggregate expenditures curve should be shifted upward to get the economy to full employment. The government can eliminate a recessionary gap of, say, $10 billion by increasing its spending by that amount.

Government spending, like investment spending, contributes directly to aggregate expenditures. Furthermore, a change in government spending has the same multiplied effect on equilibrium domestic product as do changes in investment.

Changes in tax rates also affect domestic product, but not in the same direct way because taxes are not a component of aggregate expenditures. However, changes in taxes affect disposable income and therefore affect consumption. For example, an increase in tax rates reduces the disposable income of the public, thereby discouraging consumption. As a result, the consumption function is lowered, and the aggregate expenditure function is likewise lowered.

An increase in tax rates also has a second important effect on the consumption function and aggregate expenditures. Not only do these functions become *lower*; they also become *flatter*. The reason is that an increase of, say, 10% in taxes will take more income from the public if domestic product is large than if it is small. Therefore, the larger is domestic product—that is, the further we go to the right in the 45° diagram—the greater will be the depressing effect of taxes on consumption.

The leakage of spending into imports also tends to rise automatically when domestic product and income rise, and to fall when product and income fall. The *marginal propensity to import* (MPM) is a measure of the fraction of an increase in income which leaks out as additional imports. Just like a proportional tax, the import leakage makes the consumption and aggregate expenditure functions flatter: As with taxes, the import leakage becomes larger as domestic product and income increase. In an economy with a high tax rate and a high marginal propensity to import, the aggregate expenditure function is quite flat. As a result, the multiplier is small. Fluctuations in investment or government spending have a weakened effect on equilibrium domestic product. Because the existence of imports and taxes means that the multiplier is smaller, the economy is *stabilized automatically*.

The action of taxes as an automatic stabilizer means that government deficits automatically tend to increase during recessions. Tax rates do not have to be adjusted for taxes to have a stabilizing effect.

While these "automatic deficits" help to stabilize the economy, they introduce two important complications into fiscal policy. First, they present a *trap* for the policy maker. If the government follows a superficially plausible strategy of trying to balance the budget every year, it will end up destabilizing the economy. As the economy swings into recession, deficits will automatically appear. If the authorities raise taxes or cut spending in an attempt to balance the budget, they will be following precisely the wrong fiscal policy; they will be depressing aggregate expenditures further, and adding to the depth of the recession. The Canadian government fell into this trap in the 1930s when they imposed a substantial tax increase. This added to the downward momentum of the economy. One of Keynes' major objectives was to warn against such blunders. He argued that it is important for fiscal policy to be *aimed at balancing the economy, not the budget*.

The second complication is the problem of *measuring*

fiscal policy. Deficits *automatically* increase during a recession. Just because deficits rise during recessions, we should not conclude that the authorities are following counter-cyclical fiscal policies; they may be doing nothing. In order to determine what is happening to fiscal *policy,* some measure other than the actual budgetary surplus or deficit is needed. The *full-employment budget* provides such a measure. This budget gives a measure of the deficit or surplus that would occur with current tax rates and spending programs *if* the economy were at full employment. Because the full-employment budget is always measured at full employment (regardless of where actual output is), it does not automatically swing into deficit when the economy moves into a recession. However, the size of the deficit or surplus does change when tax rates or spending programs are changed. In brief, the full-employment budget changes when policies change; it does not change when the economy falls into recession. It, therefore, may be taken as a *measure of fiscal policy.*

(A related concept, the *cyclically adjusted budget*, is sometimes also used to measure fiscal policy. It is similar to the full-employment budget in the sense that it also changes only when policy changes, not as a result of fluctuations in the economy. But it differs from the full-employment budget by measuring the deficit as it would be at the *average* level of cyclical unemployment, not as it would be at *full* employment.)

Keynesian economists showed how the old objective of balancing the actual budget could lead to the wrong policies. But if the government is not held responsible for balancing the budget, what will restrain their spending? One possibility would be to have a guideline that would require restraint, while avoiding the trap of balancing the budget every year. Suggested guidelines include: (1) balancing the full-employment budget every year, (2) balancing the actual budget over the business cycle, with surpluses during prosperity to offset the deficits during recessions, or (3) limiting federal government spending to some fixed percentage of GDP. While all of these options have been discussed, none has become a firm basis for policy. The question of restraint has become increasingly important in recent years. Government deficits have grown rapidly during the 1980s, and have been running at above $30 billion per year.

When the government runs deficits, it borrows the difference between its expenditures and receipts. That is, it issues bonds or shorter-term securities. A $30 billion deficit, therefore, leads to a $30 billion increase in the national debt. The high deficits of recent years have made the national debt soar. A national debt is different from a personal or corporate debt, because we "owe most of it to ourselves." That is, even though we as taxpayers have to pay interest on the debt, we also receive most of the interest payments. We may not always be aware of this, because some of the interest payments are not obvious to us. For example, government bonds may be held by our pension funds, and the interest is paid into our pension funds without our necessarily being aware of the fact.

However, the national debt does raise a number of problems, particularly if it is increasing rapidly:

1. Some of the debt may *not* represent what we owe to ourselves; some government bonds may be held by foreigners. In this case, the nation is less well off. In the future, we will be taxed to make interest payments to foreign countries.

2. Even when we own our government's bonds, and pay interest to ourselves, the debt is not problem-free. To pay the interest, the government levies taxes. The public has an incentive to alter its behaviour to avoid the taxes. When this happens, the economy generally becomes less efficient. This decrease in efficiency is known as the *excess burden* of taxes.

3. If the national debt rises high enough, the government may find it very difficult to collect enough taxes to pay the interest. It may simply borrow more and more, to service the ever-growing debt. In other words, the debt may *grow on itself*. This is an issue which has attracted much greater attention during the 1980s because of the combination of rising debt and high interest rates.

4. Finally, as interest payments balloon, the government may be tempted to print money to meet these payments. If it does so to any great extent, this will add to inflationary pressures in the economy. (The government prints money via a complicated procedure. The government issues bonds, and the Bank of Canada prints money to buy these bonds. This is a subject that will be studied in the next few chapters.)

IMPORTANT TERMS: MATCH THE COLUMNS

Match each term in the first column with the corresponding phrase in the second column.

_____	1.	Recessionary gap
_____	2.	Output gap
_____	3.	Excess burden of tax
_____	4.	Injections
_____	5.	Leakages
_____	6.	Net exports
_____	7.	Marginal propensity to import
_____	8.	Deficit
_____	9.	Full-employment surplus
_____	10.	Automatic stabilizer
_____	11.	Policy trap

a. Negative surplus

b. The decrease in economic efficiency when people change their behaviour to reduce their taxes

c. Any tax or spending program that makes the budgetary deficit rise during recession, even if no policy change is made

d. The amount added to aggregate expenditures to account for goods and services purchased or sold by Canadian residents in foreign markets

e. Vertical distance from the aggregate expenditures function up to the 45° line, measured at full-employment domestic product

f. $R_{FE} - G_{FE}$

g. The annually balanced budget

h. Exports and government purchases of goods and services

i. Full-employment domestic product − actual domestic product

j. The proportion of an increase in income that goes to buying foreign goods and services

k. Taxes and imports

TRUE-FALSE

T F 1. An increase in government spending of $100 million will increase equilibrium domestic product by more than $100 million.

T F 2. If Americans increase their purchases of snowmobiles produced in Canada, equilibrium domestic product in Canada will increase by more than the increased revenue of the snowmobile producers.

T F 3. An increase in tax rates reduces equilibrium domestic product.

T F 4. An across-the-board increase in income taxes by, say, 5% has an effect similar to an increase in a lump-sum tax: It causes the consumption function to move down, but it does not change its slope.

T F 5. If the marginal propensity to import increases, the the aggregate expenditure schedule becomes steeper and the multiplier becomes larger.

T F 6. An automatic stabilizer acts to stabilize the size of the government's surplus or deficit.

T F 7. A decline into recession causes an increase in the deficit in the actual budget.

T F 8. If the government tries to balance the full-employment budget every year, it will fall into a policy trap; it will increase the severity of recessions by raising tax rates or cutting spending during recessions.

T F 9. When the economy moves into a recession, the actual budget automatically moves toward deficit, but the full-employment budget does not.

T F 10. An increase in government spending to build roads will move both the actual budget and the full-employment budget toward deficit.

T F 11. A cyclically balanced budget requires the full-employment budget to be balanced every year.

T F 12. Foreign-held debt imposes no burden, because we pay foreigners with exports of goods and services, and exports make the economy stronger.

MULTIPLE CHOICE

1. The recessionary gap is
    a. the amount by which actual GDP falls short of equilibrium GDP
    b. the amount by which actual GDP falls short of full-employment GDP
    c. the vertical distance from the aggregate expenditures line to the 45° line, measured at equilibrium domestic product
    d. the vertical distance from the aggregate expenditures line to the 45° line, measured at the full-employment domestic product
    e. the vertical distance from equilibrium domestic product to the aggregate expenditures function

2. When the economy is in equilibrium, the vertical distance between the aggregate expenditures function and the 45° line is equal to
    a. the output gap
    b. the recessionary gap
    c. investment demand
    d. saving
    e. zero

3. Suppose that the recessionary gap is $10 billion, and it is expected to remain at that amount into the future if no action is taken. The appropriate policy to eliminate this $10 billion gap is
    a. a cut in taxes of $10 billion
    b. a cut in government spending of $10 billion
    c. an increase in taxes of $10 billion
    d. an increase in government spending of $10 billion
    e. an increase in government spending of $10 billion x the multiplier

4. There is a relationship between the recessionary gap and the output gap. Specifically, the output gap is the recessionary gap
    a. times the multiplier
    b. divided by the multiplier
    c. times the average tax rate
    d. divided by the average tax rate
    e. minus the average tax rate

5. Suppose that MPC equals 0.75 and that all taxes are lump-sum taxes. If domestic product is $300 billion and full-employment domestic product is $340 billion, then the output gap is
    a. $10 billion
    b. $40 billion
    c. $60 billion
    d. $70 billion
    e. $160 billion

6. To stimulate aggregate expenditures during a severe recession, the appropriate fiscal policy is

    a. an increase in taxes and/or an increase in government spending
    b. an increase in taxes and/or a decrease in government spending
    c. a decrease in taxes and/or an increase in government spending
    d. a decrease in taxes and/or a decrease in government spending
    e. a decrease in government purchases and/or a decrease in transfer payments

7. A $10 billion increase in government spending for goods and services has
    a. the same effect on aggregate expenditures as a $10 billion increase in taxes
    b. the same effect on aggregate expenditures as a $10 billion cut in taxes
    c. a weaker effect on aggregate expenditures than a $10 billion cut in taxes
    d. a stronger effect on aggregate expenditures than a $10 billion cut in taxes
    e. no affect on aggregate expenditures; it affects only the "supply side" of the economy

8. In a diagram with aggregate expenditures on the vertical axis and domestic product on the horizontal axis, an across-the-board cut of one-half in all income tax rates will cause the consumption function to become
    a. lower, with no change in slope
    b. lower and flatter
    c. lower and steeper
    d. higher and flatter
    e. higher and steeper

9. An increase in income tax rates
    a. makes the aggregate expenditures function steeper, and therefore lowers the size of the multiplier
    b. makes the aggregate expenditures function steeper, and therefore raises the size of the multiplier
    c. makes the aggregate expenditures function flatter, and therefore lowers the size of the multiplier
    d. makes the aggregate expenditures function flatter, and therefore raises the size of the multiplier
    e. lowers aggregate expenditures, but has no effect on the size of the multiplier

10. When we include international transactions in our model of the economy, the multiplier becomes
    a. larger, because exports are an injection
    b. larger, because imports are an injection
    c. larger, because of the interaction between taxes and imports

d. smaller, because the aggregate expenditures function now slopes downward

e. smaller, because the leakage into imports increases as domestic product increases

11. When we include the government and international transactions in our model of the economy, equilibrium occurs when

a. $S + T + M = I^* + G + X$

b. $S + T + X = I^* + G + M$

c. $S + T + X + M = I^* + G$

d. $S + G + M = I^* + T + X$

e. $S + G + X = I^* + T + M$

12. Suppose that net exports are zero at the initial equilibrium domestic product. Suppose now that Canadian exports to foreign countries suddenly increase by $5 billion. Then

a. equilibrium domestic product will increase by more than $5 billion

b. at the new equilibrium domestic product, net exports will be less than $5 billion

c. the aggregate expenditure schedule shifts upward

d. at the new equilibrium, savings will be higher than before

e. all of the above

13. An illustration of the term "automatic stabilizer" is provided by

a. the tendency of tax collections to rise as the economy moves into a recession

b. the tendency of tax collections to fall as the economy moves into a recession

c. increases in tax rates as the economy moves into a recession

d. decreases in tax rates as the economy moves into a recession

e. public works designed to get the economy out of a depression

14. In which of the following cases does the government fall into a "policy trap" and make the economy more unstable?

a. It cuts taxes as the economy falls into a recession, since its deficits will increase as a result.

b. It increases tax rates as the economy falls into a recession, since it will depress aggregate expenditures.

c. It increases spending as the economy falls into a recession, since its deficits will increase as a result.

d. It attempts to balance the full-employment budget every year, since this will strongly destabilize aggregate expenditures.

e. It moves toward a full-employment deficit during recessions, since this will strongly destabilize aggregate expenditures.

15. The principal purpose of the full-employment budget is to measure

a. changes in fiscal policy

b. the size of the recessionary gap

c. the size of the output gap

d. the cut in taxes needed to get the economy to full employment

e. the increase in taxes needed to get the economy to full employment

16. The full-employment budget

a. differs from the actual budget because it does not include transfer payments

b. differs from the actual budget because it includes transfer payments, whereas the actual budget does not

c. is in surplus whenever the economy falls short of full employment

d. is more likely to show a surplus than is the actual budget

e. is less likely to show a surplus than is the actual budget

17. Suppose that a tax cut improves the efficiency of the economy and shifts the aggregate supply curve to the right. The most likely results are

a. an increase in both output and inflation

b. an increase in output, but lower inflation

c. a decrease in output, but higher inflation

d. a decrease in both output and inflation

e. there is no basis for a conclusion; each of the above is equally likely

18. The term, "excess burden of taxes," refers to which of the following?

a. taxes become burdensome whenever they exceed 10% of GDP

b. personal income taxes are more obvious and, therefore, more burdensome than taxes on corporate profits

c. personal income taxes are more obvious and, therefore, more burdensome than sales taxes

d. people may alter their behaviour to avoid paying taxes, thereby reducing the efficiency of the economy

e. taxes must be raised, not only to repay the principal on the government debt, but also to pay interest

19. The federal government cannot "go broke" because

a. it has the power to tax

b. it has the power to issue bonds whenever needed to repay its debt

c. it has the power to print money, and bonds are repayable in money

d. it has gold stocks equivalent to its long-term debt outstanding

e. the constitution limits the size of the debt

20. A number of guidelines have been proposed as a way of exerting restraint on the government. Which of the following possible guidelines provides the greatest opportunity for an active fiscal policy aimed at reducing the amplitude of business fluctuations?
   a. balance the actual budget every year
   b. balance the full-employment budget every year

c. balance the actual budget over the business cycle
   d. allow the government to increase spending whenever an increase in tax receipts pushes the budget into surplus
   e. none of the above allow any active countercyclical fiscal policy

EXERCISES

1. Figure 10.1 below shows a consumption function in an economy with no taxes. Its equation is $C = 200 + 0.5DI$, where units are billions of dollars and DI stands for disposable income. In the no-tax economy, $DI = Y$. The MPC equals _____. Now suppose that the government imposes a *lump-sum* tax of $200 billion. When $Y = $400 billion$, $DI = \$$ _____ billion, and $C = \$$ _____ billion. When $Y = $600 billion$, $DI = \$$ _____ billion, and $C = \$$ _____ billion. Plot this consumption function in the same diagram. The new consumption function is (flatter than, steeper than, has the same slope as) the initial consumption function.

Now suppose that the lump-sum tax is eliminated and replaced with a proportional tax: $T = (1/3)DI$. The marginal tax rate is _____. When $Y = $300 billion$, $T = \$$ _____ billion, $DI = \$$ _____ billion, and $C = \$$ _____ billion. When $Y = $600 billion$, $T = \$$ _____ billion, $DI = \$$ _____ billion, and $C = \$$ _____ billion. Plot this new consumption function on the same diagram. This new consumption function is (flatter than, steeper than, has the same slope as) the initial consumption function. How do you account

for the different behaviour of the slope here, compared to what happened when a tax was imposed in the previous paragraph?

2. Figure 10.2 shows aggregate expenditures and its components. In this economy, equilibrium is at point _____, with domestic product = _____. At this equilibrium, government purchases of goods and services plus net exports $(G + X - M)$ amounts to distance _____, $I^* = $ _____, and $I = $ _____. Personal saving (S) equals $(DE, DF,$ we don't have enough information to say).

Now, suppose that domestic product is at the disequilibrium amount Y_4. $I^* = $ _____, while $I = $ _____, and undesired inventory (accumulation, decumulation) = _____.

Now, suppose that this disequilibrium quantity Y_4 represents the full employment output. There is a recessionary gap equal to distance _____. The appropriate fiscal policy is an (increase, decrease) in government purchases of goods and services amounting to distance _____.

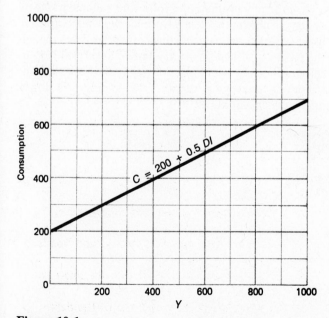

Figure 10.1

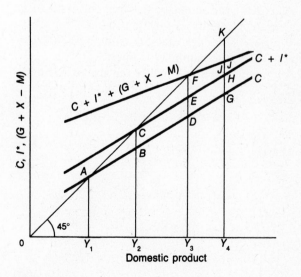

Figure 10.2

3. The government's tax revenues increase as domestic product increases, and fall during recessions. This means that the budget automatically tends to move into (surplus, deficit) during recession.

The automatic (surpluses, deficits) during recessions introduce two major complications into fiscal policy. First, they present a (opportunity, trap) for the policy maker. If the government follows a superficially plausible strategy of trying to balance the budget (every year, over the business cycle), it will end up (stabilizing, destabilizing) the economy. As the economy swings into recession, (surpluses, deficits) will automatically appear. If the authorities (raise, lower) taxes or (raise, lower) spending in an attempt to balance the budget, they will be following the (correct, wrong) fiscal policy; they will be (slowing the decline of expenditures, depressing aggregate expenditures further), and (adding to, reducing) the depth of the recession. This was illustrated most clearly in (1932/3, 1942/3, 1961, 1981) when tax rates were (increased, cut) substantially. This (reduced, added to) the downward momentum of the economy. One of Keynes' major objectives was to (show how fiscal policy could be used in this manner to restore full employment, warn against such blunders). He argued that it was important for fiscal policy to be aimed at balancing the (budget, economy, both, neither).

The second complication is the problem of measuring fiscal policy. (Surpluses, Deficits) *automatically* increase during a recession. Just because (surpluses, deficits) rise during recessions, we should not conclude that the authorities are following counter-cyclical fiscal policies; they may be doing nothing. In order to determine what is happening to fiscal *policy,* some measure other than the actual budgetary surplus or deficit is needed. The (actual, full-employment, long-term) budget provides such a measure. This budget gives a measure of the deficit or surplus that would occur with current tax rates and spending programs *if* the economy were at (equilibrium, full employment). Because it is always measured at (equilibrium, full employment), this budget does not automatically swing into (surplus, deficit) when the economy moves into a recession. However, the size of the deficit or surplus does change when tax rates or spending programs are changed. In brief, this budget changes when policies change; it does not change when the economy falls into recession. It therefore may be taken as a measure of fiscal policy.

Keynesian economists showed how the old objective of balancing the (actual, full-employment) budget could lead to the wrong policies. But if the government is not held responsible for balancing this budget, what will restrain their spending? One possibility would be to have a guideline which would require restraint, while avoiding the trap of balancing the (actual, full-employment) budget every year. Suggested guidelines include

(1)_____

(2)_____

or

(3) _____

ESSAY QUESTIONS

1. For each of the following, state whether you agree or disagree, and explain why:

a. A tax acts as an automatic stabilizer only if it makes the aggregate expenditures function flatter.

b. Whenever the aggregate expenditures function becomes flatter, the multiplier is lower.

c. Automatic stabilizers reduce the size of the multiplier.

2. Critically evaluate the following statement: "Any system of unemployment insurance will be completely useless as a way of reducing business cycles. Even though the payment of benefits to the unemployed will help to raise aggregate expenditures during recessions, the contributions (taxes) to support the system will lower aggregate expenditures."

ANSWERS

Important Terms: 1e, 2i, 3b, 4h, 5k, 6d, 7j, 8a, 9f, 10c, 11g
True-False: 1T, 2T, 3T, 4F, 5F, 6F, 7T, 8F, 9T, 10T, 11F, 12F
Multiple Choice: 1d, 2e, 3d, 4a, 5b, 6c, 7d, 8e, 9c, 10e, 11a, 12e, 13b, 14b, 15a, 16d, 17b, 18d, 19c, 20c
Exercises: **1.** 0.5, $200, $300, $400, $400, has the same slope as, 1/3, $100, $200, $300, $200, $400, $400, flatter than, here the tax increases with Y while it did not do so with the lump-sum tax in the previous paragraph.
2. F, Y_3, EF, DE, DE, we don't have enough information to say [Note: the reason is that, in equilibrium, I^* + G = S + T. The diagram tells us what G and I^* are, but we can't tell what S is unless we also know T.], GH, GH + JK, accumulation, JK, JK, increase, JK.
3. [Note: this exercise is based partly on the chapter highlights section.] deficit. deficits, trap, every year, destabilizing, deficits, raise, lower, wrong, depressing aggregate expenditures further, adding to, 1932/3, increased, added to, warn against such blunders, economy. Deficits, deficits, full-employment, full employment, full employment, deficit. actual, actual, (1) balancing the full-employment budget every year, (2) balancing the actual budget over the business cycle, with surpluses during prosperity to offset the deficits during recessions, or (3) limiting government spending to a fixed percentage of GDP.

ANSWERS TO SELECTED REVIEW QUESTIONS FROM THE TEXT

10-1. This question asks for the presentation of Figure 10-2, without the higher, dashed AE_2 line. The output gap is the larger; it is the recessionary gap times the multiplier.

10-3. The first sentence is at least partially true, although the Depression was also the result of policy blunders. The statement might be rewritten as follows:

A market economy can suffer large-scale unemployment, as was the case during the Great Depression. Military spending can reduce unemployment. But military spending should be considered on its own merits, not simply as a way of stimulating employment. Other government spending or tax cuts can be used to stimulate aggregate expenditures to the target level instead. There is no need at all for military spending for the purposes of economic stabilization; capitalism does not require militarism to survive.

10-4. **(a)** With the export function in Figure 10-7(a) shifting up, the net export function and the AE function in Figures 10-7(b) and 10-7(c) would also shift up, so equilibrium output would be higher.

(b) The import function would shift up, and the export function down, so the net export function and AE function in panels (b) and (c) would shift down. This would *reduce* equilibrium output.

10-6. **(a)** The actual budget will move into deficit, as the fall in total output and income reduces the government's tax receipts. The full-employment budget will not be affected by the recession, since this budget is calculated to include the revenues the government would receive if the economy were still at full employment.

(b) The full-employment budget will now move into deficit, since an increase in spending or a cut in tax rates will show up in that budget. The actual budget will also be affected negatively by the fiscal policy: It will move more sharply into deficit. To the extent that the fiscal policy actions are successful in combatting the recession, the negative effect on the actual budget will be softened, since economic recovery will work toward higher tax revenues.

10-8. **(a)** If the extent of foreign ownership of private capital rises because Canadians use more of their savings to acquire government debt, future generations' consumption of imported goods will have to be reduced, since more of Canada's export earnings will go to paying foreigners a return on the capital they own in Canada.

(b) Yes, but if there were no foreign capital in Canada, then the private-sector capital stock here would most likely be smaller if the government debt was large.

Across

4. a way to combat a depression (2 words)
7, 10. This can be a trap for fiscal policy makers.
14. type of investment
15. When government runs a deficit, the national _____ increases.
18. no (slang)
19. what you do with disposable income that you do not spend on consumption
20. change in saving, divided by change in disposable income
23. change in equilibrium national product, divided by change in government spending for goods and services
26. precious stone
28. one of the factors of production
29. investment or government spending
32. He said an increase in real holdings of money leads to an increase in consumption. (Appendix to Chapter 10)
33. C + 1* + G + X − M (2 words)
35. largest component of national product

Down

1. saving and taxes
2. huge bodies of water
3. national income + sales tax
5. He was a U.S. oil billionaire.
6. a banned insecticide
8. one (German)
9. This carries the code of life (abbrev.).
10. to _____ or not to _____
11. To reduce this, deficit spending may be desirable.
12. move
13. make a mistake
16. university degree
17. a popular type of entertainment (abbrev.)
21. should precede action
22. transgression
24. small picture case worn as pendant
25. remove errors from a manuscript
26. NNP + depreciation
27. Russian-made jet fighter plane
30. number (abbrev.)
31. famous student of psychology
34. Government spending can be used to fill recessionary _____.

Chapter 11

■ ■

Money and the Banking System

MAJOR PURPOSE

The major purpose of this chapter is to explain how the banking system creates money. The details of money creation, as set out in the various tables in this chapter, are important. A number of specific conclusions are also important: (1) Even though the banking system can create money equal to a multiple of its reserves, an individual bank cannot do so. (2) Instead, an individual bank receiving a deposit of $100 can create money by lending only a fraction of this $100 (specifically, $100 x 0.8, if the required reserve ratio is 0.2). (3) The bank sees nothing particularly magical or peculiar about such loans, even though they result in an increase in the money stock. (4) Fractional-reserve banking developed as a natural result of the desire to make profits. (5) Fractional-reserve banks can be subject to runs. Because each bank holds reserves equal to only a fraction of its deposit liabilities, no bank can withstand an all-out run without outside help, no matter how sound the bank was originally. (6) Bank runs are not only unfortunate for the banks and individual depositors who are too late to get their funds; they also can have strong adverse effects on the economy. Because reserves are being withdrawn from the base of the monetary pyramid, bank runs cause strong downward pressures on the money stock. One of the major tasks of the monetary authorities is to prevent bank runs and instability of the monetary supply, as we shall see in the next chapter.

LEARNING OBJECTIVES

After you have studied this chapter in the textbook and study guide, you should be able to
- Describe the three basic functions of money
- Explain the differences between M1, M2, M2+, and M3
- Explain why a bank might want to hold only fractional reserves, rather than reserves equal to 100% of its deposit liabilities
- Explain why fractional-reserve banking leads to the risk of a bank run, and why no bank can withstand a severe run without outside help
- Explain in detail how an individual bank responds to an increase in its reserves, and how the overall banking system can increase money by a multiple of the increase in reserves. (The explanation requires use of balance sheets.)
- State the formula for the deposit multiplier
- Give two reasons that the actual expansion of deposits is likely to be less than indicated by this formula

HIGHLIGHTS OF THE CHAPTER

This chapter introduces the basic concepts of money and banking, as a background for studying monetary policy in the next chapter.

Money performs three interrelated functions:

1. It is a *medium of exchange*; that is, it is used to buy goods and services.

2. It is a *standard of value*; that is, we keep accounts, quote prices, and sign contracts in dollar terms.

3. It is a *store of value*; that is, you can hold money for future purchases rather than spending it right away.

The basic definition of the money stock, M1, includes items which are used as money in everyday transactions—coins, paper currency, and demand deposits in chartered banks. Each of these items represents wealth to the holder; if you have $100 in your pocket, you are better off than you would be without it. In this way, money is different from a credit card, which represents a convenient way to run up debt, rather than an asset. Thus, even though credit cards (and the corresponding lines of credit) are often used to make purchases, lines of credit are not included in the money stock.

M2 includes M1 plus all chequable deposits, as well as savings ("notice") deposits, and term deposits held by individuals, in the chartered banks. Although such assets are not used in an unrestricted way to make purchases, they can be quickly switched into M1. Thus, they can have a powerful effect on people's spending behaviour. When we are concerned about the relationship between "money" and aggregate demand, we often use the broader definition of money, M2.

Even broader concepts of money are M3, which includes large non-personal (corporate) term deposits, as well as some deposits denominated in foreign currency, in the chartered banks, and M2 + which includes not only deposits in the chartered banks but also deposits that the public holds with trust and mortgage loan companies and shares in credit unions and in Quebec's *caisses populaires*.

Chartered banks and similar financial institutions—such as trust and mortgage loan companies—accept deposits, using most of the proceeds to make loans. They hold reserves equal to only a fraction of their deposit liabilities. *Fractional-reserve banking* developed centuries ago, when financial institutions realized that they could cover their costs and make profits from the interest on loans. Through history, fractional-reserve banks have been plagued by the problem of runs, which have not only been dangerous for them, but have also disrupted the economy. One conspicuous example occurred in the United States in 1932/33, when the banking system collapsed, adding to the downslide into the Depression.

Even in olden times, when there were no *required* reserve ratios, banks kept reserves to use as working balances and to meet unexpected withdrawals; such reserves provided some protection against a run. Now, the function of reserves is not to provide protection against a run, but rather, to give the authorities control over the money stock. The *Bank Act*, which contains the legislation that governs the operations of Canada's chartered banks, requires the banks to hold reserves equivalent to specified percentages of demand and notice deposit liabilities. If the required reserve ratio is, say, 0.10, then a $100 withdrawal from a bank deposit will reduce the required reserves by only $10. The other $90 will have to be obtained elsewhere by the bank, most likely by reducing its portfolio of loans or bonds. In other words, reserves in this case would only provide one-tenth of the funds needed to meet the withdrawal.

If there is a required reserve ratio, R, specified by law, then the banking system as a whole can increase its deposit liabilities by as much as $1/R$ times any increase in its reserves. Tables 11-4 to 11-9 in the text explain in detail how banks do this. These tables are not repeated here, but they are of central importance in any study of the monetary system. They often appear on examinations. Students should go over them particularly carefully, together with the balance sheets in the exercises below. Warning: *The multiple expansion of bank deposits is one of the most important and difficult concepts in introductory economics.*

The deposit multiplier, $D = 1/R$, shows the *maximum* increase in deposits that can occur when the banking system acquires additional reserves. In practice, the actual increase is likely to be much less, for two reasons. Most important is that, as people acquire more bank deposit money, they are likely to want to hold some of the additional money in the form of currency. When they make withdrawals from their banks, the reserves of banks are reduced. The second reason is that banks may hold *excess reserves*—that is, reserves over and above the amounts required by law—rather than lending all they are permitted. In recent years, excess reserves have been very small: The reserves that banks have been *required* to hold have been larger than the amounts of cash they would have *voluntarily* held for purposes of meeting their customers' withdrawal needs. As will be discussed in the next chapter, under proposed legislative changes in the late 1980s, chartered banks will no longer be legally required to hold specific amounts of reserves. However, this does not mean that the deposit multiplier will become infinitely large, since banks will still want to hold a certain amount of cash reserves to meet their customers' needs and, therefore, will continue to limit their lending to only a fraction of the money they receive as deposits.

During the Great Depression of the 1930s, chartered banks held very large amounts of excess reserves. There were two reasons for this. First, interest rates were very low, which meant that bankers didn't forgo much interest when they kept excess reserves. Second, bankers were frightened to lend to businesses, since so many businesses were going bankrupt. The failure of banks to lend more of their excess reserves was unfortunate, since more lending and more money would have promoted economic recovery. We here have one illustration of the difference between what is good for an individual or an institution and what is good for the economy as a whole. Risky bank lending would have increased the money stock and contributed to economic recovery. But it could have meant financial suicide for any bank making risky loans. Bankers cannot be expected to commit suicide for the public good. It is up to the Bank of Canada, not up to individual banks, to see that the money stock is at the right level to keep aggregate demand close to its desired path. How the Bank of Canada does this will be studied in the next chapter.

(A second example of the conflict between what is good for the individual and what is good for the overall economy occurs during a bank run. Each individual has an incentive to be first in line. But severe bank runs can disrupt the economy.)

IMPORTANT TERMS: MATCH THE COLUMNS

Match each term in the first column with the corresponding phrase in the second column.

_____	1.	Currency	**a.** Assets − net worth
_____	2.	M1	**b.** Coins, paper currency, plus most demand, notice, and term deposits in chartered banks and trust and mortgage loan companies
_____	3.	M2	
_____	4.	M2+	
_____	5.	Liquid assets	**c.** Deposit liabilities $\times R$
_____	6.	Liabilities	**d.** Major reason for risk of runs
_____	7.	What a single bank can prudently lend	**e.** Actual reserves − required reserves
			f. Coins, paper currency, demand deposits, plus most notice and term deposits in chartered banks
_____	8.	Required reserves	**g.** Coins, paper currency, and demand deposits
_____	9.	Maximum increase in deposits	**h.** Increase in reserves $\times 1/R$
_____	10.	Fractional-reserve banking	**i.** Short-term government securities
			j. Coins and bills

TRUE-FALSE

T F 1. Demand deposits held by manufacturing corporations—such as Canadian General Electric—are included in the money stock (M1).

T F 2. Reserve deposits held by the Bank of Montreal in the Bank of Canada are included in the money stock (M1).

T F 3. Fractional-reserve banking was invented by the U.S. Federal Reserve.

T F 4. In the modern Canadian banking system, most chartered banks' reserves are held in the form of gold.

T F 5. When Canadian General Electric deposits $100,000 in the Bank of Nova Scotia, the resulting deposit appears as an asset on CGE's balance sheet, and the same deposit appears as a liability on the Bank of Nova Scotia's balance sheet.

T F 6. If a chartered bank receives a deposit of currency, then its actual reserves and excess reserves both increase by the same amount (specifically, by the amount of the deposit).

T F 7. If a chartered bank receives the deposit of a cheque drawn against an account in another bank, then its actual reserves and its excess reserves both increase as a consequence.

T F 8. A bank may prudently lend the amount of its excess reserves $\times 1/R$.

T F 9. Banks are more likely to hold excess reserves during a depression than during prosperity.

T F 10. Bank deposits are normally equal to reserves $\times 1/R$. However, they can be larger than that during depressions, when more money is needed to stimulate recovery.

T F 11. If there were no legal reserve requirements on chartered banks, then they would normally lend out 100% of any additional funds they received as deposits from the public.

MULTIPLE CHOICE

1. Between 1929 and 1933, during the early part of the Great Depression
   a. the quantity of money rose, but aggregate demand nonetheless collapsed
   b. the quantity of money fell, but prices nevertheless rose moderately
   c. there was hyperinflation, even though the money stock fell
   d. the quantity of money fell, and this contributed to the downturn
   e. the quantity of money increased at a slow, steady rate, as advocated by monetarists, but the Depression nevertheless occurred

2. Even though credit cards are used by many people in making purchases, they are not included in M1. A major reason is that
   a. credit cards are a way of going into debt, whereas the components of M1 represent assets
   b. credit cards had not yet been invented when money was defined
   c. some credit cards are issued by stores (such as Sears), whereas all money is issued by banks
   d. credit cards are much less liquid than M1
   e. credit cards don't affect consumer expenditures, whereas M1 does

3. Which of the following is included in the M2 definition of money?
   a. chequable deposits in trust and mortgage loan companies
   b. daily interest savings (notice) deposits in chartered banks
   c. U.S. dollar deposits of Canadian residents held in chartered banks
   d. Treasury bills held by chartered banks
   e. none of the above

4. Demand deposits are included in the money stock M1
   a. only if they are owned by individuals
   b. if they are owned by individuals or non-bank corporations (such as Bell Canada or a local car dealer)
   c. if they are owned by individuals, other banks, or the Bank of Canada
   d. if they are owned by individuals, other banks, or the federal government
   e. if they are owned by individuals, the Bank of Canada, or the federal government

5. Suppose we know M1, and want to calculate M2. To do so, which of the following must be added to M1?
   a. coins

   b. paper currency
   c. demand deposits
   d. notice deposits in chartered banks
   e. daily interest deposits in trust companies

6. In the balance sheet of a business
   a. Assets = Liabilities
   b. Assets = Liabilities + Net Worth
   c. Assets = Liabilities − Net Worth
   d. Liabilities = Assets + Net Worth
   e. any of the above may be correct; it depends on the health of the business

7. The primary reason the activities of early goldsmiths developed into "fractional reserve banking" was the desire to
   a. keep the money stock down to a fraction of its earlier level, in order to restrain inflation
   b. increase the quantity of money, in order to finance the growth of trade
   c. provide a more stable money system, in order to reduce the size of business fluctuations
   d. provide a broader range of financial services to their customers
   e. increase profits, by lending out some of the gold deposited with them

8. A bank run is most likely to occur at a time when
   a. government surpluses are high
   b. tax rates are high
   c. many non-bank businesses are going bankrupt
   d. investment by non-bank businesses is large
   e. banks have reserves equal to 100% of their deposit liabilities

9. During a bank run, there can be a conflict between the interests of the individual and the interests of the society as a whole. Specifically
   a. each depositor has an incentive to get in line, even though bank runs can weaken the economy
   b. each depositor has an incentive to make additional deposits because of the high interest rates, but high interest rates are undesirable for the society as a whole
   c. it is even more important for society than for the individual depositor that unsound banks be closed down
   d. even though a run at a specific bank causes a contraction at that bank, the overall economy nevertheless expands because of the improved competitive position of other banks
   e. all of the above

10. The Bank of Canada performs all the following functions *except one*. Which is the exception? The Bank

a. issues paper currency
b. conducts fiscal policy
c. controls the quantity of money in Canada
d. acts as the federal government's bank
e. acts as a bankers' bank

11. In the balance sheet of the typical chartered bank, the largest asset is
a. reserve deposits
b. ioans
c. demand deposits
d. time deposits
e. net worth

12. Chartered banks have been required by law to hold reserves. These reserves have been specified as percentages of a bank's
a. total assets
b. total liabilities
c. deposit liabilities
d. holdings of government securities
e. net worth

13. Suppose that the required reserve ratio is 10% and that a person deposits $100 of currency in his or her bank. Then that single bank can create
a. $80 in additional money by lending $80
b. $90 in additional money by lending $90
c. $100 in additional money by lending $100
d. $1,000 in additional money by lending $1,000
e. no additional money; it takes the actions of the whole banking system to create more money, not just one bank

14. Suppose that the required reserve ratio of a chartered bank is represented by the fraction R. Suppose that this chartered bank receives a deposit of currency of $100. Then, as a result, *this single chartered bank* can make a loan of as much as
a. $100/R$
b. $100 \times R$
c. $100/(1 - R)$
d. $100 \times (1 - R)$

15. When a chartered bank makes a loan to the local drug store
a. the bank's assets increase
b. the bank's liabilities increase
c. the money stock increases
d. the amount of demand deposits increases
e. all of the above

16. Suppose that someone in Toronto, who banks at the Bank of Montreal, sends a cheque for $1,000 to someone in Calgary, who deposits it in the Royal Bank. The required reserve ratio is R. In the process of cheque clearing, the reserves of the Bank of Montreal will
a. increase by $1,000, while those of the Royal Bank will decrease by $1,000

b. decrease by $1,000, while those of the Royal Bank will increase by $1,000
c. increase by $1,000 \times R$, while those of the Royal Bank will decrease by $1,000 \times R$
d. decrease by $1,000 \times R$, while those of the Royal Bank will increase by $1,000 \times R$
e. increase by $1,000 divided by R, while those of the Royal Bank will decrease by $1,000 divided by R

17. An increase in the required reserve ratio on demand deposits would most likely cause
a. an increase in M1
b. a decrease in M1
c. an increase in demand deposits
d. an increase in bank profits
e. an increase in the deposit multiplier

18. The monetary system is sometimes said to form an inverted pyramid. By this, we mean that
a. a large quantity of bank deposit money can be built on a small quantity of reserves
b. a large quantity of reserves can be built on a small quantity of bank deposit money
c. a large quantity of currency can be built on a small quantity of bank deposit money
d. bank deposits are the largest component of M1
e. currency is the largest component of M1

19. The deposit multiplier, $1/R$, represents the *maximum* amount by which the banking system may increase deposits as a result of an initial increase in bank reserves. (R is the required reserve ratio.) In practice, the actual increase is likely to be less than shown by this multiplier, since
a. a single bank can increase deposits by less than can the banking system as a whole
b. a single bank can increase deposits by more than can the banking system as a whole
c. as the banks expand their loans, the public will decide to deposit more currency in their bank accounts
d. banks may hold less than the required reserve ratio; with a smaller actual reserve ratio, the expansion of deposits is likewise smaller
e. banks may hold excess reserves, and the public may decide to hold more currency as the quantity of money increases

20. Banks are most likely to hold significant quantities of excess reserves when
a. their profits are high
b. the economy is in a boom
c. the economy is growing slowly and steadily
d. the economy is in a mild recession
e. the economy is in a depression

EXERCISES

1a. If I deposit $100,000 in currency into a demand deposit in bank A and the required reserve ratio is 20%, then the immediate increase in bank A's total reserves is $ _____ and the immediate increase in bank A's required reserves is $ _____. Thus, the immediate increase in bank A's excess reserves is $ _____. As a result of this transaction, the total amount of currency in the hands of the public has [increased by $ _____, decreased by $ _____, not changed], the total amount of bank deposits held by the public has [increased by $ _____, decreased by $ _____, not changed], and the total amount of M1 has [increased by $ _____, decreased by $ _____, not changed].

b. Suppose bank A now lends all its new excess reserves. The borrower writes a cheque against the proceeds of the loan, and this cheque is deposited in a demand deposit in bank B. When this loan is made and this cheque is deposited and cleared, the effect is to make bank A's total reserves [increase by $ _____, decrease by $ _____, remain unchanged], to make bank A's required reserves [increase by $ _____, decrease by $ _____, remain unchanged], to make bank A's excess reserves [increase by $ _____, decrease by $ _____, remain unchanged], to make bank B's total reserves [increase by $ _____, decrease by $ _____, remain unchanged], to make bank B's required reserves [increase by $ _____, decrease by $ _____, remain unchanged], and to make bank B's excess reserves [increase by $ _____, decrease by $ _____, remain unchanged]. As a result of this loan, the total amount of bank deposits has [increased by $ _____, decreased by $ _____, not changed].

c. If the process of lending continues until all excess reserves have been eliminated throughout the banking system then, as a result of the whole process, starting with my initial deposit, the total quantity of currency in the hands of the public will have [increased by $ _____, decreased by $ _____, not changed], the total quantity of bank deposits in the hands of the public will have [increased by $ _____, decreased by $ _____, not changed], the total quantity of M1 in the hands of the public will have [increased by $ _____, decreased by $ _____, not changed], and the total quantity of M2 in the hands of the public will have [increased by $ _____, decreased by $ _____, not changed].

2. Show what happens as a direct result of each of the following transactions by filling in the appropriate numbers for that transaction in the balance sheet. Each balance sheet should represent the *change* in assets and liabilities of *all* banks as a group. In each case, suppose that the required reserve ratio on demand deposits is 20% and on all other deposits is 10%. Each transaction should be considered separately from all the others.

a. Someone deposits $25,000 in currency into a demand deposit.

b. Someone withdraws $100,000 in currency from a non-chequable savings account.

c. Someone switches $200,000 from a demand deposit to a non-chequable savings deposit.

d. A bank lends $40,000 to someone who immediately takes the proceeds of the loan in the form of currency.

e. A bank lends $100,000 to someone who uses that $100,000 to pay off a loan to someone who puts the $100,000 into a non-chequable savings deposit.

BALANCE SHEET A

Change in Assets		Change in Liabilities	
Loans	_____		
Total reserves	_____		
		Demand deposits _____	
Required reserves	_____	Other deposits _____	
Excess reserves _____			

BALANCE SHEET B

Change in Assets		Change in Liabilities	
Loans	_____		
Total reserves	_____		
		Demand deposits _____	
Required reserves	_____	Other deposits _____	
Excess reserves _____			

BALANCE SHEET C

Change in Assets		Change in Liabilities	
Loans	_____		
Total reserves	_____		
		Demand deposits	_____
Required reserves	_____		
		Other deposits	_____
Excess reserves	_____		

BALANCE SHEET D

Change in Assets		Change in Liabilities	
Loans	_____		
Total reserves	_____		
		Demand deposits	_____
Required reserves	_____		
		Other deposits	_____
Excess reserves	_____		

BALANCE SHEET E

Change in Assets		Change in Liabilities	
Loans	_____		
Total reserves	_____		
		Demand deposits	_____
Required reserves	_____		
		Other deposits	_____
Excess reserves	_____		

ESSAY QUESTIONS

1. Why are bank runs most likely to occur during a depression or severe recession? Are bank runs most damaging to the economy at such times, or would they be more damaging during a period of prosperity? Why?

2. In both Canada and the United States, deposits in most banks and institutions such as trust and mortgage loan companies are now covered by government-sponsored insurance. If your bank or trust company doesn't have the money, the insurance will make good, up to a maximum of $60,000 per deposit in Canada in the late 1980s. As a result, runs on financial institutions have been much less common than they were during the 1930s, prior to deposit insurance. Nevertheless, runs still occasionally occur. Why do you suppose they still do?

3. By his term "invisible hand," Adam Smith suggested that self-interested actions tend to benefit society. This chapter has explained two cases where pursuit of self-interest led to undesirable results for the society as a whole. What are these two cases, and why does self-interest lead to socially undesirable outcomes? Can you think of any way to deal with these problems?

4. Individual bankers often argue, "We don't create money; we just lend money that has already been deposited with us." Is this correct? If so, explain why. If not, explain why not.

ANSWERS

Important Terms: 1j, 2g, 3f, 4b, 5i, 6a, 7e, 8c, 9h, 10d
True-False: 1T, 2F, 3F, 4F, 5T, 6F, 7T, 8F, 9T, 10F, 11F
Multiple Choice: 1d, 2a, 3b, 4b, 5d, 6b, 7e, 8c, 9a, 10b, 11b, 12c, 13b, 14d, 15e, 16b, 17b, 18a, 19e, 20e
Exercises: 1a. $100,000, $20,000, $80,000, decreased by $100,000, increased by $100,000, not changed

1b. decrease by $80,000, remain unchanged, decrease by $80,000, increase by $80,000, increase by $16,000, increase by $64,000. increased by $80,000

1c. decreased by $100,000, increased by $500,000, increased by $400,000, increased by $400,000 (note: M1 is included in M2)

BALANCE SHEET A

Change in Assets		Change in Liabilities	
Loans	0		
Total reserves	25,000		
		Demand deposits	25,000
Required reserves	5,000		
		Other deposits	0
Excess reserves	20,000		

BALANCE SHEET B

Change in Assets		Change in Liabilities	
Loans	0		
Total reserves	− 100,000		
		Demand deposits	0
Required reserves	− 10,000		
		Other deposits	− 100,000
Excess reserves	− 90,000		

BALANCE SHEET C

Change in Assets		Change in Liabilities	
Loans	0		
Total reserves	0		
		Demand deposits	− 200,000
Required reserves	− 20,000		
		Other deposits	− 200,000
Excess reserves	+ 20,000		

BALANCE SHEET D

Change in Assets		Change in Liabilities	
Loans	+ 40,000		
Total reserves	− 40,000		
		Demand deposits	0
Required reserves	0		
		Other deposits	0
Excess reserves	− 40,000		

BALANCE SHEET E

Change in Assets		Change in Liabilities	
Loans	100,000		
Total reserves	0		
		Demand deposits	0
Required reserves	+ 10,000		
		Other deposits	100,000
Excess reserves	− 10,000		

ANSWERS TO SELECTED REVIEW QUESTIONS FROM THE TEXT

11-1. (a)

THE CORPORATION

Assets		Liabilities
Currency	– $100,000	No change
Chequing deposit	+ $100,000	

BANK OF NOVA SCOTIA

Assets		Liabilities	
Reserves of		Chequing deposits	$100,000
currency	$100,000		

(b) The money stock is not changed. The corporation has no more money; it simply exchanges $100,000 in one form of money (currency) for $100,000 in another form (a chequing deposit). (The reserves of currency held by the bank are not included in the money stock.)

(c) It can lend its excess reserves; that is, $90,000. Direct effect of loan on bank's balance sheet:

BANK OF NOVA SCOTIA

Assets		Liabilities	
Loans	$90,000	Chequing deposit	
		of farmer	$90,000

Net effect of all transactions, including the clearing of the farmer's cheque:

BANK OF NOVA SCOTIA

Assets		Liabilities	
Reserves	$10,000	Chequing deposit	
Loans	$90,000	of corporation	$100,000

(d) The maximum increase in chequing deposits is $100,000 divided by 10% — that is, $1 million. The maximum amount of bank lending is $900,000. (There is a bank loan corresponding with each increase in chequing deposits, except the first deposit of $100,000.) The maximum increase in the money stock is $900,000. (The initial deposit of $100,000 represents a change in the composition of the public's money stock, not a net increase; see part (b) of this question.)

11-2. Initially, there will be no problem, since the changes in the bank's balance sheet as a result of the deposit and the loan will be the following:

BANK A

Assets		Liabilities	
Reserves	$100,000	Chequing deposits	
Loans	$100,000	of initial depositor	$100,000
		of borrower	$100,000

Chequing deposits have gone up by $200,000. But reserves have gone up by $100,000 and, therefore, they are adequate for the moment. But the borrower is likely to spend the money, writing a cheque against the deposit of $100,000. If, as is likely, the cheque is deposited in a second bank and is cleared, then the effects thus far on Bank A's balance sheet will be as follows:

BANK A

Assets		Liabilities	
Reserves	0	Chequing deposits	
Loans	$100,000	of initial depositor	$100,000
		of borrower	0

Unless the bank initially had excess reserves (not shown), it is now in a situation of inadequate reserves. Its chequing deposits are up by $100,000; therefore, its required reserves are up by $20,000 (if the required reserve ratio is 20%). But its actual reserves are back to where they were at the beginning. With less-than-required reserves, the bank must liquidate loans or other earning assets (or borrow) in order to meet reserve requirements.

11-3. There will be a change in the composition of the money stock (with more chequing deposits, but less currency), but no net change in the quantity of money. The initial effects of the deposit will be as follows:

DEPOSITOR'S BALANCE SHEET

Assets		Liabilities
Currency	– $100,000	No change
Chequing deposit	+ $100,000	

BANK A

Assets		Liabilities
Reserves of		Chequing deposits $100,000
currency	$100,000	

This will also be the final effect. With a 100% reserve requirement, Bank A will be unable to make loans as a result of the deposit. (The deposit has created no excess reserves.)

11-5. It can lend $400,000. The single bank is the total banking system and, therefore, it can safely lend more than its initial excess reserves, since cheques written by borrowers will be deposited in this single bank and will not cause a reserve loss. (Insofar as the public holds more currency as its chequing deposits rise, the total lending can be less than the $400,000.)

Chapter 12

■ ■

The Bank of Canada and the Tools of Monetary Policy

MAJOR PURPOSE

There are two major tools for controlling aggregate demand—fiscal policy and monetary policy. Fiscal policy, which involves changes in tax rates and in government spending, is in the hands of the government. Monetary policy, which involves changes in the rate of growth of the money stock, is in the hands of the Bank of Canada. The major purpose of this chapter is to explain how the Bank of Canada can influence the money stock.

As we saw in Chapter 11, most of the money stock consists of deposits in chartered banks (and other similar institutions if we use the M2 + concept). The amount of money that banks can create depends on the quantity of reserves that they own and on the required reserve ratio. The Bank of Canada has three principal tools with which it can influence the quantity of money:

1. It can *purchase government securities* on the open market.

2. It can *purchase foreign currencies* from Canadian chartered banks or non-bank corporations or individuals.

3. As the government's bank, the Bank of Canada can *transfer federal government deposits* to the chartered banks.

Through these three types of transactions, the Bank of Canada can directly increase the reserves of chartered banks and, therefore, influence the money stock. In addition, there are two indirect methods through which the Bank can affect the money stock:

4. It can *change the Bank rate* (and the rate it charges on loans to investment dealers). Since the reserves of chartered banks increase when they borrow from the Bank of Canada (or when the investment dealers borrow from the Bank of Canada), changes in the Bank rate indirectly influence the quantity of reserves in the banking system and, hence, the money stock.

5. Before 1967, the Bank of Canada had the power to use *changes in the required reserve ratio* as a tool for deliberately controlling the money stock; such changes influence the quantity of deposit money that can be created on any given base of cash reserves.

LEARNING OBJECTIVES

After you have studied this chapter in the textbook and study guide, you should be able to

- Describe the organization of the Bank of Canada
- Describe how the Bank of Canada can use each of its major tools to affect the size of the money stock
- Explain how open market operations change the balance sheets of the chartered banks and the Bank of Canada
- Explain how open market operations affect not only the size of the money stock, but also interest rates
- Give an example which shows why the yield (interest rate) on a Treasury bill falls when its price rises
- Explain why a restrictive monetary policy usually does not involve an open market sale, but rather just a reduction in the rate of purchases on the open market
- Explain how Bank of Canada purchases and sales of foreign currencies and transfers of federal government deposits to and from chartered banks influence the size of the money stock

- Explain how Bank of Canada loans to chartered banks or to investment dealers influence the size of the money stock
- Explain why the Bank rate is usually set high enough to be a "penalty rate"
- Explain why the Bank of Canada did not use changes in the required reserve ratio as a policy tool even when it had the legal power to do so
- Explain why government-sponsored deposit insurance reduces the risk of a run on banks

HIGHLIGHTS OF THE CHAPTER

The Bank of Canada is Canada's central bank. It is the "bankers' bank," and it is responsible for controlling the quantity of money.

The Bank of Canada is formally owned by the federal government. It is managed by a government-appointed board of directors, which, in turn, appoints the Bank's governor and deputy governor, subject to the government's approval. While the Bank of Canada retains a considerable degree of independence in its day-to-day management of monetary policy, the present Bank Act clearly specifies that the federal government has final responsibility for the overall conduct of monetary policy: If a fundamental conflict develops between the government and the governor of the Bank of Canada, the governor is obliged to resign.

Open market operations, sales and purchases of foreign currencies, and transfers of federal government deposits to the chartered banks are the tools most frequently used by the Bank of Canada to influence the money stock.

Consider first open-market operations. When the Bank of Canada buys securities worth, say, $10 million on the open market, chartered bank reserves increase by the same $10 million. Because the banks have additional excess reserves, they are able to make loans; the money stock can increase by a multiple of the $10 million. As we saw in Chapter 11, the *maximum* increase in the money stock is the $10 million times $1/R$, where R is the required reserve ratio. (For simplicity, we disregard the complication that the present Bank Act stipulates different reserve ratios for demand deposits and other deposits.) However, in practice, the actual increase is not likely to be this great. As banks make loans and the quantity of money increases, the public is likely to want not only more bank deposits, but more currency too. People, therefore, withdraw some currency from their bank accounts. When they do so, the reserves of banks decline and the amount of money they can create likewise declines.

The maximum increase in the money stock depends on the size of the open market operation ($10 million in the above example) and on the required reserve ratio. It does not depend on whether a chartered bank, a non-bank cor-poration, or an individual sells the securities to the Bank of Canada. However, the details of the way in which the money supply increases will vary, depending on who the seller is. If a non-bank corporation—such as Molson's Ltd.—or an individual is the seller, then the money stock will go up immediately as a result of the open market purchase. For example, if Molson's sells the $10 million in securities which the Bank of Canada buys, Molson's will deposit the proceeds from the sale in its chartered bank, and its holdings of money will, therefore, increase by $10 million. Molson's bank will now have larger deposit liabilities, and its required reserves will rise—by $10 million times the required reserve ratio. If this ratio is, say, 15%, the bank will have $8.5 million of excess reserves (the $10 million addition to reserves less the increase of $1.5 million in required reserves). It will safely be able to lend the $8.5 million. There will be a series of expansions: $10 million + ($10 × 0.85) million + ($10 × 0.85^2) million, and so on.

On the other hand, if a chartered bank sells the $10 million in securities, there is no initial increase in the quantity of money, since the bank deposits held by the public have not been affected. Required reserves likewise remain unchanged, but the chartered banks have $10 million in excess reserves. They can, therefore, lend the full $10 million, again initiating an expansion of $10 million + ($10 × 0.85) million + ($10 × 0.85^2) million, and so on. Although the initial, first-round effects of the two types of transaction are different, their ultimate effects on the money stock will be the same.

Thus, when the Bank of Canada buys securities on the open market, the money stock increases. If the Bank *sold* securities on the open market, it would likewise cause a multiple *decrease* in the money stock. However, this would cause very tight monetary conditions. In our growing economy, the money stock can grow at a moderate rate without causing inflation. Therefore, when the Bank of Canada wants to tighten monetary conditions, it normally does not sell securities. Instead, it simply reduces the rate of purchases on the open market.

When it buys securities on the open market, the Bank of Canada bids their prices up. But this is just another way of saying that it bids interest rates down. As a result of the Bank's purchase, the chartered banks have excess reserves. As they make loans or buy bonds with these reserves, the banks bid interest rates down even further.

Bank of Canada purchases of *foreign currencies* from Canadian residents influence the money stock in precisely the same way as purchases of government securities. Again, the ultimate effect does not depend on whether the foreign currency is bought from a chartered bank or from a non-bank corporation or individual.

Unlike open-market operations or Bank of Canada transactions in foreign currencies, transfers of federal government deposits to the chartered banks do not directly influence the money stock, since federal government deposits in the chartered banks are not counted as part of the money stock. However, such deposit transfers create excess cash reserves in the chartered banks. When these excess reserves are lent out, the money stock increases, just as in the case of Bank of Canada purchases of government securities or foreign currencies.

Changes in the Bank rate are another major tool of the Bank of Canada. By cutting the Bank rate, the Bank of Canada encourages chartered banks to borrow more. When they borrow more, their reserves increase. Thus, a cut in the Bank rate is an expansionary policy; increases in the rate are a restrictive policy. The Bank of Canada is sometimes spoken of as the *lender of last resort*; the chartered banks can go to it to borrow reserves if they are temporarily short and cannot get funds elsewhere.

The Bank of Canada also makes loans to authorized investment dealers. A reduction in the rate that the Bank charges on such loans can also be used as a way of increasing chartered bank reserves: With a lower rate on loans from the Bank of Canada, investment dealers have an incentive to borrow from the Bank, using the proceeds to repay some of the loans they have taken from the chartered banks. As they do this, the reserves of the chartered banks increase, and the money stock expands.

Another possible tool with which a central bank can control the money stock is a change in the required reserve ratio. As we have seen in Chapter 11, chartered bank deposits can be as much as $1/R$ times reserves, where R is the required reserve ratio. By changing R, the Bank of Canada can thus change the size of the deposit multiplier. Relatively small changes in R can have a powerful effect on the size of the money stock. Partly because of the fear that even small changes in required cash reserve ratios might cause disruptions in the monetary system, the Bank of Canada never used this tool to control the money stock even when it had the authority to do so before 1967; since that year, the required ratios of cash reserves have been laid down in the Bank Act so that the Bank of Canada has not had the power to change them. On the other hand, the Act does allow the Bank of Canada to impose a minimum ratio of *secondary* reserves on the chartered banks, with secondary reserves being defined to include Treasury bills, loans to investment dealers, and excess cash reserves. However, while changes in the secondary reserve ratio may force chartered banks to rearrange the asset side of their balance sheets, it is unlikely to have any major effect on the stock of money.

In the late 1980s, proposals to abolish legal reserve requirements on chartered banks were being actively considered. (The banks argued that the existing reserve requirements made it more difficult for them to compete with institutions such as trust and mortgage loan companies that were not subject to legal reserve requirements.) Although economists argued that the Bank of Canada would still retain ultimate control over the money stock (since banks would *voluntarily* hold a certain portion of their assets as reserves, even if they were not *legally* required to do so), critics of these proposals feared that abolishing the legal reserve requirements would make it *more difficult* for the Bank to control the money stock with precision.

Finally, the Bank of Canada can influence chartered bank behaviour by *moral suasion*—informal suggestions to chartered banks to take certain kinds of action and refrain from others. Moral suasion has been used by the Bank of Canada on many occasions. However, it has most often been used as a way of accomplishing special policy objectives (such as increasing bank lending to house building, or assisting financial institutions in difficulty), rather than as a device for controlling the money stock.

When the Bank of Canada purchases securities on the open market, it creates money "out of thin air." Our money is not backed by gold. Money retains its value because the Bank of Canada limits its supply; money is scarce. Deposits in chartered banks and similar financial institutions are backed not only by the assets of these institutions, but also by the Canada Deposit Insurance Corporation. Insurance is important for individual depositors; it offers them protection. It is also important for the stability of the system as a whole: Deposit insurance greatly reduces the risk of a run on banks and other institutions such as trust companies.

At times in our history, money has also been backed by *gold* (and silver). This system had one great advantage, in that it limited the amount of money that could be created, and thus acted as a restraint on reckless, inflationary expansions in the money stock. However, it had two great defects: (1) Increases in the quantity of gold played a function similar to open market purchases in the present system; they increased bank reserves, and permitted a multiple increase in the money stock. However, there was no assurance that the amount of gold mined or imported from abroad would provide the amount of money needed for a full-employment, non-inflationary economy. (2) The banking system was vulnerable to runs. Whenever gold reserves were withdrawn from the base of the monetary pyramid, there was a powerful contractionary effect on the quantity of money. In other words, the gold standard could make financial crises and recessions worse—as it did in some countries in the early 1930s. This was the major reason for the abandonment of the gold standard.

IMPORTANT TERMS: MATCH THE COLUMNS

Match each term in the first column with the corresponding phrase in the second column.

_____	1. The Bank of Canada
_____	2. Open market operation
_____	3. Example of restrictive policy
_____	4. Example of an expansive policy
_____	5. The Government of Canada
_____	6. The Bank rate
_____	7. Prime rate
_____	8. Price of a Treasury bill
_____	9. Authorized investment dealer
_____	10. Legal tender
_____	11. Fiat money
_____	12. Secondary reserves

a. Money unbacked by gold or silver; it is money because the government says so

b. Like banks, these firms can borrow from the Bank of Canada

c. Interest rate on Bank of Canada's loans to chartered banks

d. Creditors must accept this money in repayment of debts

e. This rises when interest rate falls

f. Canada's central bank

g. Includes Treasury bills and loans to investment dealers

h. Reduction of Bank rate

i. Purchase or sale of government securities by the Bank of Canada

j. A bank's publicly announced interest rate for short-term loans

k. This institution initially issued securities bought or sold in open market operations

l. Increase in the required reserve ratio

TRUE-FALSE

T F   1. During the early years of the Great Depression, there was no central bank in Canada.

T F   2. Changes in required cash reserve ratios are commonly used tools of monetary policy.

T F   3. If the required reserve ratio of the chartered banks is 10%, then an open market purchase of $1 million by the Bank of Canada permits the banks to increase their deposits by a maximum of $10 million.

T F   4. The appropriate strategy for the Bank of Canada during a depression is to sell government bonds, to make low-risk, sound assets available for the chartered banks to buy.

T F   5. When chartered banks repay their borrowings from the Bank of Canada, the result is an increase in their excess reserves.

T F   6. When the Bank of Canada sells securities to the chartered banks, it increases their earning assets and, thus, makes possible an increase in the money stock.

T F   7. When the Bank of Canada increases its purchases of government securities, it is engaging in an expansionary act; when it sells government securities, it is engaging in a restrictive act.

T F   8. If the interest rate doubles, then the price of a treasury bill falls by 50%.

T F   9. Bank of Canada notes (Canada's paper currency) are backed dollar for dollar with gold held by the federal government in the Exchange Fund Account.

T F   10. The existence of government-sponsored insurance for depositors in banks and similar institutions reduces the danger of runs on such institutions. Indeed, one of the major purposes of such insurance is to reduce this danger.

T F   11. Since 1980, the Bank rate has usually been higher than the interest rate on Treasury bills.

T F   12. Changes in the secondary reserve ratio have a powerful effect on the money stock, and have almost never been used as a tool of monetary policy by the Bank of Canada.

MULTIPLE CHOICE

1. The Bank of Canada cannot do one of the following. Which one?
   a. change the tax rate on profits
   b. change the Bank rate
   c. change the required secondary reserve ratio
   d. buy and sell foreign currencies
   e. buy securities on the open market

2. When the Bank of Canada purchases securities on the open market, the securities it buys are:
   a. common stock of the corporations whose stocks are included in the TSE 300 industrial average
   b. corporate bonds
   c. securities issued by provincial governments
   d. securities issued by the federal government
   e. any of the above; since it is a transaction on "the open market," the Bank of Canada buys whatever is offered for sale at the best price

3. As a result of an open market operation by the Bank of Canada, the amount of bank deposit creation will be larger, the higher is the:
   a. required reserve ratio
   b. Bank rate
   c. fraction of securities purchased from chartered banks, rather than the general public
   d. fraction of securities purchased from the general public, rather than from chartered banks
   e. volume of securities purchased by the Bank of Canada

4. If the Bank of Canada purchases $100,000 of government securities on the open market and the required reserve ratio is 20%, then the maximum increase in chartered bank reserves is:
   a. $20,000
   b. $100,000
   c. $200,000
   d. $400,000
   e. $500,000

5. When the Bank of Canada purchases a $100,000 Treasury bill from a manufacturing corporation, and that corporation deposits the proceeds in a demand deposit in its bank (Bank A), then:
   a. Bank A's total reserves rise by $100,000
   b. Bank A's excess reserves rise by $100,000
   c. Bank A can safely lend $100,000
   d. the liabilities of the Bank of Canada increase by $500,000
   e. all of the above

6. Suppose that (a) the Bank of Canada purchases a $100,000 government security on the open market, (b) the required reserve ratio is 20%, (c) Molson's sells the security, and (d) Molson's deposits the proceeds from the sale in its chartered bank. The effect of this single transaction will be to increase the excess reserves of the chartered banking system banks by:
   a. $20,000
   b. $80,000
   c. $100,000
   d. $200,000
   e. $500,000

7. Suppose that (a) the Bank of Canada purchases a $100,000 government security on the open market, (b) the required reserve ratio is 20%, (c) Molson's sells the security, and (d) Molson's deposits the proceeds from the sale in its chartered bank. The effect of this single transaction will be to increase the money stock by:
   a. zero
   b. $20,000
   c. $100,000
   d. $200,000
   e. $500,000

8. When the Bank of Canada purchases a $100,000 Treasury bill from a chartered bank, as a result:
   a. the bank's total reserves rise by $100,000
   b. the bank's excess reserves rise by $100,000
   c. the bank can safely lend $100,000
   d. the Bank of Canada's assets increase by $100,000
   e. all of the above

9. During a depression, the best strategy of the Bank of Canada is to:
   a. sell government bonds, to make low-risk, sound assets available for chartered banks to buy
   b. sell government bonds, in order to reduce the size of the government's deficits
   c. sell government bonds, in order to increase aggregate demand
   d. buy government securities
   e. exhort banks not to lend to businesses, in order to reduce their risks of loss

10. The Bank of Canada would *tighten* monetary conditions by *lowering*:
   a. required reserve ratios
   b. the prime rate
   c. the Bank rate
   d. the interest rate on Treasury bills
   e. the rate at which it is buying securities on the open market

11. The Bank rate refers to:
    a. the penalty paid by risky bank borrowers; that is, the amount of interest they pay in excess of the prime rate
    b. the rate at which banks write off bad loans
    c. the rate at which assets lose their real value as a result of inflation
    d. the rate at which money loses its value as a result of inflation
    e. the rate of interest that the Bank of Canada charges on loans to chartered banks

12. If the required reserve ratio is 20%, and if chartered banks borrow $100 million from the Bank of Canada, then the effect on chartered bank reserves is:
    a. an increase of $100 million
    b. an increase of $500 million
    c. a decrease of $100 million
    d. a decrease of $500 million
    e. no change

13. If the price of a Treasury bill falls, then:
    a. all interest rates certainly fall
    b. all interest rates probably fall
    c. the interest rate on this bill certainly falls
    d. the interest rate on this bill probably rises
    e. the interest rate on this bill certainly rises

14. If the price of a $100,000 Treasury bill with 1 month to maturity is $99,000, then the annual yield on that bill is approximately:
    a. 1%
    b. 3%
    c. 4%
    d. 6%
    e. 12%

15. When the Bank of Canada purchases Treasury bills on the open market:
    a. the quantity of chartered bank reserves falls
    b. the interest rate on Treasury bills rises
    c. the price of Treasury bills rises
    d. the risk premium on business loans usually rises
    e. required reserves of banks fall

16. If the Bank of Canada transfers federal government deposits from the chartered banks to the Bank of Canada, the result is:
    a. a decrease in chartered bank reserves and, therefore, a decrease in the money stock
    b. a decrease in the money stock but no change in chartered bank reserves
    c. a lower interest rate on government securities
    d. an increase in foreign currency reserves as the Bank will use the funds to buy more foreign money
    e. a decrease in the Bank rate

17. When the Bank of Canada makes loans to authorized investment dealers, this:
    a. contributes to financial instability because the investment dealers often experience difficulty in repaying the loans
    b. has little effect on the money stock because it does not change chartered bank reserves
    c. increases the prime rate
    d. tends to lower the prices of government securities because the Bank of Canada has to sell government securities to raise the funds that it lends to the investment dealers
    e. affects the money stock in about the same way as Bank of Canada loans to the chartered banks would do

18. The Bank of Canada issues paper currency which acts as money in Canada. It is most accurate to say that this money is "backed" by Bank of Canada assets in the form of:
    a. loans to chartered banks
    b. federal government securities
    c. gold (or gold certificates)
    d. required reserves of the chartered banks
    e. the value of the Bank of Canada building in Ottawa

19. Under the old gold standard system:
    a. the need for gold reserves limited the creation of money
    b. the knowledge that all money was backed 100% by gold created confidence in the government and the central bank
    c. the knowledge that money was backed partly by gold created confidence and prevented runs on banks
    d. the government was forbidden to issue bonds unless it held 100% backing for those bonds in the form of gold
    e. the money stock was just a small fraction of the quantity of gold

20. If the Bank rate were to fall below the Treasury bill rate, chartered banks would be tempted to:
    a. increase their holdings of excess reserves
    b. sell their Treasury bills in order to pay off their loans from the Bank of Canada
    c. call in loans in order to lend to the Bank of Canada
    d. borrow from the Bank of Canada to buy Treasury bills
    e. increase their investments in the stock market

EXERCISES

1. Suppose that the required reserve ratio on all deposits is 20%.

a. In balance sheets A, show the initial effects of an open market purchase of $10 million in government securities by the Bank of Canada. The seller is a manufacturing corporation that deposits the proceeds immediately in its bank.

b. In balance sheets B, show the ultimate effects of the above transaction after the maximum expansion of loans and deposits. Assume that banks keep all increases in reserves in the form of deposits in the Bank of Canada.

c. In balance sheets C, show the initial effects of an open market purchase of $10 million in government securities by the Bank of Canada. The seller is a chartered bank. (Is the initial change in the money stock the same as in part **a**? Why or why not?)

d. In balance sheets D, show the ultimate effects of the transaction in part **c**, after the maximum expansion of loans and deposits. Assume that banks keep all increases in reserves in the form of deposits in the Bank of Canada. (Compare the results with the results in **b**.)

BALANCE SHEETS A

Bank of Canada			All chartered banks			
	Bank of Canada notes	_____	Loans	_____	Deposits	_____
			Total reserves	_____		
Federal government securities _____						
	Deposits of chartered banks	_____	Required reserves	_____		
	Net Worth	_____	Excess reserves	_____		

BALANCE SHEETS B

Bank of Canada			All chartered banks			
	Bank of Canada notes	_____	Loans	_____	Deposits	_____
			Total reserves	_____		
Federal government securities _____						
	Deposits of chartered banks	_____	Required reserves	_____		
	Net Worth	_____	Excess reserves	_____		

BALANCE SHEETS C

Bank of Canada			All chartered banks			
	Bank of Canada notes	_____	Loans	_____	Deposits	_____
			Government securities	_____		
			Total reserves	_____		
Federal government securities _____						
	Deposits of chartered banks	_____	Required reserves	_____		
	Net Worth	_____	Excess reserves	_____		

BALANCE SHEETS D

Bank of Canada		All chartered banks		
	Bank of Canada notes _____	Loans _____		Deposits _____
		Government securities _____		
		Total reserves _____		
Federal government securities _____	Deposits of chartered banks _____	Required reserves _____		
	Net Worth _____	Excess reserves _____		

2. (This exercise is only for those who have studied Box 12-1 in the textbook.) Consider a bond with a face value of $100 and with an annual coupon of $10. In the table below, fill in the approximate price of the bond under different assumptions regarding its term to maturity and current market rates of interest. What does this example suggest regarding the relationship between (a) the term to maturity and (b) the size of price changes in response to a change in interest rates?

Term to Maturity

Rate of interest	1 year	2 years	Perpetuity
8%	_____	_____	_____
10%	_____	_____	_____
12%	_____	_____	_____

ESSAY QUESTIONS

1. At present, the Bank of Canada pays no interest on the balances that the chartered banks have deposited with it. Some economists have suggested that the Bank of Canada *should* pay interest on these deposits; in their view, such a policy change would be better than the proposed change under which legal reserve requirements on chartered banks would be abolished.

Discuss the ways in which these two policy proposals are similar, and how they are different.

2. In the United States, financial institutions called Savings and Loan associations (S&Ls) have traditionally held most of their assets in the form of mortgages on homes, with initial terms of 25 or 30 years. Suppose that many mortgages are made when interest rates are 8%. Then suppose that interest rates in the financial markets rise to 12%. What happens to the value of the mortgages held by an S&L? Suppose the S&L continues to offer low interest rates to depositors, because that is all it can afford to pay since it is receiving low interest on mortgages made in previous years. If it does so, what is likely to happen? Do you see why many S&Ls ran into difficulty when interest rates soared in the late 1970s and early 1980s?

In Canada, some trust companies with large mortgage portfolios experienced similar problems. However, the problems were not as severe as those of the S&Ls in the United States. Can you explain why?

ANSWERS

Important Terms: 1f, 2i, 3l, 4h, 5k, 6c, 7j, 8e, 9b, 10d, 11a, 12g
True-False: 1T, 2F, 3T, 4F, 5F, 6F, 7T, 8F, 9F, 10T, 11T, 12F
Multiple Choice: 1a, 2d, 3e, 4b, 5a, 6b, 7c, 8e, 9d, 10e, 11e, 12a, 13e, 14e, 15c, 16a, 17e, 18b, 19a, 20d

Exercises:

1.

BALANCE SHEETS A

Bank of Canada		All chartered banks	
Federal government securities $10 million	Bank of Canada notes 0	Loans 0	Deposits $10 million
	Deposits of chartered banks $10 million	Total reserves $10 million	
	Net Worth 0	Required reserves $2 million	
		Excess reserves $8 million	

BALANCE SHEETS B

Bank of Canada		All chartered banks	
Federal government securities $10 million	Bank of Canada notes 0	Loans $40 million	Deposits $50 million
	Deposits of chartered banks $10 million	Total reserves $10 million	
	Net Worth 0	Required reserves $10 million	
		Excess reserves 0	

BALANCE SHEETS C

Bank of Canada		All chartered banks	
Federal government securities $10 million	Bank of Canada notes 0	Loans 0	Deposits 0
	Deposits of chartered banks $10 million	Government securities −$10 million	
	Net Worth 0	Total reserves $10 million	
		Required reserves 0	
		Excess reserves $10 million	

BALANCE SHEETS D

Bank of Canada		All chartered banks	
Federal government securities $10 million	Bank of Canada notes 0	Loans $50 million	Deposits $50 million
	Deposits of chartered banks $10 million	Government securities −$10 million	
	Net Worth 0	Total reserves $10 million	
		Required reserves $10 million	
		Excess reserves 0	

2. The exact answers are:

Term to Maturity

Rate of Interest	1 year	2 years	Perpetuity
8%	$101.85	$103.57	$125.00
10%	$100.00	$100.00	$100.00
12%	$ 98.21	$ 96.62	$ 83.33

The longer the term to maturity, the greater is the change in price of the bond for any given change in market interest rates. (Note: market interest rates on long-term bonds generally fluctuate much less than market rates on shorter-term securities. This dampens the fluctuations in long-term bond prices somewhat. Nevertheless, long-term bond prices still fluctuate much more than the prices of shorter-term securities.)

ANSWERS TO SELECTED REVIEW QUESTIONS FROM THE TEXT

12-3. The Treasury bill is selling at a discount of about 4% below its face value. Since the bill has only a quarter of a year to go until it matures, this discount represents an annual interest rate of about 16%.

If the price falls to $95,000, the discount will be about 5%. That is, the annual rate of interest on this bill will now be about 20%.

Note that a fall in the price of the bill means an increase in the interest rate or yield.

12-5. It is indeed desirable for the money stock to be increased during a depression. But this should be done by the Bank, not by counterfeiters. If, for some reason, the Bank can't or won't act, the government can increase the money stock: It can borrow from the Bank (or print money directly) to pay income tax rebates to the public, or to pay for additional government expenditures. (This would represent a combined monetary and fiscal action.)

12-6. In a sense, Bank of Canada notes are backed by the assets of the Bank of Canada, principally government securities. But this is not what gives Bank of Canada notes their value. Rather, they are valuable because they are scarce, relative to the demand for them.

Across

2. Italian city
7. animal associated with rising stock market, or with nonsense
9. indefinite article
10. Reserves are a _____ of deposit liabilities.
13, 15, 16. responsible for monetary policy
17. led a rebellion in Western Canada in the 1800s
18. built for defence
20. interjection
21. Telepathy is an example of this. (abbrev.)
23. To raise taxes in a depression would be an example of this.
26. shape, sometimes used to explain monetary instability under the gold standard
29. third person singular
32, 33. central bank of the United States
34. smallest units of paper money in Canada
35. give an account
37. Egyptian god
38. a charge for service rendered
39. currency of South Africa
40. not small
42. a stiff, boring writing style
44. former Middle East group of countries (abbrev.)
45. computer measure of information
46. not far
48. Moral _____ is sometimes used by the Bank of Canada.
49. in parliament, those who vote "yes"

Down

1. weapon used to fence with
2. part of a window made of glass
3. sometimes gets twisted
4. visitor from another world? (abbrev.)
5. what dogs say in cartoons
6. agreement
7. constrictor
8. beneath
11. black sticky substance
12. return on a loan
14. what we breathe
19. either... _____ ...
22. heavenly body
24. Dr. Jekyll's alter ego
25. African river
26. The Bank of Canada rate is usually a _____ rate.
27. Chartered banks are required to hold these.
28. open _____ operations
29. denotes present location
30. type of bill that can be counted as part of chartered banks' secondary reserves
31. In this country, Bank of Canada notes are legal _____.
32. preposition meaning "on behalf of"
33. fish eggs
36. Persian language
41. poem of praise
43. place where a traveller can eat and sleep
47. helps those with a drinking problem (abbrev.)

Chapter 13

■ ■

Monetary Policy and Fiscal Policy: Which Is the Key to Aggregate Demand?

MAJOR PURPOSE

One of the important controversies of recent decades has been over the relative importance of monetary and fiscal policies. If the economy is heading into an inflationary boom or into a recession, should we turn to fiscal policy to stabilize the economy? Or to monetary policy? Most economists would now say that a *combination* of monetary and fiscal policies is best. However, there has been a sharp debate between Keynesians—who have often emphasized fiscal policy—and monetarists, who have emphasized that money is the key to aggregate demand. The purpose of this chapter is to review the highlights of this debate, and suggest that it is unwise to rely exclusively on either monetary or fiscal policy.

LEARNING OBJECTIVES

After you have studied this chapter in the textbook and study guide, you should be able to
- Explain the three steps in the Keynesian explanation of how a change in the quantity of money can cause a change in aggregate demand
- Explain how problems at two of these three steps might mean that aggregate demand will not change much as a result of a change in the quantity of money
- Explain how, at the first step, the quantity of money and people's willingness to hold money determine the rate of interest
- Explain what the investment demand curve means, and remember what "price" is measured on the vertical axis
- Explain the key propositions of monetarists, and the major points of disagreement between monetarists and Keynesians
- Explain how deficit spending may lead to a decrease in investment and/or in net exports
- Explain why, in spite of the strength of the case for using both policies, Canada has nevertheless relied mostly on monetary policy as a demand-management tool in recent years

HIGHLIGHTS OF THE CHAPTER

This chapter deals with the controversy over the relative importance of monetary and fiscal policies. Although most economists take an intermediate position, two extreme views may be identified. One position—the position of strong Keynesians, particularly during the 1950s and 1960s—is that fiscal policy is very important, while monetary policy has little or no effect. The other extreme position—the strong monetarist view—is just the opposite. An earlier chapter explained the Keynesian view of how fiscal policy affects aggregate expenditures. This chapter rounds out the discussion by explaining (1) the reasons that strong Keynesians have dismissed monetary policy, (2) the monetarist view as to why monetary policy is important, and (3) the monetarist view as to why fiscal policy does not have much effect on aggregate demand. This chapter also explains why the historical evidence does not give unqualified support to either extreme view; we are left with a case for using both monetary and fiscal policies.

The Keynesian View of Monetary Policy

In the Keynesian view, there are three links in the chain of events whereby an open market purchase can increase aggregate demand. At the *first link,* an open market purchase can cause a *fall in interest rates.* In Chapter 12, we have already seen why. Specifically, the increase in the Bank of Canada's demand for bonds will work to bid up the prices of bonds—that is, to bid down interest rates. With excess reserves, chartered banks will be anxious to make loans; this will create additional downward pressure on interest rates. This chapter explains this first link (between an expansive monetary policy and a fall in interest rates) in more detail.

To see how monetary policy affects interest rates, Keynesian economists look at the demand for and supply of money. By the supply of money, they mean the quantity which exists in the economy. By the demand, they mean the *willingness* of people to hold money. This willingness depends in part on interest rates—the lower are interest rates, the more money people are willing to hold. This is reflected in the downward slope of the demand curve in Figure 13-2 in the text.

Now, suppose that the economy is initially in equilibrium, and that the Bank of Canada then increases the quantity of money. At the existing interest rate, people now have more money than they are willing to hold. They try to reduce their money balances. How do they do so? The answer is: by buying bonds. As people buy bonds, bond prices rise. That is, interest rates fall. Once the interest rate has fallen to its equilibrium, people no longer have more money than they are willing to hold; the demand for bonds levels off. (Note that, overall, people don't actually reduce their money balances. Instead, they bid down the interest rate until they are willing to hold the quantity of money in existence.)

The *second link* represents the *effect that a change in the interest rate has on investment.* Interest represents one of the expenses that businesses face in deciding whether to buy machinery or make other investments. If interest rates fall, the costs of investment will accordingly fall, and businesses will be more eager to make investments. The increase in investment as interest rates fall is illustrated by the *investment demand curve.* For example, consider the investment demand curve in Figure 13-3 in the text. If the interest rate is 8%, businesses want to undertake $20 billion in investment. Then, if the interest rate falls to 6% as a result of an expansive monetary policy, businesses will want to increase investment by $5 billion (*ceteris paribus*). In other words, the policy leads to an increase in investment at this second step.

At *the third step*, an increase in investment has a *multiplied effect on aggregate demand.* The theory of the multiplier was explained in detail in Chapter 9.

Keynesian economists foresee two situations in which monetary policy may not have much effect. First, Keynes himself saw a problem at the first step. He was skeptical that monetary policy could be used as a way out of the Depression of the 1930s. Interest rates were already very low, and there was not much prospect that they could be lowered significantly with monetary policy. After all, there is a downward limit on interest rates: They cannot be pushed below zero. In other words, in the special case of the Depression when interest rates were already low, Keynes believed that the authorities could not rely on monetary policy. They would have to use fiscal policy to get the economy out of the Depression.

Some of his followers had a more general skepticism regarding monetary policy; they doubted its effectiveness even during more normal times. Specifically, they foresaw a problem at the second step. They believed that the investment demand curve might be almost vertical. As a result, they were skeptical that changes in interest rates would lead to a significant change in investment. Even if monetary policy did change interest rates at step 1, there might be very little change in investment at step 2.

(The skepticism of some Keynesians over monetary policy lasted through the 1960s. Now, however, almost all Keynesians see an important role for monetary policy. The recent difficulties in actually using fiscal policy—explained toward the end of the chapter—have increased their interest in monetary policy. There has been a move away from polar views and toward more central views.)

The Monetarist View of Monetary Policy

The monetarist view begins with the equation of exchange: $MV = PQ$, where M is the stock of money, V is the velocity of money, P is the average level of prices, and Q is the quantity of output (that is, real domestic product). This equation is not a "theory," because it is simply true *by definition*. Specifically, V is defined as PQ/M. However, a theory has been built on this equation. This theory—the *quantity theory*—is the proposition that V is stable. If this is so, then a change in the quantity of M will cause an approximately proportional change in PQ, and monetary policy has a strong and predictable effect on nominal GDP.

Monetarism is built on the quantity theory. Five key propositions of monetarism are:

1. The money supply, M, is the most important determinant of aggregate demand and nominal domestic product, PQ.

2. In the *long run*, real GDP tends to move to its full-employment level. Consequently, the only long-run effect of M is on P, not on Q.

3. However, in the short run, an increase (decrease) in M can cause *both* P and Q to increase (decrease).

4. If M is increased at a slow, stable rate, then aggregate demand will also increase at a slow, stable rate.

5. Such a slow, stable increase in aggregate demand is the best way to reduce the magnitude of business cycles and keep inflation down. Therefore, the central bank should follow a monetary rule, aiming for a slow, steady increase in M.

The Monetarist View of Fiscal Policy

Monetarists doubt that fiscal policy has a strong and predictable effect on aggregate demand. The major reason for this is because of *crowding out*. Suppose that the government spends more, and finances the resulting deficit by borrowing from the public. Interest rates will rise. As a result, businesses will move upward to the left along the investment demand curve; desired investment will decline. Thus, the government spending will crowd out investment; the net effect on aggregate demand will be smaller than foreseen in the simple discussion of Chapter 10. The strength of the crowding-out effect will depend on the slope of the investment demand curve. The flatter it is, the more investment will decrease for any increase in the interest rate. Monetarists generally believe that the investment demand curve is quite flat. As a result, they foresee a strong crowding-out effect, with little or no net effect of fiscal policy on aggregate demand.

This crowding out argument is based on the assumption that the government sells bonds *to the public*. In this case, there will be no effect on the money stock; this will be an example of *pure fiscal policy*. If, on the other hand, the Bank of Canada buys the additional government bonds, interest rates may be kept down and investment and aggregate demand will increase. But the money stock will rise, and a monetarist will consider money, not government spending, to be the cause of the increase in aggregate demand. Thus, if we want to distinguish between the Keynesian and monetarist viewpoints, we should look at a *pure* fiscal policy—a change in G or in tax rates with no change in M—and compare it with what we might call a *pure* monetary policy: an open market operation and a change in M with no change in fiscal policy. If an expansive fiscal policy is accompanied by an increase in M, there is no disagreement: Aggregate demand will increase. Keynesians will generally attribute the increase to fiscal policy, and monetarists to a change in M.

A second reason that deficit spending may have a weak effect on aggregate demand has attracted considerable attention in recent years. An increase in deficit spending by the government can cause an increase in interest rates, encouraging foreigners to buy Canadian bonds and bidding up the price of the Canadian dollar in terms of foreign currencies. Canadian exports are discouraged, and imports stimulated. In other words, a budgetary deficit can cause a deficit in international trade, with the trade deficit offsetting the stimulative effects of the government's deficit spending.

The events of the past quarter-century do not give unqualified support to either the strong monetarist or to the strong Keynesian view. Strong Keynesians were shaken by the events of the late 1960s, when money, not fiscal policy, appeared to be the major engine driving aggregate demand. During the past 15 years, large changes in the velocity of money have shaken the beliefs of strong monetarists.

Now, there is widespread uncertainty over the relative effectiveness of monetary and fiscal policies. Because we do not know exactly how the economy operates, it makes sense to diversify—to use some of each policy, rather than putting all our eggs in one basket. But, while the importance of diversification is widely recognized, we have, in fact, placed almost exclusive reliance on monetary policy as a demand-management tool in recent years. The reason is that fiscal policy is caught in a political impasse. Many people believe that smaller deficits would be desirable, but there is little agreement on how to achieve that goal.

IMPORTANT TERMS: MATCH THE COLUMNS

Match each term in first column with the corresponding phrase in the second column.

_____	**1.**	Investment demand curve
_____	**2.**	More investment
_____	**3.**	Equation of exchange
_____	**4.**	Velocity
_____	**5.**	Quantity theory
_____	**6.**	Crowding out
_____	**7.**	Pure fiscal policy
_____	**8.**	Decline in net exports

a. $MV = PQ$
b. Possibly, a result of a government budget deficit
c. Proposition that V is stable
d. Relationship between the interest rate and I^*
e. Change in G with no change in the rate of growth of M
f. Caused by a lower rate of interest
g. More G leads to higher i, which leads to less I^*
h. PQ/M

TRUE-FALSE

T F   1. If interest rates fall, people will be willing to hold a larger quantity of money.

T F   2. According to Keynes, interest rates might be low during a depression. He argued that in this case, expansive monetary policy would not be an effective tool for promoting recovery.

T F   3. The flatter is the investment demand curve, the more effective is monetary policy as a way of controlling aggregate demand.

T F   4. Keynesians generally argue that, while the equation of exchange is correct (MV does equal PQ), it is not the best way to analyse changes in demand and output; the equation $Y = C + I^* + G + X - M$ is a better place to begin.

T F   5. According to the quantity theory of money, V is stable through time and PQ, therefore, changes by about the same percentage as M.

T F   6. According to quantity theorists, a change in M will have little or no effect on P in the long run.

T F   7. According to quantity theorists, a change in M will have a greater effect on P in the long run than in the short run.

T F   8. The stronger is the crowding-out effect, the more powerful will be the effect of fiscal policy on aggregate demand.

T F   9. The flatter is the investment demand curve, the more effective is fiscal policy as a way of controlling aggregate demand.

T F 10. According to monetarists, fiscal policy can have a powerful effect on aggregate demand, provided that changes in government spending are financed by borrowing from the central bank.

MULTIPLE CHOICE

1. According to the Keynesian approach, the effectiveness of monetary policy on aggregate expenditures should be analysed by looking at three steps. These three steps include each of the following except one. That one is
  a. the effect of monetary policy on the rate of interest
  b. the effect of a change in the interest rate on open market purchases by the Bank of Canada
  c. the effect of a change in the interest rate on desired investment
  d. the effect of a change in desired investment on aggregate expenditures

2. Which of the following is most likely to *decrease* when the quantity of money *increases*?

  a. P
  b. Q
  c. $P \times Q$
  d. the interest rate
  e. the quantity of money demanded

3. In the Keynesian approach to monetary policy, if the quantity of money exceeds the quantity demanded, the most likely result is a
  a. fall in the interest rate
  b. rise in the interest rate
  c. fall in investment
  d. fall in domestic product
  e. fall in the size of the multiplier

4. Suppose that the amount of money people have exceeds the quantity that they want to hold. Then,

according to Keynesian theory, they will try to get rid of excess money balances by
   a. saving more
   b. buying more goods
   c. buying more services
   d. switching from bank deposits to currency
   e. switching from money into bonds or other financial assets

5. The investment demand curve shows the relationship between
   a. the rate of interest and the quantity of bonds that people are willing to hold
   b. the rate of interest and the quantity of money that people want to invest in bonds
   c. the interest rate and desired investment
   d. the interest rate and actual investment
   e. the investment demand curve shows all of the above

6. Keynes believed that an expansive monetary policy might not be very effective as a way to stimulate the economy out of a depression. Monetary policy was most likely to be *ineffective* if
   a. V were stable
   b. the investment demand curve were flat
   c. the demand curve for money were steep
   d. interest rates were already very high
   e. interest rates were already very low

7. The quantity theory of money is the proposition that
   a. $MV = PQ$
   b. $MQ = PV$
   c. P is stable
   d. V is stable
   e. according to the quantity theory, all of the above must be true

8. Most Keynesians argue that the equation of exchange, $MV = PQ$
   a. is incorrect, because V does not equal PQ/M
   b. is incorrect, because V is unstable
   c. is incorrect, because M does not equal PQ/V
   d. is incorrect, because M is unstable
   e. is correct, but is not the most enlightening place to begin macroeconomic theory, because V is unstable

9. Keynesians and monetarists are most likely to agree that
   a. monetary policy is more effective than fiscal policy
   b. fiscal policy is more effective than monetary policy
   c. neither fiscal nor monetary policy can effect Q; the only effect will be on P
   d. the investment demand curve is generally steep
   e. $V = PQ/M$

10. According to the quantity theory of money, a rise in the quantity of money causes an increase in
   a. the ratio of demand deposits to currency
   b. the ratio of currency to demand deposits
   c. the gold stock
   d. $P \times Q$
   e. Q/P

11. According to the quantity theory of money, a rise in the quantity of money causes
   a. a rise in P in the long run, and also, possibly, a rise in Q in the short run
   b. a rise in Q in the long run, and also, possibly, a rise in P in the short run
   c. a fall in P in the short run, and a rise in Q in the long run
   d. a rise in both P and Q in both the long run and the short run
   e. a rise in Q in the long run, with no change in P

12. Suppose that the amount of money people have exceeds the quantity that they want to hold. Then, monetarists emphasize that they will try to get rid of excess money balances by
   a. saving more
   b. buying bonds
   c. buying goods
   d. switching from currency to bank deposits
   e. switching from bank deposits to currency

13. Which of the following views is most likely to be held by a monetarist?
   a. a decrease in the rate of growth of the money stock will cause the level of domestic product to stay below the full-employment level permanently
   b. the money stock should be increased at a steady, constant rate
   c. desired investment is quite unresponsive to changes in the rate of interest
   d. the quantity of money demanded responds strongly to changes in the rate of interest
   e. fiscal policy has a powerful effect on aggregate demand

14. The "crowding-out" effect of fiscal policy applies to which of the following ideas?
   a. an increase in G leads to an increase in interest rates, which leads to an increase in I^*
   b. an increase in G leads to a decrease in interest rates, which leads to an increase in I^*
   c. an increase in G leads to an increase in interest rates, which leads to a decline in I^*
   d. an increase in G leads to an increase in I^*, which leads to an increase in interest rates
   e. an increase in G leads to an increase in I^*, which leads to a decrease in interest rates

15. If the investment demand curve is quite flat, then we would expect the effects on aggregate demand of
  a. monetary policy to be strong while fiscal policy is weak
  b. fiscal policy to be strong while monetary policy is weak
  c. both monetary and fiscal policies to be strong
  d. both monetary and fiscal policies to be weak

16. By "pure" fiscal policies, economists mean
  a. fiscal policies uninfluenced by special interests
  b. fiscal policies where all changes take place in the non-defence sectors of the government's budget
  c. fiscal policies concentrated in the defence sectors of the government's budget, because these have little effect on the productive capacity of the economy
  d. changes in government spending or tax rates unaccompanied by changes in the rate of growth of the money stock
  e. changes in government spending or tax rates while interest rates are held constant

17. Deficit spending by the Canadian government can lead to a decline in Canada's net exports by the following sequence of events
  a. budget deficits cause a rise in interest rates, which causes a rise in the price of the Canadian dollar in terms of foreign currencies, which causes a rise in imports
  b. budget deficits cause a rise in interest rates, which causes a fall in the price of the Canadian dollar in terms of foreign currencies, which causes a rise in imports
  c. budget deficits cause a rise in interest rates, which causes a fall in the price of the Canadian dollar in terms of foreign currencies, which causes a fall in imports
  d. budget deficits cause a fall in interest rates, which causes a fall in the price of the Canadian dollar in terms of foreign currencies, which causes a rise in imports
  e. budget deficits cause a fall in interest rates, which causes a fall in the price of the Cana-

dian dollar in terms of foreign currencies, which causes a fall in imports

18. During the period 1975-85,
  a. the velocity of M1 and that of M2 both rose substantially
  b. the velocity of M1 rose substantially and the velocity of M2 remained fairly stable
  c. the velocity of both M1 and M2 fell gradually
  d. the velocity of M2 rose substantially while that of M1 remained fairly stable
  e. *PQ* was fairly constant, even though velocity fluctuated

19. During the last half of the 1980s,
  a. fiscal and monetary policies were both used actively to stabilize the economy
  b. fiscal policy was the primary demand-management tool used by the authorities
  c. monetary policy was the primary demand-management tool used by the authorities
  d. both fiscal policy and monetary policy were held rigidly constant by political constraints
  e. both fiscal and monetary policies were very restrictive, and the result was a major recession in 1987/1988

20. Fiscal policy was stuck in a "gridlock" in the late 1980s; monetary policy was the only macroeconomic "game in town." The reason was
  a. the Bank of Canada's firm commitment to high interest rates meant that the government could not afford to run deficits
  b. the Bank of Canada's firm commitment to low interest rates meant that the fiscal policy could not become expansive without the danger of hyperinflation
  c. there were large surpluses; the conservative government's firm commitment to new taxes to "soak the rich" meant that the surpluses would become even larger
  d. the federal deficit was increased by large outflows of Canadian funds to the United States
  e. there were large deficits, and considerable political opposition to substantial tax increases

EXERCISES

1. According to the Keynesian approach, money can affect aggregate demand as a result of a three-step process. Specifically, an increase in the quantity of money will lead to:
  a. _____ ; which in turn will cause
  b. _____ ; which in turn will lead to
  c. _____ .

Keynesians foresee no problem at the third step. However, problems might occur at each of the first two steps. Specifically, there might be a problem at the first step, particularly if (interest rates were already very low, interest rates were already high, the rate of inflation were high). There also could be a major problem at the second step, if (the demand for money, the investment demand curve, the consumption function) were steep.

In Keynesian theory, if the amount of money people have exceeds the quantity that they want to hold, they will (buy bonds, buy goods, save more). As a result, (prices will rise, interest rates will fall). Monetarists foresee a different response. If the amount of money people have exceeds the quantity that they want to hold, they will (buy bonds, buy goods, save more). As a result, (aggregate demand will increase, interest rates will fall). In the short run, monetarists believe that this will lead to (higher P, higher Q, both); in the long run, it will cause (higher P, higher Q, both). Monetarism is based on the quantity theory of money. That is, it is based on the view that (M, V, P, Q, all of them) is/are stable.

2. Suppose that the investment demand curve is very steep. This suggests that monetary policy will be (effective, weak). Specifically, suppose the Bank of Canada engages in a very restrictive policy, selling Treasury bills on the open market. As a result, the prices of bills will (fall, rise), and their interest rates or yields will (fall, rise). This will lead to an (increase, decrease) in I^*, with the size of this effect being very (large, small) because of the steepness of the investment demand curve.

3. In Figure 13.1 below, the curves labelled A and B are two alternative ways the investment demand curve may be drawn. Of the two, curve (A, B) is the one in which I^* is most responsive to changes in the rate of interest. According to curve A, when the rate of interest is 10%, I^* will be _____ ; when the rate of interest is 5%, I^* will be _____. According to curve B, when the rate of interest is 10%, I^* will be _____ ; when the rate of interest is 5%, I^* will be _____. If the two economies are identical except for the investment demand, then monetary policy will be more powerful in

(A, B), and fiscal policy will be more powerful in (A, B).

Figure 13.2 shows the 45° line and the line indicating consumption expenditures plus government expenditures for goods and services in either economy A or B. (Assume there are no international transactions.) The slope of this line is equal to _____. This means that the multiplier is equal to _____. [If you have trouble with this point, refer back to Chapter 9.] Suppose that the interest rate in economy A is 10%. Draw the aggregate expenditures line ($C + I^* + G$) for economy A. The equilibrium is at a domestic product of _____. Now suppose that the interest rate decreases to 5%. I^* will (increase, decrease) from _____ to _____ in economy A. Draw in a new aggregate expenditures line. The new equilibrium domestic product is _____. From your last two answers, confirm the size of the multiplier shown earlier in the paragraph.

Now go through the same exercise for economy B. That is, draw in the aggregate expenditures line when the interest rate is equal to 10%, and then when it is equal to 5%. As a result of the fall in the interest rate, investment (increases, decreases) from _____ to _____, and equilibrium domestic product (increases, decreases) from _____ to _____. By comparing answers, we see that the multiplier is (higher than in A, lower than in A, the same as in A). [Do you see why this is so?] A fall in interest rates from 10% to 5% has (a more powerful, a less powerful, the same) effect on domestic product in economy B, compared to economy A.

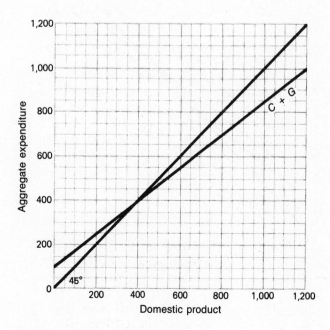

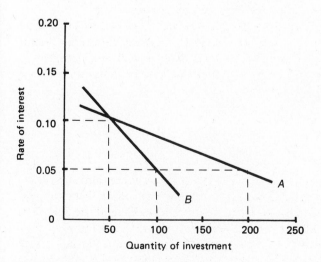

Figure 13.1

Figure 13.2

ESSAY QUESTIONS

1. One reason for using both monetary and fiscal policies together is that diversification spreads the benefit or pain. For each of the following policies, explain who the major gainers and losers are, and why.

   a. expansive monetary policy

   b. expansive fiscal policy

   c. restrictive monetary policy

   d. restrictive fiscal policy

2. Suppose one economist told you that the investment demand curve was quite steep, and another told you it was quite flat. Which is more likely to be a monetarist, and which a Keynesian? Explain.

3. "The equation of exchange, $MV = PQ$, is a tautology. Therefore it is useless in helping us understand how the economy works." Evaluate this statement. Also evaluate the following: "The basic Keynesian equation, Aggregate expenditures $= C + I^* + G + X - M$, is also a tautology. Therefore, it is also useless in helping us understand how the economy works."

ANSWERS

Important Terms: **1d, 2f, 3a, 4h, 5c, 6g, 7e, 8b**

True-False: **1T, 2T, 3T, 4T, 5T, 6F, 7T, 8F, 9F, 10T**

Multiple Choice: **1b, 2d, 3a, 4e, 5c, 6e, 7d, 8e, 9e, 10d, 11a, 12c, 13b, 14c, 15a, 16d, 17a, 18b, 19c, 20e**

Exercises: **1a.** a fall in the interest rate **b.** a rise in desired investment **c.** a multiplied increase in domestic product, interest rates were already very low, the investment demand curve, buy bonds, interest rates will fall, buy goods, aggregate demand will increase, both, higher *P, V*

2. weak, fall, rise, decrease, small

3. *A*, 50, 200, 50, 100, *A, B*, 0.75, 4, 600, increase, 50, 200, 1200, increases, 50, 100, increases, 600, 800, the same as in *A* (because the multiplier depends on the slope of the aggregate expenditures function, which is the same in the two countries), less powerful

Figure 13.2 completed

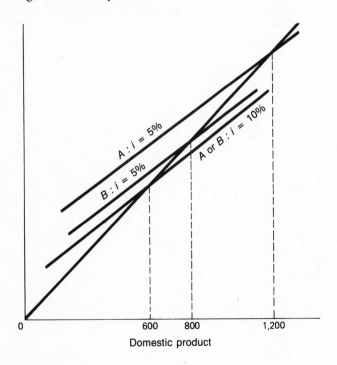

ANSWERS TO SELECTED REVIEW QUESTIONS FROM THE TEXT

13-1. (a) i. The effect of monetary policy on interest rates. **ii.** The effect of a change in interest rates on desired investment. **iii.** The effect of a change in investment on aggregate expenditures (the multiplier). (See Figures 13-1 and 13-4.)

13-2. The quantity of money demanded should be greater at any interest rate, since the opportunity cost of holding money — in terms of interest forgone — is less. If chequing deposits were to pay the same rate of interest as government securities, then the demand for money might become very great and very unresponsive to the rate of interest. In fact, however, interest rates on "money" held in the form of chequing deposits are well below rates on securities. And, as the general level of interest rates rises, the gap between the rate on securities and on chequing deposits increases. Thus, the demand for money continues to slope downward and to the right, although it is further to the right than it would be without the payment of interest on chequing deposits.

13-4. A strong Keynesian draws a steep investment demand curve. As a result, a change in monetary policy will have little effect on investment, even if it succeeds in changing the interest rate substantially. A strong monetarist, in contrast, draws a much flatter investment demand curve. Consequently, monetarists doubt the strength of fiscal policies as a way of controlling aggregate demand. For example, an increase in government spending, involving a deficit (or smaller surplus) will tend to push up interest rates. With higher interest rates, investment will fall sharply. Thus, the effects of more government spending will tend to be offset by the decline in private investment.

13-5. Yes. The equation of exchange must be accepted as valid, since its terms (specifically, V) are defined in such a way that it is true by definition. (That is, it is a truism.) But the quantity theory involves a proposition that need not be true; that is, the proposition that V is stable. Keynesians often argue that, while the equation of exchange is undoubtedly true, it is not an enlightening way to study macroeconomics: A change in the quantity of money might have very weak effects on aggregate demand, since it might simply be offset by a movement of V in the opposite direction.

Similarly, quantity theorists may argue that, while the basic Keynesian equation is undoubtedly true ($Y = C + I + G + X - M$), it is not an enlightening place to begin the analysis of policy, since an increase in G can lead to a fall in I (the crowding-out effect).

Chapter 14

■ ■

Stabilization Policy with International Transactions

MAJOR PURPOSE

The major purpose of this chapter is to explain the relationship between *macroeconomic policy* and the *international payments system* which reflects Canada's transactions, in the form of trade and investment flows, with foreign countries. Canada's international economic relations are reflected in our *balance-of-payments accounts*, which provide a record of all transactions between Canadian residents and foreign residents on current account (sales and purchases of goods and services) and capital account (transactions involving foreign or Canadian assets). All such transactions affect the *exchange market* in which Canadian dollars are exchanged for foreign currencies, at prices which constitute the *exchange rates* between the Canadian dollar and these foreign currencies.

A well-functioning system of international payments helps make the economy more efficient by facilitating international trade and capital flows. Thus, trying to keep the international payments system operating smoothly is an important government policy objective in itself. At the same time, disturbances in the payments system sometimes cause problems in the domestic economy. For a country with extensive international transactions, therefore, there is a close relationship between international payments and macroeconomic policy.

The nature of this relationship depends to a large extent on the exchange rate system that a country is using. If the country is committed to maintaining *fixed* or *pegged* exchange rates, its policy makers may sometimes be forced to use the tools of macroeconomic policy to stabilize exchange rates rather than for the purpose of stabilizing the domestic economy. For example, a deficit country may have to follow restrictive policies even though it may already be suffering from high unemployment. On the other hand, a system of *floating* or *flexible* exchange rates provides countries with a *greater degree of flexibility* to follow the aggregate demand policies they think best for their domestic economies. (However, it also puts less pressure on individual countries to control their domestic inflation rates.)

The exchange rate system may influence the relative effectiveness of monetary and fiscal policies in controlling aggregate demand. In particular, under a system of flexible exchange rates, monetary policy tends to be especially powerful, while the effectiveness of fiscal policy may be weakened in such a system. Conversely, fiscal policy tends to be more powerful under fixed exchange rates.

LEARNING OBJECTIVES

After you have studied this chapter in the textbook and study guide, you should be able to

- Identify three sources of demand for a country's currency on the foreign exchange markets, and three sources of supply
- Explain what foreign exchange rates are and how they influence the amounts of a country's currency supplied and demanded in foreign exchange markets
- Describe the most important accounts in Canada's balance of payments and explain what is meant by a deficit or surplus in the overall balance of payments
- Describe four options open to a government when the demand or supply for its currency shifts

• Explain why intervention in the exchange market does not provide a permanent solution to disequilibrium in the foreign exchange market
• Explain the advantages and disadvantages of fixed or pegged exchange rates
• Describe how monetary and fiscal policies influence the current account and the capital account in the balance of payments
• Explain why the effectiveness of either monetary or fiscal policy depends on whether Canada is on fixed or flexible exchange rates

HIGHLIGHTS OF THE CHAPTER

This chapter focuses on the relationship between a country's macroeconomic policies and its international transactions. In particular, it deals with the issue of whether Canadian policy makers should strive to maintain fixed exchange rates between the Canadian dollar and foreign currencies such as the U.S. dollar, or whether it is a better policy to let exchange rates float freely. There is also a discussion of some of the problems created for Canadian stabilization policies (such as monetary and fiscal policies) by the strong interdependence between the Canadian economy and the economies of foreign countries, particularly the United States, and how the relative effectiveness of the two kinds of policy is affected by the exchange rate system. As a preliminary to dealing with these issues, the chapter begins with a discussion of the mechanics of the foreign exchange market, followed by a description of Canada's balance-of-payments accounts.

The Foreign Exchange Market

International trade differs from domestic trade for two main reasons: (1) International trade must overcome barriers such as tariffs; (2) International trade involves two or more currencies (national monies). As a result of the second complication, international trade leads to transactions in the foreign exchange market, where one national currency is bought in exchange for another.

Exchange rates are determined in the foreign exchange market. The demand for Canadian dollars in the exchange market arises when people offer foreign currencies (such as U.S. dollars), in order to buy Canadian dollars. They want the Canadian dollars in order to buy (1) Canada's exports of goods, such as automobiles and newsprint; (2) Canadian services, such as hotel accommodations for tourists; and (3) Canadian assets, such as Canadian government bonds or shares in Canadian nickel mines. On the other side of the market, the supply of Canadian dollars rises when people offer Canadian dollars in order to buy foreign currencies. Canadians use foreign currencies to buy (1) imports of goods; (2) imports of services; and (3) foreign assets.

An exchange rate is the price of one currency in terms of another. An exchange rate may be quoted either way.

For example, $1 U.S. = $1.25 Can. is the same as $1 Can. = $0.80 U.S. To verify this, multiply each side of the first equation by four-fifths and switch the two sides.

An equilibrium exchange rate is one at which the quantity of currency supplied is equal to the quantity demanded. When demand for a country's currency decreases (the demand curve shifts to the left), the government has four options:

1. Buy the surplus quantity of the home currency at the existing exchange rate, in order to prevent the exchange rate from changing.

2. Decrease the supply by direct actions, such as increasing tariffs or limiting the amount of foreign assets that citizens are permitted to acquire.

3. Decrease the supply and increase the demand for the country's currency by more restrictive monetary and fiscal policies. By restraining aggregate demand, such policies will keep prices and incomes down, thereby reducing imports and stimulating exports.

4. Let the price of the currency fall to its new equilibrium.

In recent decades, most industrialized countries have avoided option **2.**, since it tends to reduce the efficiency of the world economy. Instead, countries have used either option **1.** (that is, they have tried to maintain pegged exchange rates through intervention in the exchange market), or option **4.**, allowing exchange rates to float. In looking at the choice between these two options, however, it must be kept in mind that a country on fixed or pegged exchange rates will be able to buy up the surplus of its currency in the exchange market only as long as it has enough foreign exchange reserves to do this. Thus, in reality, option **1.** is only a temporary expedient. If the shift in demand is permanent, a country will run out of foreign exchange reserves if it relies solely on option **1.** To prevent this, countries sometimes have to adjust their macroeconomic policies—that is, turn to option **3.**

Canada's Balance of Payments

Canada's balance-of-payments accounts provide a record of all transactions between Canadian residents and foreign residents during a period of time such as a year.

The *merchandise trade account* records exports (on the credit side) and imports (on the debit side) of goods. The *current account* includes exports and imports of services (including payments of interest and dividends on foreign-owned capital invested in Canada), as well as exports and imports of goods. On the credit side the *capital accounts* record foreign purchases of Canadian assets (such as stocks and bonds), as well as foreign expenditures on direct investment in Canada; on the debit side, Canadian purchases of foreign assets and direct Canadian investment in foreign countries are recorded. The net increase in Canada's official reserves of foreign currencies is added as a balancing item on the debit side. Because of the way the accounts are constructed, the total credits are always equal to total debits, including the balancing item. However, if we exclude the balancing item, we can speak of a balance-of-payments surplus (when total credits exceed the remaining debits so that there is an increase in official reserves) or a deficit (when debits exceed credits so that official reserves are decreasing).

Fixed vs. Flexible Exchange Rates

Economists who favour fixed exchange rates point to several advantages of a fixed-rate system over a system of floating or flexible exchange rates:

1. When exchange rates remain fixed, the risk of exchange rate fluctuations is eliminated in international transactions; as a result, international trade and capital flows are encouraged and the world economy becomes more efficient.

2. When a government is committed to maintaining fixed exchange rates, it will be forced to avoid inflationary policies, since a high rate of domestic price inflation would make it impossible to maintain fixed rates.

3. Exchange rate fluctuations under flexible rates sometimes aggravate domestic problems. For example, when a country's currency depreciates under a floating rate system, this adds to domestic inflation.

On the other hand, advocates of flexible exchange rates emphasize a severe disadvantage of fixed rates: The government's commitment to maintaining fixed exchange rates may sometimes force it to pursue tight monetary and fiscal policies even when domestic conditions are such that tight policies are not appropriate. (The problems that have arisen in practice during time periods when countries did try to maintain a system of fixed exchange rates, such as under the old gold standard of the 1920s and 1930s, or the IMF adjustable-peg system during 1945-73, are further discussed in Chapter 20.)

Monetary and Fiscal Policies under Fixed and Flexible Exchange Rates

The relative effectiveness of monetary and fiscal policies for stabilizing a country's economy—first discussed in Chapter 13—depends on whether the country is on fixed or flexible exchange rates. As noted in the text, fixed exchange rates may make a country lose control over its monetary policy: Monetary policy cannot be effectively used to stabilize the domestic economy if the central bank must react passively to the balance of payments. But if capital is highly mobile internationally, fixed exchange rate may *add* to the effectiveness of *fiscal* policy. As we saw in Chapter 13, the effectiveness of an expansionary fiscal policy, say, may be diminished if the increased need for government borrowing drives up interest rates and thus reduces private investment (the "crowding-out" problem). With fixed exchange rates and internationally mobile capital, however, the tendency for interest rates to rise will be counteracted by an inflow of foreign capital and (as the central bank buys foreign currencies) an increase in the domestic money supply; this will reduce both the tendency for interest rates to rise and the extent of crowding out.

With flexible exchange rates, on the other hand, *monetary* policy tends to be relatively more effective. For example, an expansionary monetary policy will reduce interest rates and, therefore, stimulate private investment, as outlined in Chapter 13. But the lower domestic interest rate will also tend to cause a capital outflow. This will lead to a depreciation in the value of the country's currency, which, in turn, stimulates exports and makes domestic goods more competitive with imports. The increased demand for exports and import-competing goods reinforces the effectiveness of monetary policy in stimulating aggregate demand. (The effectiveness of fiscal policy, by contrast, tends to be weakened by flexible exchange rates if capital is highly mobile. For example, as an expansionary fiscal policy puts upward pressure on domestic interest rates, a capital *inflow* results. But this tends to make the domestic currency *appreciate*, which reduces the demand for the country's exports and import-competing goods. Thus, the initial stimulative effect of an expansionary fiscal policy is "diluted.")

IMPORTANT TERMS: MATCH THE COLUMNS

Match each term in the first column with the corresponding phrase in the second column.

_____	1.	Foreign exchange
_____	2.	Exchange rate
_____	3.	Current account
_____	4.	Capital account
_____	5.	Foreign exchange reserve
_____	6.	Deficit in the balance of payments
_____	7.	Depreciation
_____	8.	Direct investment
_____	9.	Portfolio investment
_____	10.	Dirty float

a. Shows international flows of direct and portfolio investment

b. Fall in the market price of a currency

c. International sales and purchases of bonds and short-term assets

d. Occurs when governments intervene to influence price of currency

e. Money of another country

f. Shows trade in merchandise and services

g. Price of one currency in terms of another

h. Government's holdings of foreign currency

i. Results in foreign ownership of some firms

j. When a country is losing official exchange reserves

TRUE-FALSE

T F 1. When the Japanese buy Saudi Arabian oil, this creates a supply of yen.

T F 2. If Canada cuts its tariffs, this will lead to an increase in imports and an increase in the supply of Canadian dollars on the world market.

T F 3. A restrictive monetary policy in a country will shift the supply curve for the country's currency to the right in the exchange market.

T F 4. Payments of interest and dividends by Canadian residents to foreign owners of stocks and bonds issued by Canadian firms are included in the capital account in the balance of payments.

T F 5. A country's overall balance-of-payments accounts can show a deficit or a surplus only if there was a change in the country's foreign exchange reserves.

T F 6. A foreign takeover of a previously Canadian-owned firm is recorded as a long-term capital inflow in Canada's balance-of-payments accounts.

T F 7. An expansionary fiscal policy usually tends to cause deficits in both the current account and the capital account.

T F 8. A fixed exchange rate usually increases the effectiveness of fiscal policy because it reduces the tendency for government spending to crowd out private investment.

T F 9. The reason an expansionary monetary policy tends to be highly effective under flexible exchange rates is that it usually causes an appreciation of the domestic currency, making imported goods cheaper.

T F 10. With flexible exchange rates, central banks have more freedom to combat recessions than they do under fixed or pegged exchange rates.

MULTIPLE CHOICE

1. Which of the following is a source of demand for the Canadian dollar on the foreign exchange markets?
   a. purchases of foreign currencies by the Bank of Canada
   b. Canadian demand for foreign goods
   c. Canadian demand for foreign services
   d. Canadian investment in foreign countries
   e. foreign demand for Canadian exports

2. Which of the following leads to a decline in the demand for British pounds on the foreign exchange markets?
   a. a decrease in British purchases of German chemicals
   b. an increase in the number of U.S. tourists in Britain
   c. a switch by U.S. consumers from British to Japanese cars

d. an increase in U.S. purchases of British cars

e. an increase in British sales of textiles to Canada

3. Which of the following is likely to cause a rightward shift in the supply curve for Canadian dollars in the exchange market?

a. A Canadian firm sells subway cars to the city of Los Angeles

b. A Canadian citizen spends a year coaching a hockey team in Switzerland

c. A Canadian businessperson buys enough shares to gain control of a U.S. retail firm

d. Ontario Hydro sells bonds in New York to finance a new project

e. All of the above affect only the demand curve for Canadian dollars

4. Suppose that a British machine costs £400,000, while the exchange rate is £1 = $2.00. Then the price of that machine, in dollars, is:

a. $800,000

b. $600,000

c. $400,000

d. $200,000

e. $100,000

5. Suppose that, as a result of changing preferences, Canadian winter vacationers increase their spending in Mexico by C$100 million, and decrease their spending in the United States by the same amount. The result of this change is likely to be:

a. an increase in the price of Mexican pesos in terms of U.S. dollars

b. an increase in the price of Mexican pesos in terms of Canadian dollars

c. an increase in the price of Canadian dollars in terms of U.S. dollars

d. a decrease in the price of Canadian dollars in terms of Mexican pesos

e. all of the above

6. In Canada's balance of payments, exports of Canadian goods to Japan are entered as a:

a. positive (credit) item

b. negative (debit) item

c. long-term capital account item

d. short-term capital account item

e. change in reserves

7. In the balance-of-payments accounts of the United States, an increase in U.S. official reserve holdings of German marks is entered as:

a. a positive (credit) item

b. a negative (debit) item

c. a current account item

d. a statistical discrepancy

e. direct investment

8. Which of the following transactions is *not* recorded in the capital accounts of Canada's balance-of-payments statistics?

a. a deposit by a Canadian executive of $1500 in an account with a New York bank

b. purchases by the Bank of Canada of $10 million worth of German marks from a Canadian chartered bank

c. payment by an American firm of a debt to a Canadian supplier

d. contributions by an American resident to a Canadian foundation for the protection of Arctic wildlife

e. an American takeover of a Canadian auto parts firm

9. Suppose a Canadian chartered bank lends $20 million to a Swiss businessperson who uses the funds to take over a previously Canadian-owned small manufacturing company. In the balance-of-payments statistics, this would be recorded as:

a. a portfolio capital outflow and a direct foreign investment in Canada

b. only the loan would appear in Canada's balance-of-payments accounts; the takeover would appear in Switzerland's balance-of-payments accounts

c. a Canadian portfolio investment and an outflow of ownership capital from Canada

d. a Canadian import of services

e. **a.** and **d.**

10. An expansionary monetary policy:

a. tends to move both the current account and the capital account toward deficit

b. has little effect on the domestic economy if exchange rates are flexible

c. tends to move the capital account toward a surplus but may cause either a surplus or a deficit in the current account

d. will work under flexible exchange rates only if the Bank of Canada takes steps to prevent the balance-of-payments deficit from affecting Canada's money supply

e. tends to expand the thickness of your wallet

11. Under flexible exchange rates, the restrictive effects of a contractionary fiscal policy tend to be:

a. partially offset by an increase in investment but reinforced by a decrease in net exports

b. partially offset by an increase in net exports but reinforced by a decrease in investment

c. stronger than they would be under fixed exchange rates

d. partially offset by increases in both investment and net exports

e. strengthened by an increase in Canada's foreign exchange reserves

12. If Canada is on flexible exchange rates and the Bank of Canada follows a policy of clean floating, then open market purchases of Treasury bills by the Bank of Canada will have a tendency to:
   a. cause Canadian interest rates to rise
   b. cause an appreciation of the U.S. dollar in terms of Canadian dollars
   c. cause investment to fall
   d. cause Canadian net exports to fall
   e. none of the above

13. Under flexible exchange rates, a contractionary monetary policy will have a tendency to:
   a. reduce exports and increase imports
   b. reduce both exports and imports
   c. increase net investment but reduce net exports
   d. increase net exports but reduce investment
   e. increase gross investment but reduce net investment

14. Under flexible exchange rates, an expansionary fiscal policy tends to:
   a. crowd out imports
   b. have an ambiguous effect, since it is likely to increase both imports and exports
   c. cause the Canadian dollar to depreciate
   d. crowd out net exports

   e. crowd out investment but stimulate net exports

15. Under fixed or pegged exchange rates, and when capital is highly mobile, a reduction in the federal government's budget deficit:
   a. tends to make bond prices fall
   b. tends to make both the supply and demand curves for Canadian dollars in the exchange market shift to the right
   c. would cause an appreciation of the Canadian dollar
   d. tends to make the money supply in Canada increase
   e. tends to create a capital outflow from Canada

16. A "dirty float" is called "dirty" because:
   a. it is unfair to foreign countries
   b. it is unfair to exporters
   c. it is unfair to importers
   d. it is not "clean"; that is, the central bank intervenes in exchange markets to influence exchange rates
   e. it is not "clean"; that is, the central bank departs from the rule of aiming for a steady growth in the money stock

Note: the following four questions are partially based on the appendix to Chapter 14.

17. Suppose that the price of the Canadian dollar rises on the foreign exchange markets. This will:
   a. encourage Canadian exports, and slow down inflation
   b. discourage Canadian exports, and make inflation worse
   c. discourage Canadian exports, and slow down inflation
   d. encourage Canadian exports, and make inflation worse
   e. encourage Canadian exports, and ease the Canadian problem of unemployment

18. Which of the following discourage exports of Canadian goods, and encourage imports of foreign goods into Canada?
   a. Canadian inflation and a depreciation of our dollar
   b. foreign inflation and a depreciation of our dollar
   c. Canadian inflation and an appreciation of our dollar
   d. foreign inflation and an appreciation of our dollar
   e. a depreciation of the Canadian dollar, and an appreciation of foreign currencies

19. Under flexible exchange rates, which of the following would be a "vicious circle" for Canada?

   a. Canadian inflation causes an appreciation of the dollar on the exchange markets, which causes higher Canadian inflation, which causes more appreciation of the dollar
   b. Canadian inflation causes a depreciation of the dollar on the exchange markets, which causes higher Canadian inflation, which causes more depreciation of the dollar
   c. higher Canadian interest rates lead to a depreciation of the Canadian dollar, which causes even higher interest rates
   d. lower Canadian interest rates lead to an appreciation of the dollar, which causes even lower interest rates
   e. lower Canadian interest rates lead to an appreciation of the dollar, which causes Canadian interest rates to rebound sharply

20. With fixed exchange rates, an increase in the rate of inflation in the United States would tend to:
   a. shift the supply curve for Canadian dollars in the exchange market to the left
   b. shift the demand curve for Canadian dollars in the exchange market to the right
   c. cause an increase in Canada's official foreign exchange reserves
   d. increase the inflation rate in Canada
   e. all of the above

EXERCISES

1. The data in Table 14.1 describe the demand and supply of pounds in the foreign exchange market. Plot the demand and supply curves in Figure 14.1, and label the demand curve D_1.

a. The equilibrium exchange rate is $ _____ per pound, or £ _____ per dollar. The equilibrium quantity of pounds sold is £ _____ million, in exchange for $ _____ million.

Table 14.1

Exchange rate	Quantity demanded	Quantity supplied
($ per £)	(£ millions)	(£ millions)
$1.25	100	40
$1.50	90	50
$1.75	80	60
$2.00	70	70
$2.25	60	80
$2.50	50	90
$2.75	40	100
$3.00	30	110
$3.25	20	120

b. Suppose now that the demand for pounds decreases by £20 million at each exchange rate. Plot the new demand curve, and label it D_2. The new equilibrium exchange rate is $ _____ per pound. The equilibrium quantity of pounds sold is now £ _____ million, in exchange for $ _____ million. If the British government wanted to hold the exchange rate at its previous equilibrium (in part a.), it would have to (buy, sell) £ _____ million on the foreign exchange markets; that is, it would have to (buy, sell) $ _____ million.

2. Suppose the Bank of Canada sells government securities in the open market. This [increases, decreases] the reserves of chartered banks, [increases, decreases] the stock of money in Canada, and [raises, lowers] Canadian interest rates. As a result, Canada will experience an increased capital [inflow, outflow], and there will be a tendency toward a balance-of-payments [deficit, surplus].

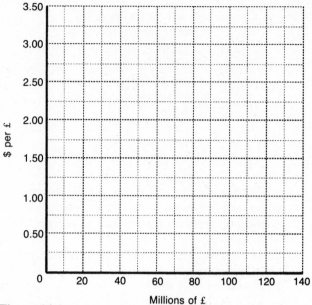

Figure 14.1

If exchange rates are [fixed, flexible], this tendency will force the Bank of Canada to intervene in the foreign exchange markets, [selling, buying] Canadian dollars in exchange for foreign currencies. As a result, there will now be a tendency for chartered bank reserves to [increase, decrease], and this will [counteract, reinforce] the effect of the original sale of government securities.

If exchange rates are [fixed, flexible], the change in Canadian interest rates resulting from the Bank of Canada sale of government securities will tend to make the Canadian dollar [appreciate, depreciate]. As a result, net exports will [increase, decrease]. The effect of the original open market sale is to make domestic investment [increase, decrease]. The change in net exports, therefore, [reinforces, counteracts] the effect of the change in investment on aggregate demand. This exercise, therefore, shows that monetary policy is most likely to be a powerful economic policy tool under a system of [fixed, flexible] exchange rates.

ESSAY QUESTIONS

1. Many countries in the world are heavily dependent on a single primary product for their export earnings. Suppose a country in this position suddenly faces a substantial decline in the world demand for its export good.

Explain what is likely to happen to the supply and demand curves for the country's currency in the exchange market. Discuss what macroeconomic problems this would be likely to give rise to, and what policy responses might be appropriate, (a) if the country was on fixed exchange rates; (b) if it was on flexible exchange rates.

2. During the 1980s, Canada was on flexible exchange rates, and even though it was not an entirely clean float,

the Bank of Canada did not usually intervene in the foreign exchange market in a major way. Nevertheless, some critics argued that the Bank of Canada was still allowing monetary policy to be essentially determined by international considerations. Specifically, the critics suggested that the Bank was trying to conduct monetary policy in such a way that the exchange rate between the U.S. dollar and the Canadian dollar would remain stable even without direct Bank of Canada intervention in the exchange market. Discuss how this can be done, and what the consequences of such a policy might be for the stability of the domestic economy.

ANSWERS

Important Terms: 1e, 2g, 3f, 4a, 5h, 6j, 7b, 8i, 9c, 10d
True-False: 1T, 2T, 3F, 4F, 5T, 6T, 7F, 8T, 9F, 10T
Multiple Choice: 1e, 2c, 3c, 4a, 5e, 6a, 7b, 8d, 9a, 10a, 11d, 12b, 13a, 14d, 15e, 16d, 17c, 18c, 19b, 20e
Exercises: **1a.** $2.00, £0.50, £70 m, $140 m **b.** $1.75, £60 m, $105 m, buy, £20 m, sell, $40 m
Figure 14.1 completed

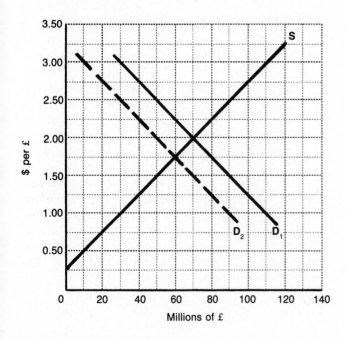

2. decreases, decreases, raises, inflow, surplus, fixed, selling, increase, counteract, flexible, appreciate, decrease, decrease, reinforces, flexible

ANSWERS TO SELECTED REVIEW QUESTIONS FROM THE TEXT

14-1. The government can buy Canadian dollars with its foreign exchange reserves to keep up the price of our dollar. It can allow the exchange value of our dollar to decline, that is, it can allow a depreciation. It can restrict Canadian imports or other expenditures in foreign countries in order to reduce the supply of Canadian dollars to the foreign exchange market, and thus bring the quantity supplied back in line with the quantity demanded at the original exchange rate. It could introduce restrictive demand policies at home, decreasing the supply of Canadian dollars to the foreign exchange market.

14-2. With pegged or fixed exchange rates, a balance-of-payments surplus means that the country's central bank must buy foreign currencies — that is, supply more Canadian dollars — in order to stabilize the exchange rate. As it does this, the domestic money stock will rise, unless the central bank succeeds in completely "sterilizing" the effects of its purchases of foreign currencies.

14-3.

Positive Item	Negative Item
(a) Exports of $100 million	Imports of $100 million
(b) Increased Canadian bank deposits of foreign nationals	Purchase of foreign factory by Canadian firm
(c) Increased Canadian bank deposits of foreign nationals	Dividend payments to foreigners
(d) Export of Canadian services	Decreased Canadian bank deposits of foreign nationals
(e) Export of Canadian machine	Increased lending to foreign firms by Canadian nationals

14-4. In each case, the positive item is listed first:
  (a) current; current
  (b) capital; capital
  (c) capital; current
  (d) current; capital
  (e) current; capital

14-5. Under fixed exchange rates, the central bank must stand ready to alter the supply of money in response to shifts in demand, so as to maintain a stable "price." Therefore, it loses control over the domestic money stock, so it is inappropriate to consider monetary policy in these circumstances.

Under flexible exchange rates, expansionary monetary policies stimulate trade through a depreciation of the home currency (raising exports and reducing imports).

Part Four

Aggregate Supply: Theory and Policy Issues

Chapter 15

∎∎∎∎∎∎∎∎∎∎∎∎∎∎∎∎∎∎∎∎∎∎∎∎∎∎∎∎∎∎

Aggregate Supply: The Inflation and Unemployment Problems

MAJOR PURPOSE

For several decades following the Great Depression, macroeconomists concentrated on the management of aggregate demand. When the economy was declining into a recession, they advocated expansive demand policies to keep output and employment at high levels. When inflationary pressures were strong, they advocated tighter policies to restrain demand and keep inflation down.

However, during the past two decades, the economy has from time to time given conflicting signals. There have been bouts of *stagflation*—that is, periods when high unemployment was combined with rapid inflation. The high unemployment suggested that demand should be expanded; the rapid inflation indicated the opposite. To understand this complex economy, we must look not only at aggregate demand, but also at aggregate supply. Our purpose in Chapter 15 is to study aggregate supply and, in doing so, to explore stagflation.

In the study of aggregate supply, economists generally begin with a diagram with the two macroeconomic problems—unemployment and inflation—on the axes. The smooth curve traced out by historical data during some periods, such as the 1960s, is known as a *Phillips curve*. However, the Phillips curve has not been stable in recent decades. One of the major purposes of this chapter is to try to explain why the Phillips curve shifts.

LEARNING OBJECTIVES

After you have studied this chapter in the textbook and study guide, you should be able to
- Summarize Canada's experience with inflation and unemployment since 1960
- Explain why demand-management authorities sometimes feel that they face a policy dilemma
- Explain the two major reasons why the Phillips curve can shift upward
- Explain the difference between cost-push inflation and demand-pull inflation, and explain why cost-push inflation can lead to higher prices *and* higher unemployment
- Explain why demand-management authorities face a very difficult problem when there is a large upward shift in the Phillips curve (such as in the early and late 1970s)
- Explain why inflation can accelerate to higher and higher rates if the authorities try to keep unemployment below the natural rate
- Explain why many economists believe that the long-run Phillips curve is vertical
- Explain why Milton Friedman argues that, "There is *always* a *temporary* trade-off between inflation and unemployment; there is no *permanent* trade-off."
- Explain why the process of reducing inflation can be painful

HIGHLIGHTS OF THE CHAPTER

When the demand for a specific commodity—such as wheat—changes, there is a movement *along* the supply curve (as illustrated in Figure 4-7 in the textbook). Similarly, when *aggregate* demand changes, the economy moves along the *aggregate* supply curve. Thus, when we study aggregate supply in this chapter, we are studying how the economy responds to a change in aggregate demand. This is an important and puzzling topic. From time to time, the economy has suffered from *stagflation*—a combination of high unemployment and high inflation. In such circumstances, it is not clear what the authorities should do. If they take steps to increase aggregate demand in an attempt to increase output and employment, they may get more inflation instead. If they restrain demand in an attempt to reduce inflation, they may get more unemployment. Making sense of the aggregate supply puzzle is an important topic; it is the main purpose of this chapter.

To study aggregate supply, it is possible to use the aggregate supply curve introduced in Chapter 8, with real domestic product on the horizontal axis and the average level of prices (*P*) on the vertical axis. However, this is not the approach most commonly used. Instead, economists generally begin with a diagram with the two macroeconomic problems—unemployment and inflation—on the axes.

When historical data are plotted on such a diagram (Figure 15-3 in the text) two main conclusions stand out:

1. For most of the 1960s, the points trace out a smooth curve, sloping upward to the left. This is known as a *Phillips curve*.

2. Since 1970, the observations have been above and to the right of that Phillips curve. We have gotten more unemployment *and* more inflation. Strong movements in a "northeast" direction (upward and to the right) occurred during the 1971-75 period and also in 1977/78.

During the 1960s, when most economists believed that the Phillips curve being traced out by the data represented a stable relationship, authorities felt trapped on the horns of a *dilemma*. If they expanded aggregate demand briskly, they would get more output and employment. But inflation would rise. On the other hand, if they restrained demand in order to keep inflation down, the unemployment rate would remain high. They hoped to escape from this dilemma by using expansive aggregate demand policies to reduce unemployment, and incomes policies to directly restrain inflation. (Incomes policies will be studied in Chapter 19.) They were not entirely successful. Inflation, in fact, did increase as output expanded and unemployment declined. The economy moved upward as it moved to the left in Figure 15-3 in the text.

Shifts in the Phillips Curve

Even worse problems were to come in the 1970s, as both inflation and unemployment increased. Two of the three strong movements to the "northeast" in Figure 15-3 coincided with the spiralling price of oil on the international markets. This suggests one explanation for the stagflation since 1970: Rising oil prices shifted the Phillips curve upward, and meant more inflation combined with more unemployment. Inflation was caused by the *upward push of costs*.

Oil prices certainly do not provide the whole explanation, however. The first major movements to the northeast, in 1967-69 and again in 1971/72, occurred while international oil prices were stable at a very low level. In fact, there was something of a glut on the international oil market.

To explain this early episode of stagflation, we must look elsewhere. The *accelerationist* theory provides the most generally accepted explanation.

The Accelerationist Theory

The accelerationist theory, put forward in the late 1960s by Phelps and Friedman, has one core idea. The Phillips curve—such as that observed in the 1960s—is fundamentally *unstable*. If the authorities attempt to reduce the unemployment rate to a very low level, they will succeed, but *only temporarily*. In particular, they will succeed only during the interval between the time when demand is expanded and the time when contracts are renegotiated to take the resulting inflation into account. When people renegotiate contracts, they will demand compensation for inflation; wages and other contractual prices will be adjusted upward. Inflation will accelerate; a *wage-price spiral* will gain momentum. This is illustrated by points *H*, *J*, and *K* in Figure 15-7 of the text. At each of these points, actual inflation is higher than people expected when they negotiated contracts. For example, at *H*, people expected zero inflation (as illustrated by the Phillips curve), but get 2% instead. They then renegotiate contracts on the expectation of 2% inflation. But, with higher costs, businesses raise prices; the economy moves to *J*. People expect 2% inflation; they get 4% instead.

How, then, can we return to macroeconomic equilibrium, once the wage-price spiral has begun? *Equilibrium occurs only when people get the amount of inflation they expected.* This happens if the rate of inflation stabilizes. For inflation to stabilize, the authorities must depart from their single-minded attempt to keep unemployment low; they must introduce a degree of restraint in aggregate demand policies. As restraint occurs, businesses will find it hard to raise prices more and more rapidly; inflation will indeed level off. However, as it becomes harder to sell goods, output will increase more slowly and the unemployment rate will rise.

Once people get the amount of inflation they expect, the unemployment rate will move back to its *natural* or *equilibrium* rate, illustrated by point *N* in Figure 15-8 of the text. A central proposition of the accelerationist theory is that this equilibrium rate of unemployment *doesn't depend on the rate of inflation*; once people adjust completely to inflation, the inflation rate doesn't affect their behaviour. They are neither more nor less willing to work, and businesses are neither more nor less willing to hire them. Because the equilibrium rate of unemployment isn't affected by inflation—once people have gotten used to it—*the long-run Phillips curve is vertical* (Figure 15-9). In the short run, the central bank can lower the rate of unemployment by an inflationary policy. But in the long run, their willingness to accept an inflation rate of, say, 6% will not result in any gain in output and employment.

There is a *short-run trade-off* between the goals of low inflation and low unemployment, but there is *no long-run trade-off*.

Just as low unemployment is associated with an acceleration of inflation, so high unemployment is associated with a deceleration of inflation. If aggregate demand is too low to buy the goods and services being offered at the current rate of inflation, output will fall and businesses will settle for smaller increases in price. This is illustrated by point *V* in Figure 15-10 of the text. *V* is not a good place to be; the unemployed are being used as cannon fodder in the war against inflation. In order to avoid painful periods at points like *V*, it is important to stop the inflationary spiral from gathering momentum in the first place. To those who asked in the 1970s how we might get out of stagflation, there was only one easy—although unsatisfactory—answer: Go back to 1965 and do it right this time. Stop inflation from accelerating in the first place. But, of course, we could not go back to 1965 again. In fact, the economy was dragged through the severe recession of 1982 before the inflation rate was brought down to 4%—a rate that was still much higher than that of the period from 1955 to 1965.

IMPORTANT TERMS: MATCH THE COLUMNS

Match each term in the first column with the corresponding phrase in the second column.

_____ **1.** Phillips curve	**a.** When expected and actual inflation are equal
_____ **2.** Trade-off	**b.** View that there is trade-off in the short run, but not in the long run
_____ **3.** Stagflation	**c.** Unemployment greater than the natural rate
_____ **4.** Cost-push inflation	**d.** Choice between conflicting goals
_____ **5.** Natural rate of unemployment	**e.** When inflation leads to higher wage settlements which contribute to inflation
_____ **6.** Accelerationist theory	**f.** High unemployment combined with high inflation
_____ **7.** Market power inflation	**g.** Equilibrium rate of unemployment
_____ **8.** A likely cost of reducing inflation	**h.** Relationship between inflation and unemployment
_____ **9.** Stable inflation	**i.** Another term for cost-push inflation
_____ **10.** Wage-price spiral	**j.** The rise in the international price of oil is an example

TRUE-FALSE

T F   1. According to the aggregate supply function of simple Keynesian theory, large-scale unemployment or rapid inflation can exist, but not simultaneously.

T F   2. Canadian data for most of the 1960s trace out a reasonably smooth Phillips curve, but the data for the 1970s do not.

T F   3. The short-run Phillips curve shifted down in the 1970s but by 1981/82, it was back to where it had been in the early 1960s.

T F   4. Those who emphasize cost-push inflation are more likely to believe that market power is important than are advocates of the accelerationist theory.

T F   **5.** Even when the unemployment rate is at its natural level, there is still frictional unemployment.

T F   **6.** A high point on the long-run Phillips curve represents a higher rate of inflation than does a low point.

T F   **7.** A high point on the long-run Phillips curve represents a higher rate of unemployment than does a low point.

T F   **8.** According to the accelerationist theory, the economy can be in equilibrium only when the inflation rate is zero; any positive rate of inflation will tend to accelerate.

T F   **9.** If the long-run Phillips curve is vertical, then there is no long-run trade-off between the objectives of price stability and high employment. A low unemployment rate cannot be "bought" over the long run by a willingness to accept inflation.

MULTIPLE CHOICE

1. In the horizontal range of the Keynesian aggregate supply function, the rate of inflation is:
  a. zero
  b. rising
  c. high and constant
  d. equal to the natural rate
  e. less than the natural rate

2. If we compare Canada's experience since the 1970s with that of the early 1960s, we find that, on average:
  a. the rate of unemployment and the rate of inflation have both been lower since 1970 than during the early 1960s
  b. the rate of unemployment has been lower since 1970 than during the early 1960s, but the rate of inflation has been higher
  c. the rate of inflation has been lower since 1970 than during the early 1960s, but the rate of unemployment has been higher
  d. the rate of unemployment and the rate of inflation have both been higher since 1970 than during the 1960s

3. In Canada, "double-digit" inflation (that is, inflation of 10% or more) occurred in:
  a. every year from 1966 to 1975
  b. every year from 1973 to 1981
  c. 1971-1973
  d. 1971/72, and 1982
  e. 1974/75, and 1980-1982

4. The Phillips curve traced out by the Canadian data of the 1960s suggested that there was a policy "trade-off." Specifically, there seemed to be a conflict between achieving the goal of high employment and the goal of:
  a. an equitable distribution of income
  b. allocative efficiency
  c. technological efficiency
  d. high growth
  e. low inflation

5. Cost-push inflation is different from demand-pull inflation because:

  a. demand-pull inflation involves a rise in every price, whereas cost-push inflation involves a rise in prices only in industries with monopoly power
  b. demand-pull inflation involves a rise in every price, whereas cost-push inflation involves only a rise in the prices of goods, not services
  c. when demand-pull inflation begins, it represents a movement along a short-run Phillips curve, but cost-push inflation is an upward shift of the short-run Phillips curve
  d. demand-pull inflation is accompanied by a rise in unemployment rate, but cost-push inflation by a fall in unemployment
  e. demand-pull inflation is accompanied by a fall in output, but cost-push inflation by an increase in output

6. Economists are most likely to conclude that "cost-push" inflation is occurring when a rise in the rate of inflation is accompanied by an increase in:
  a. output
  b. the rate of growth of output
  c. the unemployment rate
  d. government deficits
  e. the money stock

7. Which of the following is an important assumption of cost-push theories of inflation?
  a. there is perfect competition
  b. market power is an important feature of the economy
  c. unemployment is below the natural rate
  d. an increase in the money stock is the most important cause of inflation
  e. government deficits are the most important cause of inflation

8. A point to the left of the long-run Phillips curve is unstable because:
  a. workers and others have underestimated inflation; they will demand higher wages and prices when new contracts are written
  b. workers and others have overestimated infla-

tion; they will be willing to settle for lower wages and prices when new contracts are written
   c. monetary policy is unsustainably tight
   d. fiscal policy is unsustainably tight
   e. the unemployment rate is above its natural rate

9. Suppose two points, A and B, are on the long-run Phillips curve. B is higher than A. Then, the *real* wage at B is:
   a. higher than at A
   b. the same as at A
   c. lower than at A
   d. falling, and so is the real wage at A and every other point on the long-run Phillips curve
   e. rising, even though the real wage is falling at A

10. According to the accelerationist theory (that is, the natural rate hypothesis), the short-run Phillips curve shifts whenever there is a change in:
   a. the natural rate of inflation
   b. the natural rate of acceleration of inflation
   c. expectations of inflation
   d. the degree of unionization of the labour force
   e. the rate at which innovations are being used by businesses

11. According to the accelerationist theory, equilibrium can exist only when:
   a. the unemployment rate is at its natural rate
   b. the inflation rate is zero, since any non-zero rate of inflation will tend to accelerate
   c. the expected inflation rate is zero, since inflation will accelerate otherwise
   d. the growth of the money stock is zero, since inflation will accelerate otherwise
   e. all of the above conditions are met

12. Which of the following is an assumption of the accelerationist theory of inflation?
   a. there is downward rigidity in nominal wages
   b. inflation is caused mainly by unions
   c. inflation is caused mainly by OPEC
   d. inflation is caused mainly by an acceleration in investment
   e. people's expectations of inflation have an important effect on the contracts they negotiate

13. Suppose we draw a diagram with both a short-run Phillips curve and a long-run Phillips curve. At the point where they intersect:
   a. the inflation rate is zero
   b. the unemployment rate is zero
   c. actual inflation is the same as expected inflation
   d. inflation is accelerating
   e. the rate of unemployment is rising

The next three questions are based on Figure 15.1.

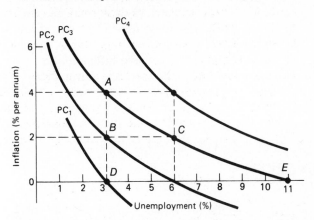

Figure 15.1

14. In Figure 15.1, the natural rate of unemployment is 6%. Which of the points represents an equilibrium?
   a. *A*
   b. *B*
   c. *C*
   d. *D*
   e. *E*

15. In Figure 15.1, the natural rate of unemployment is 6%. Suppose that the economy is at point *A* on Phillips curve PC$_3$. To get to that point, contracts have been based on an expected rate of inflation of:
   a. zero
   b. 2%
   c. 3%
   d. 4%
   e. 6%

16. In Figure 15.1, the natural rate of unemployment is 6%. Last year, the economy was at point *A* on short-run Phillips curve PC$_3$. If contracts are now renegotiated, which of the short-run Phillips curves is most likely to result?
   a. PC$_1$
   b. PC$_2$
   c. PC$_3$
   d. PC$_4$
   e. either PC$_1$ or PC$_2$, but we can't be sure which

17. According to the accelerationist theory, the unemployment rate will be greater than the natural rate when inflation is:
   a. greater than people expected
   b. less than people expected
   c. low and steady
   d. high and steady
   e. zero

18. According to the accelerationist theory (that is, the natural rate hypothesis),

a. inflation will accelerate whenever the unemployment rate deviates from the natural rate
b. the short-run and long-run Phillips curves are both vertical
c. there is a trade-off between inflation and unemployment in the long run, but not the short

d. aggregate demand policies should be fine tuned in order to prevent inflation from accelerating
e. an attempt to reduce inflation with more restrictive monetary policies will result in above-normal unemployment during a transition period

EXERCISES

1. Figure 15.2, shown here, represents the Phillips curve for year 1, when the expected rate of inflation is zero. The natural rate of unemployment is _____ %. If unemployment is at the natural rate, the rate of inflation will be _____ in year 1. If, alternatively, the unemployment rate is 3%, the actual rate of inflation will be (more, less) than the expected rate by _____ %.

Suppose now that the expected rate of inflation is 2% in year 2. Draw the Phillips curve for year 2 in Figure 15.2. If the rate of unemployment is still 3% in year 2, the rate of inflation will be _____ %.

If, on the other hand, inflation is 3% in year 2, the rate of unemployment will be slightly more than _____ %. Now suppose that the rate of inflation is kept at 3% indefinitely, into years 3, 4, 5.... The expected rate of inflation will eventually become _____ %, and the rate of unemployment will move to _____ %. Alternatively, if aggregate demand policies are aimed at keeping the unemployment rate at 3%, the rate of inflation will _____.

2a. Suppose that the economy is initially at point A on Phillips curve 1 in Figure 15.3. Then the curve shifts to Phillips curve 2. If policy makers pursue restrictive monetary and fiscal policies that keep the rate of inflation from increasing, then unemployment will (increase, decrease) by amount _____. If, on the other hand, they keep the rate of unemployment stable by following more expansive policies, then inflation will (increase, decrease), by amount _____.

2b. Suppose this shift in the Phillips curve is caused by workers observing a rate of inflation higher than they expected. Then, according to the natural rate theory, the rate of unemployment at A was (more than, less than, the same as) the natural rate. The attempt by the policy makers to go to point C will cause the Phillips curve to _____ when contracts are renegotiated.

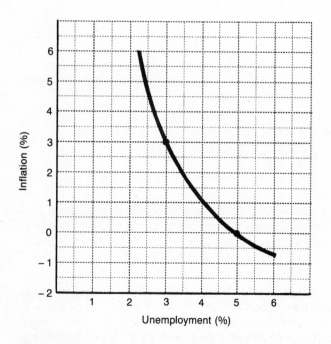

Figure 15.2

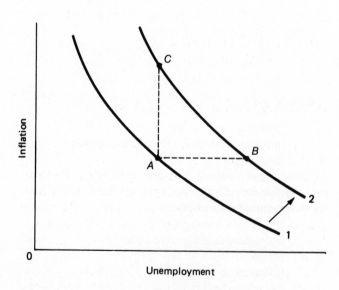

Figure 15.3

ESSAY QUESTIONS

1. According to the accelerationist theory, the rate of unemployment cannot be kept permanently below the natural rate by an expansive aggregate demand policy. Explain why. Can the rate be kept permanently above the natural rate by a restrictive aggregate demand policy? Explain why or why not.

2. The short-run Phillips curve indicates that when unemployment rises, inflation should fall. But, in some years, both inflation *and* unemployment rise. How would an accelerationist explain this? Is there any other explanation?

ANSWERS

Important Terms: 1h, 2d, 3f, 4j, 5g, 6b, 7i, 8c, 9a, 10e
True-False: 1T, 2T, 3F, 4T, 5T, 6T, 7F, 8F, 9T
Multiple Choice: 1a, 2d, 3e, 4e, 5c, 6c, 7b, 8a, 9b, 10c, 11a, 12e, 13c, 14c, 15b, 16d, 17b, 18e
Exercises: **1.** 5, 0, more, 3. 5. 4, 3, 5, become more and more rapid
Figure 15.2 completed

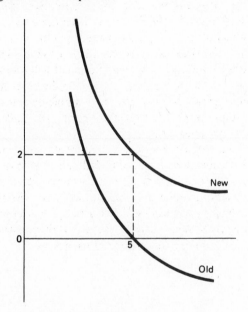

2a. increase, *AB*, increase, *AC*
2b. less than, shift further up

ANSWERS TO SELECTED REVIEW QUESTIONS FROM THE TEXT

15-2. (a) This is correct, as illustrated by points *G, N, R,* and *T* in Figure 15-9.

(b) ... the rate of unemployment will be less than natural rate whenever inflation is greater than the expected rate (for example, point *H* in Figure 15-9), and it will be greater than the natural rate whenever inflation is less than the expected rate (for example, point *V* in Figure 15-10).

(c) ... is no trade-off in the long run. Such a trade-off occurs only in the short run, when the actual rate of inflation can deviate from the expected rate.

(d) long-run trends in demand certainly affect prices.

15-3. If prices rise more than wages as a result of an increase in aggregate demand, profits per unit (and total profits) would rise; moreover, the higher prices and relatively less high wages would induce firms to increase output and employ more workers.

15-4. This is the cost-push case where prices rise because of an increase in (non-labour) input costs. In this case, firms' profit margins would have less of a tendency to rise (and might even fall); as a result, output and employment might fall instead.

15-5. Presumably, this was because there were no strong expectations of higher inflation during that extended period. This was not unreasonable, given the historical experience. Inflation occurred at some times, and deflation at others (particularly in the period between the two world wars). It was only with the development of modern tools of aggregate-demand management, which practically eliminated periods of falling demand and greatly increased the long-run trend of demand, that inflation became ingrained in the economy and became built into people's expectations.

Chapter 16

■■■■■■■■■■■■■■■■■■■■■■■■■■■■■■■■■

How Does Inflation Cause Problems?

MAJOR PURPOSE

In Chapter 15, we have seen how wage contracts can be adjusted to take account of inflation. The theory of the vertical Phillips curve is based on the view that inflation won't have any effect on the unemployment rate, once people get used to the inflation and adjust to it. This chapter deals with the way in which individuals, businesses, and the government adjust to an inflationary environment. By adjusting, they reduce the effects of inflation on real magnitudes, such as real output and real wages. However, even after two-and-a-half decades of rather rapid inflation, the economy has not adjusted fully to inflation; inflation has significant real consequences. The purpose of this chapter is to study the ways in which the economy does and does not adjust to inflation.

One important set of adjustments is in the market for bonds and other debt instruments. Unanticipated inflation hurts bondholders; they are repaid in less valuable dollars. If they anticipate inflation, however, they can adjust for it. They can withdraw from the bond market until interest rates rise to compensate for inflation. However, even if this happens, with real interest rates remaining constant, inflation can still have important consequences for borrowers and lenders. In particular, the combination of high inflation and high nominal rates of interest means that debt is front-loaded—payments in the early years are high, in real terms. As a result, young people have difficulty buying their first homes.

Another important issue is the effect of inflation on the tax system. Some of the effects of inflation can be offset by *indexation* of tax brackets, deductions, etc. Such indexation has existed in Canada since 1974, and was introduced in the United States in the mid-1980s. However, there are other important effects, such as those arising from the taxation of nominal interest, that are not so easily dealt with. Inflation continues to cause quirks and distortions in the tax system.

LEARNING OBJECTIVES

After you have studied this chapter in the textbook and study guide, you should be able to
  • Explain why unanticipated inflation has much stronger effects on the economy than anticipated inflation
  • Give examples of those who lose from unanticipated inflation, and those who gain
  • Explain how the real rate of interest is related to the nominal rate of interest and the expected rate of inflation (equation 16-1)
  • Explain how the behaviour of borrowers and lenders tends to stabilize real interest rates
  • Give an example of how the after-tax real rate of interest may be negative, even though the pre-tax real rate has remained constant in the face of higher inflation
  • Explain how borrowers—and particularly purchasers of first homes—can be adversely affected by inflation, even if the real rate of interest remains constant
  • Explain the difference between a variable-rate mortgage and a graduated-payment mortgage, and explain how they are designed to deal with different problems

• Explain why a high, uncertain rate of inflation can cause problems in the bond market
• Explain the problems that can arise if the government uses the real government deficit as a measure of fiscal policy, or if the Bank of Canada uses the real quantity of money as a measure of monetary policy

HIGHLIGHTS OF THE CHAPTER

In Chapter 15, we began to see how the economy can adjust to inflation. As inflation continues, people come to expect it and change their behaviour accordingly. For example, labour unions bargain for a higher nominal wage to compensate for the increase they have come to expect in the cost of living. If people's expectations are accurate, then the inflation need not affect real wages; it will be taken into account by both workers (who will demand higher money wages) and employers (who will be willing to pay higher money wages). Also, the rate of unemployment may be unaffected; this was the idea behind the vertical long-run Phillips curve of Chapter 15.

The Real Rate of Interest

Adjustments like this may occur not only in the labour market, but also in other markets. Among the most important markets affected by inflation are the markets for corporate bonds, government bonds, mortgages, and other debt instruments. Owners of bonds can be severely hurt by inflation; they are repaid in dollars with smaller value. If they anticipate inflation, they can take steps to protect themselves. They can switch out of bonds and into other assets, such as common stock or real estate. When they do so, bond prices fall; that is, interest rates rise. The rise in interest rates is reinforced by the eagerness of borrowers. Because they will be able to repay in less valuable dollars, they have an incentive to borrow more as inflation increases.

The *real rate of interest* is the rate of interest after account is taken of inflation. It is (approximately) the nominal rate of interest less the expected rate of inflation. For example, if the nominal interest rate is 10%, someone lending $100 today will be repaid $110 in one year's time. If the rate of inflation is 10% during that year, the $110 will buy no more than the $100 would have bought originally. In real terms, the lender has no gain. The nominal interest rate of 10% is no more than enough to compensate for the 10% inflation; the real interest rate is zero (10%-10%). This is not very good from the lender's viewpoint. Lenders are therefore reluctant to make loans, causing a further rise in interest rate. When this happens, the real interest rate becomes positive. Many observers of financial markets believe that the behaviour

of lenders and borrowers will act to stabilize the real interest rate. Until the early 1970s, evidence suggested that the real interest rate was in fact quite stable. In the early 1980s, however, real interest rates were high by historical standards, both in Canada and the United States.

Even if the real interest rate is constant and inflation is perfectly anticipated, a combination of high inflation and a high nominal interest rate can have an important effect on borrowers and lenders. There are two main reasons for this. One has to do with front loading; the other has to do with the tax system.

The Duration of Debt: Front Loading

Bonds, mortgages, and other types of debt usually specify a constant *nominal* rate of interest. In a world of zero inflation, a nominal interest rate of 3% represents a real rate of 3%. Someone who has issued a bond with a face value of $100,000 will pay $3,000 in interest each year.

Suppose now that inflation accelerates to 10%, with the nominal rate of interest keeping step at 13%. Someone issuing a $100,000 bond now has to pay $13,000 in interest per year. This $13,000 includes $10,000 to compensate for the loss of value by the $100,000 principal over the year. The remaining $3,000 represents a real interest payment. In a sense, $10,000 of the $13,000 may be looked on as a partial repayment of principal. In real terms, the borrower is not only paying interest, but is also repaying part of the principal each year. Payments in early years are very high—the $13,000 represents a lot in the first year, since prices have not yet risen much. The debt is *front-loaded*.

During periods of rapid inflation and high nominal interest rates, mortgages are similarly front loaded. As a result, it is very difficult for first-time buyers to afford homes. If they take out a mortgage now, they may face a crushing burden in the early years. This problem would be solved if mortgage payments were graduated—that is, if nominal payments rose through the years to keep real payments stable. Such graduated mortgages are not generally available, nor are they likely to become available. One reason is that they would lead to a rise in the burden of mortgage payments through time if inflation unexpectedly slowed down.

Taxation and Inflation

Taxation is another reason that inflation can have lasting real consequences, even if it is perfectly anticipated. Some taxes, like sales taxes, are a constant percentage of expenditures. If all incomes and prices rise by 10%, so will the number of dollars spent on sales taxes. In real terms, there will be no change in the taxes paid.

Income taxes are different, however. The income tax schedule is progressive: tax rates rise as income rises. Thus, in the 1960s and early 1970s, there was a problem of "tax-bracket creep." When prices doubled and income doubled in money terms, people were pushed into higher tax brackets. The percentage of their incomes paid in taxes rose. In order to correct the unlegislated increase in taxes that resulted from inflation, the income tax was *indexed*, beginning in 1974. With indexing, tax brackets, exemptions, etc., rise in proportion to prices. If all prices and incomes increase at the same rate, so do tax payments.

However, inflation still has peculiar effects on taxes. Most notably, people pay taxes on their *nominal* interest. In the earlier example, with $13,000 interest on a $100,000 bond, a bond owner in the 40% bracket would pay 40% of the $13,000 in taxes, leaving only $7,800 or 7.8% after taxes. This is not enough to compensate for the 10% inflation. The *after-tax real rate of interest* is negative.

Inflation and Uncertainty

Uncertainty is another complication that prevents perfect adjustment to inflation. Periods of *rapid* inflation also tend to be periods of *erratic* inflation. Thus, bond buyers are taking a risk. High nominal interest rates may compensate for the inflation they expected when they bought the bond. But suppose that inflation speeds up unexpectedly. The bondholder will lose. Similarly, there are risks for the borrower: If inflation unexpectedly slows down, the real burden of interest payments increases. Because erratic inflation poses risks for both borrowers and lenders, a high, erratic inflation may cause the long-term bond market to dry up.

One way to deal with the problem of uncertainty is to have periodic adjustments in interest during the period of the loan. For example, most new mortgages in Canada have variable rates. Through the introduction of variable rate mortgages, the mortgage market has dealt quite effectively with the problem of *erratic* inflation. But it has not been able to deal with the front-loading problem associated with *high* rates of inflation and interest. Graduated mortgages are not generally available.

Real Magnitudes and Fiscal and Monetary Policies

Finally, this chapter considers how the government itself might respond to an inflationary situation. One question is how we should measure fiscal policy. Some argue that we should look at the changes in the real deficit of the government. When inflation is rapid—say, at 10%—then the first 10% in interest doesn't really represent interest; it represents a partial repayment of the real value of the debt. Thus, a government with a $300 billion debt and a $30 billion deficit is not running a deficit at all. In real terms, its budget is balanced; the real value of its debt is constant.

This is a rather interesting idea, but it presents a problem. Indeed, it represents a policy trap similar to the principle of the annually balanced budget. Specifically, if inflation increases, the real value of the debt declines. This causes a swing toward surplus in the real budget. If we take the real budget as our guide, we may respond by increasing government spending or cutting taxes. But these steps will increase aggregate demand and make inflation worse.

Similarly, it would be a trap for the Bank of Canada to focus on the real quantity of money. During periods of inflation, the real value of the outstanding money stock declines. If the Bank of Canada responds by increasing the amount of money in order to restore the real quantity, it will make inflation worse.

Nevertheless, the real debt and the real quantity of money are important. For example, the real quantity of money is an important determinant of how much people will buy. The problem is that real measures must be used very cautiously by policy makers. One of the problems with inflation is that it introduces an element of confusion and chaos into the debate over aggregate demand policies.

IMPORTANT TERMS: MATCH THE COLUMNS

Match each term in the first column with the corresponding phrase in the second column.

_____ 1. Anticipated inflation
_____ 2. Unanticipated inflation
_____ 3. The real rate of interest
_____ 4. Front-loading
_____ 5. Graduated-payment mortgage
_____ 6. Variable-rate mortgage
_____ 7. Indexation
_____ 8. Tax-bracket creep
_____ 9. Cap

a. A way of dealing with the problem of front-loading
b. A limit on indexation
c. This type of inflation has relatively small real effects
d. The effect of inflation in making people pay higher tax rates in an unindexed tax system
e. Automatic adjustment for inflation, as in wages
f. The nominal rate less the expected rate of inflation
g. A way of dealing with the problem of erratic inflation
h. An effect of inflation, even if real interest rates are constant
i. This type of inflation has large real effects

TRUE-FALSE

T F   1. People who have borrowed large sums gain from inflation, particularly when it is unanticipated.
T F   2. People who hold government bonds usually lose from inflation, particularly when it is accurately anticipated.
T F   3. Inflation makes lenders more eager to lend, and borrowers less eager to borrow.
T F   4. It is possible for the real rate of interest on a short-term government bill to be negative, but not the nominal rate of interest.
T F   5. Inflation provides one incentive for borrowers to borrow. The tax system provides another.
T F   6. When nominal interest rates rise, a new mortgage is "front-loaded" as a result, if monthly payments on that mortgage are constant in dollar terms throughout the life of the mortgage.
T F   7. A variable-rate mortgage eliminates the "front-loading" of mortgages.
T F   8. Once tax brackets, deductions, and exemptions are indexed, inflation has no further effect on the real taxes paid by individuals or corporations.

MULTIPLE CHOICE

1. Someone who has taken out a mortgage to buy a house will probably:
   a. lose from inflation, especially if it was unexpected when the house was bought
   b. lose from inflation, especially if it was expected when the house was bought
   c. gain from inflation, especially if it was unexpected when the house was bought
   d. gain from inflation, especially if it was expected when the house was bought
   e. lose from inflation, but only if there is no mortgage on the house

2. If the nominal rate of interest is 12% and the real rate of interest is 3%, then the expected rate of inflation is:

   a. 18%
   b. 15%
   c. 12%
   d. 9%
   e. 3%

3. Which of the following can be negative?
   a. the nominal rate of interest on short-term securities
   b. the nominal rate of interest on long-term securities
   c. the before-tax real rate of interest on short-term securities
   d. the after-tax real rate of interest on short-term securities
   e. c. and d., but not a. or b.

4. Between 1981 and 1985, real interest rates were high in Canada. The most plausible explanation for the high real rates has been:
  a. the acceleration of inflation between 1981 and 1985
  b. high unemployment
  c. a collapsing stock market
  d. rising tax rates
  e. high real interest rates in the United States

5. Consider someone in the 40% tax bracket, holding a bank account paying 8% interest. The rate of inflation is 6%. Then, the after-tax real return to that individual is:
  a. − 2%
  b. − 1.2%
  c. 0
  d. 3.6%
  e. 4.8%

6. If the tax code is fully indexed and your money income exactly kept up with inflation, then your:
  a. nominal income tax will stay the same
  b. real income tax will fall
  c. nominal income tax will rise by the same percentage as prices, keeping your real tax constant
  d. real income tax will rise by the same percentage as prices, keeping your nominal tax constant
  e. real income tax will rise, but by less than the rate of inflation

7. During periods of rapid inflation, the real value of trading on the long-term bond market generally:
  a. is high, because after-tax real interest rates are high
  b. is high, because nominal interest rates are high
  c. is low, because the real return on bonds is unpredictable
  d. is low, because the real return on bonds is low relative to the real return on short-term securities
  e. increases while inflation is accelerating, but then decreases when inflation levels out

8. Variable-rate mortgages are aimed primarily at dealing with the problem created by:
  a. the tendency of homes to depreciate
  b. high inflation
  c. erratic inflation
  d. the combined effects of inflation and taxation
  e. the tendency for real rates of interest to vary with the business cycle

9. A mortgage is most likely to be front-loaded if:
  a. nominal interest rates are high, reflecting a high rate of inflation

  b. real interest rates are high
  c. real interest rates are low
  d. inflation decelerates after the house is bought
  e. taxes rise after the house is bought

10. If you had a "graduated-payment" mortgage:
  a. real payments would rise when prices rose
  b. real payments would rise when your real income rose
  c. real payments would rise when the value of the home rose
  d. nominal payments would rise during periods of inflation, keeping real payments stable
  e. nominal payments would rise when your nominal income rose, keeping payments at a constant fraction of your income

11. Suppose that the rate of inflation is steady at 7% per annum. Then over a period of 20 years, the average price level will:
  a. double
  b. treble
  c. quadruple
  d. increase by 500%
  e. increase by 700%

12. "Graduated-payment" mortgages (GPM) and "variable-rate" mortgages (VRM) are aimed at easing two different problems. Specifically, a:
  a. GPM is aimed at reducing the problem of front-loading caused by *high* inflation, while a VRM is aimed at the problems created by *erratic* inflation
  b. GPM is aimed at reducing the problems caused by *erratic* inflation, while a VRM is aimed at the problems created by *high* inflation
  c. GPM is aimed at keeping *after-tax* interest rates stable, while a VRM is aimed at keeping *before-tax* interest rates stable
  d. GPM is aimed at keeping *before-tax* interest rates stable, while a VRM is aimed at keeping *after-tax* interest rates stable
  e. GPM is aimed at keeping *nominal* interest rates stable, while a VRM is aimed at keeping *real* interest rates stable

13. The rule of thumb most likely to stabilize real economic activity and prices is:
  a. a slow, steady increase in the real quantity of money
  b. a slow, steady increase in the nominal quantity of money
  c. a slow, steady increase in the real value of the government's debt
  d. a balanced budget every year
  e. a stable nominal rate of interest

EXERCISES

1a. Suppose that you put $200 into a savings account and keep it there for 1 year, at which time it has grown to $220. Then, the nominal rate of interest is _____ %. If you expected inflation to be 4% during the year, you anticipated a real rate of interest of _____ %. Suppose that inflation turned out to be 6% instead. Then, after the year, you would find that your real return was only _____ %.

1b. If you are in a 40% tax bracket, you will pay $ _____ in taxes. Your after-tax nominal rate of interest will be _____ %, and your after-tax real return will be _____ %.

2. Figure 16.1 shows the demand and supply for loanable funds in a non-inflationary situation. The equilibrium rate of interest is _____ %. In the same diagram, draw the supply and demand curves that would exist if everyone expected 2% inflation and the economy had adjusted completely to this rate of inflation. The equilibrium nominal rate of interest is now _____ %, and the equilibrium real rate _____ %. The equilibrium quantity of funds, in real terms, is now (more than, less than, the same as) in the the initial situation.

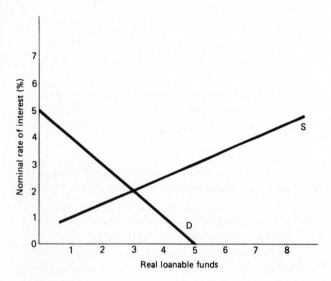

Figure 16.1

3. Table 16.1 illustrates a simple progressive income tax.

a. Suppose you have an income of $20,000 initially. Your income tax is $ _____, or _____ % of your income. You are left with an after-tax income of $ _____.

b. Now suppose that one year later, prices are 25% higher than in the initial year. Your pre-tax income has also increased by 25%, to $25,000. Thus, your real pre-tax income has (increased, decreased, remained unchanged). Your tax is now $ _____, or _____ % of your income. In real terms—that is, measured in dollars of the first year—your tax is $ _____. Thus your real tax burden has (increased, decreased, remained unchanged). Measured in current dollars, your after-tax income is $ _____. Measured in dollars of the first year, this is equal to $ _____. Thus, in real terms, your after-tax income has (increased, decreased, remained unchanged).

c. In Table 16.2, show what the income-tax schedule would be in the second year if the tax system were fully indexed.

d. If taxes were, in fact, fully indexed as shown in Table 16.2, you would pay $ _____ in taxes in the second year, leaving $ _____ in after-tax income. Measured at prices of the first year, you would pay $ _____ in taxes in the second year, leaving $ _____ in after-tax income. Thus, between the two years, when your real before-tax income was (increasing, decreasing, remaining constant), your real tax burden would (increase, decrease, remain constant).

Table 16.1

Income before tax	Tax
Less than $10,000	0
$10,000 to $20,000	10% of income over $10,000
Over $20,000	$1,000 + 20% of income over $20,000

Table 16.2

Income before tax	Tax
Less than $ ____	0
$ ____ to $ ____	10% of income over $ ____
Over $ ____	$ ____ + 20% of income over $ ____

ANSWERS

Important Terms: **1**c, **2**i, **3**f, **4**h, **5**a, **6**g, **7**e, **8**d, **9**b
True-False: **1**T, **2**F, **3**F, **4**T, **5**T, **6**T, **7**F, **8**F
Multiple Choice: **1**c, **2**d, **3**e. **4**e, **5**b, **6**c, **7**c, **8**c, **9**a, **10**d, **11**c, **12**a, **13**b
Exercises: **1a.** 10, 6, 4 **1b.** 8, 6, 0
2. 2, 4, 2, the same as

Figure 16.1 completed

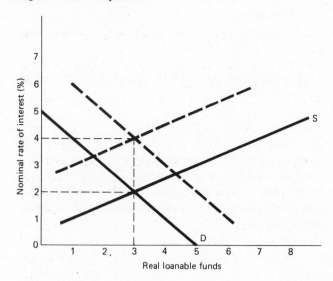

3a. $1000, 5%, $19,000 **3b.** remained unchanged, $2000 (that is, $1000 + 20% of $5000), 2/25 = 8%, $2000 × 100/125 = $1600, increased, $25,000 − $2000 = $23,000, $23,000 × 100/125 = $18,400 (also equal to $20,000 in real income less $1600 in real taxes), decreased

3c. Table 16.2 completed

Income before tax	Tax
Less than $12,500	0
$12,500 to $25,000	10% of income over $12,500
Over $25,000	$1,250 + 20% of income over $25,000

3d. $1250, $23,750, $1250 × 100/125 = $1000, $23,750 × 100/125 = $19,000, remaining constant, remain constant

ANSWERS TO SELECTED REVIEW QUESTIONS FROM THE TEXT

16-1. (a) This person would lose; the price of the house would be rising, and because the inflation was unexpected, the return on the savings account would not have become high enough to reflect the higher rate of price inflation.

(b) This person would gain: The house would rise in value, while the interest rate that he or she would have earned on the savings account would not have been high enough to fully compensate for inflation.

(c) The airline would gain: The interest payments on its debt would remain fixed, but the increased inflation rate would lead to an increase in the value of its planes.

16-2. In this case, there would be no gains or losses, because interest rates on deposits and loans would have risen enough to fully reflect price inflation.

16-3. Inflation results in a front-loading of mortgages. In other words, the burden of mortgage payments is greater in the first few years if nominal interest rates have risen to reflect inflation. It is logically possible that this

burden might be offset by a full graduation of mortgages. But the amount of graduation of mortgages thus far has been very small.

For those who already own a home, the problem is less severe, since the proceeds they receive from the sale of their first home can go toward a large down payment. Furthermore, the proceeds might be used to counteract the effects of front-loading. If the purchaser can get a large mortgage, and put the nest egg from the first home in (say) a money market fund, this nest egg can be run down in the early years of the mortgage to cover the heavy early burden. (The advantages of already owning a home are reduced, but not eliminated, if disruptions in the mortgage market make it difficult to sell a home without taking back a mortgage on it.)

16-4. (a) They will receive a windfall, as noted in the text.

(b) They will be in the opposite situation, and will face a very heavy burden of mortgage payments; also, the relative price of housing may well fall as inflation subsides. (The burden of the mortgage payments may be reduced by refinancing the mortgage.)

If homeowners have variable-rate mortgages, they will have less to gain from an acceleration of inflation, and less to lose from a deceleration.

16-8. (a) With 20% inflation, the after-tax nominal return has to be 20% if the real rate is to be zero. Consequently, the before-tax rate has to be 1000% (since 98% or $980 of every $1,000 in interest, is taken in taxes). For the real after-tax return to be 3%, the after-tax nominal rate has to be 23%, and the before-tax rate, 1150%.

(b) No (they did not rise by enough) and no.

16-9. Let ND be the new debt at the end of the fiscal year, OD the old debt at the beginning of the fiscal year, and let i be the inflation rate during the year. Then, the real deficit RD as calculated by Bossons and Dungan can be expressed as:

$$RD = [ND/(1+i)] - OD.$$

The alternative measure RD′ suggested in the question can be expressed as:

$$RD' = [ND - OD]/(1+i).$$

Clearly, RD and RD′ are not the same. For example, if the nominal deficit is zero, so that ND = OD, then RD′ is also zero, but the RD measure would show a negative real deficit (that is, a surplus), as long as price inflation was positive.

Chapter 17

■■■■■■■■■■■■■■■■■■■■■■■■■■■■■■■■

Productivity and Growth:
An International Perspective

MAJOR PURPOSE

The major purpose of this chapter is to study economic growth—that is, the increase in the productive potential of the economy. The chapter deals with two major puzzles—why the Canadian economy has grown so much more rapidly in some periods than in others, and why some nations grow so much more rapidly than others.

The key to economic growth is an increase in *productivity*, that is, an increase in output per worker (or per hour worked). Economists have been able to identify some of the reasons for changes in productivity—most notably, the increase in the *capital stock* and the improved *education* and *training* of the labour force. But economists do not have a good explanation of why productivity increased so much more slowly after 1973 than during the previous decades.

Some of the most rapidly growing nations in the world are in East Asia. These rapidly growing nations have high rates of saving and investment, and they are strongly export oriented.

LEARNING OBJECTIVES

After you have studied this chapter in the textbook and study guide, you should be able to

- Explain the relationship between total output, total number of hours worked, and productivity
- Identify the periods in the twentieth century when productivity rose most rapidly, and when it rose most slowly
- Summarize Kendrick's main conclusions regarding:
  1. The reasons for increases in output per person, 1960-73
  2. The reasons for the slowdown of the 1973-78 period
- Explain the vicious circle of poverty that can impede the growth of very poor countries
- List and explain seven problems that can make it difficult for poorer countries to develop
- Explain how ties to the international economy can help countries break out of the vicious circle
- Explain some of the secrets of success of the "four tigers" of East Asia
- Explain some of the ways in which those four economies are similar, and the ways in which they differ
- Explain how foreign borrowing can help to promote economic development in poor countries, but why it can also cause trouble
- Explain the general idea of an "industrial policy," and why some economists are skeptical of such a policy

HIGHLIGHTS OF THE CHAPTER

The average productivity of labour is equal to total output (Q) divided by the number of labour hours worked (L). To understand the growth of output, we must look at the increases in labour hours and productivity.

Figure 17-1 in the textbook shows these changes since 1926. In the decades before World War II, output grew relatively slowly on average, reflecting in part the slump in production during the Great Depression in the 1930s. Between 1940 and 1975, however, growth was relatively fast, with output increasing at an average rate of nearly 5% per year. The rate of increase in labour hours was less than 2% per year, while labour productivity grew at more than 3% per year on average. Figure 17-1 also shows the substantial decline in productivity growth that took place in the period between 1975 and the early 1980s. Following the recovery from the deep 1982 recession, however, there has been an improvement in productivity growth.

Observe in Figure 17-1 in the text that productivity has generally improved very rapidly when labour hours were growing slowly, and vice versa. With more people on the job, each works with less capital than would be the case with a lower growth in the labour force. As a result, there is a drag in output per labour hour. When the labour force increases, there are two important effects: (1) *total* output increases, since there is an increase in the labour input; and (2) output *per labour hour* decreases (or increases more slowly than it otherwise would), since the amount of capital per worker is kept down.

In a careful study, which includes several industrial countries, J.W. Kendrick has estimated the reasons for the increase in Canadian productivity for two subperiods since 1960. The first column of Table 17-1 in the text lists his estimates for the period 1960-73. The most important conclusion is that *no single item* accounted for most of the increase. There were a number of sources, each contributing small amounts to the overall increase in productivity.

The third column in Table 17-1 attempts to show the reasons for the slower productivity growth during 1973-78. The most important conclusion here is that the factors that Kendrick considered explicitly account for only part of the slowdown. Over half the decrease (1.4% at the bottom of the third column) is attributed to the unexplained residual. The reasons for the poor performance during this period remain something of a mystery. One suggestion that has sometimes been made is that a substantial part of the deterioration was due to the increase in world oil prices. Although a study by the Economic Council of Canada concluded that the oil price increase played only a minor part, the fact that productivity growth fell in most industrialized countries in the 1970s suggests that it may have been a relatively important explanation.

Canada's productivity performance in the 1980s was very mixed. Following the deep recession in 1982, both output and productivity rebounded sharply in 1983 and 1984. However, during the rest of the decade productivity growth, though higher than during the second half of the 1970s, was relatively modest by the standards of earlier decades. While the Canada/United States Free Trade Agreement that came into effect in 1989 should have a favourable effect on productivity in the 1990s, other factors, such as environmental problems, may act as a drag on productivity growth.

Growth rates in total output and productivity have varied considerably from decade to decade in individual nations; they have also varied considerably from country to country. Some nations have grown very rapidly, while others have progressed very slowly, if at all.

The very poor nations sometimes seem caught in a *vicious circle of poverty*. When incomes are very low, people have a very difficult time saving. Because almost everything that is being produced is being consumed, the nation does not have many resources to devote to investment in real capital, education, and training. With low capital formation, productivity is stagnant. In addition to low saving and investment (shown in the outer loop of Figure 17-3 in the text), a number of other problems may act as a drag on output per person and living standards: (1) slow improvements in technology, (2) small, stagnant markets that make it difficult to capture economies of scale, (3) rapid population growth that reduces the amount of capital per person, (4) social and cultural barriers to growth, (5) a lack of social capital, such as good transportation and communications systems, and (6) military conflicts.

The international economy can help countries to break out of the vicious circle by providing (1) financial capital for financing real investments, (2) technology, and (3) markets.

Four of the most rapidly growing economies are in East Asia—South Korea, Taiwan, Hong Kong, and Singapore. These nations have all had very high rates of saving and investment. They have all been strongly export oriented; much of their output has been sold abroad. They have all made extensive use of foreign technology and imported capital equipment. However, the economies have differed in some important respects. The government has been much more directly involved in the economy in South Korea than in Singapore or Hong Kong. Large conglomerates dominate the Korean economy, while small and medium-sized businesses are the core of the Taiwanese economy.

Borrowing from foreign nations can help to provide the financing for investment and growth. However, if foreign borrowing is not put to good use, it can cause major problems. Borrowers may have difficulty servicing their loans (paying interest and repaying the loans).

In North America, attitudes toward growth have been changing in recent decades. During the 1950s and early 1960s, governments actively sought to promote growth as a way of raising general living standards, reducing poverty, and keeping ahead of the Soviet Union. In the 1970s, the growth objective attracted less support, as people became more concerned about the speed with which we were using up our natural resources.

In the 1980s, the growth objective once more moved to centre stage, particularly in the United States during the Reagan administrations. However, as we begin the 1990s, there are many who argue that over the next decade, environmental protection must become increasingly recognized as an even higher priority than growth.

Some economists argue that it is desirable for the government to have an *industrial policy*—to direct investment into important industries and help them in other ways. One problem with such proposals is that they often encompass two quite different ideas, namely that the government should help (1) new, high-technology industries with high profits and good growth prospects; and (2) declining industries with low profits and poor prospects.

IMPORTANT TERMS: MATCH THE COLUMNS

Match each term in the first column with the corresponding phrase in the second column.

_____ 1. Average productivity of labour	**a.** The Soviet Union and Bulgaria
_____ 2. Technological improvement	**b.** A characteristic of the Canadian economy after 1973
_____ 3. Economies of scale	**c.** South Korea, Hong Kong, Taiwan, and Singapore
_____ 4. Slower growth	**d.** Q/L
_____ 5. Examples of First World countries	**e.** The direction of investment into specific sectors, and the assistance of these sectors in other ways
_____ 6. Examples of Second World countries	**f.** Low income leads to low saving and investment which, in turn, keeps income low
_____ 7. Examples of Third World countries	**g.** Government ownership and support of declining industries
_____ 8. Vicious circle of poverty	**h.** An increase of all inputs by 100% leads to an increase of more than 100% in output
_____ 9. Infrastructure	**i.** India, Nigeria, Peru, and Indonesia
_____ 10. The "four tigers"	**j.** Inventions and better methods of production
_____ 11. Industrial policy	**k.** France, Germany, Japan, and Canada
_____ 12. Lemon socialism	**l.** An example: the electric power system

TRUE-FALSE

T F   1. If the labour force grows at a rapid rate, this will act as a drag on productivity.

T F   2. If the labour force grows at a rapid rate, this will act as a drag on the growth of output.

T F   3. Between 1973 and 1978, productivity in Canada grew more slowly than it had previously, but the factors considered by Kendrick explained no more than half of the slowdown.

T F   4. If an economy grows at 2% each year, it will double in size in less than 25 years.

T F   5. The rapid increase in the international price of oil in 1973/1974 acted as a drag on growth, since it required some industries to retool.

T F   6. Three major reasons for an increase in output per worker are investment in real capital, investment in education and training, and improvements in technology.

T F   7. As the economy moves into a recession, output declines, and so does the rate of increase of productivity.

T F   8. The reduction in U.S. spending on R&D may have been one of the factors contributing to slower Canadian productivity growth during the 1970s.

MULTIPLE CHOICE

1. Growth of the economy causes
   a. the long-run Phillips curve to shift to the right
   b. the long-run Phillips curve to become flatter
   c. the aggregate supply curve to shift to the right
   d. an increasing gap between actual and potential GDP
   e. all of the above

2. During the 1970s, the total number of hours worked in Canada
   a. grew at a faster rate than the average since 1926, but slower than the rate of growth of total output
   b. grew at a faster rate than the average since 1926, and faster than the rate of growth of total output
   c. grew, but at a rate slower than the average since 1926
   d. stayed roughly constant
   e. decreased sharply

3. One of the factors considered in Kendrick's analysis of Canada's productivity growth during 1973-78 was changes in the quality of the labour force as measured by education. His figures show that the education of the Canadian labour force has
   a. improved, and this improvement has contributed as much to productivity as the increase in machinery and other physical capital
   b. improved, although this improvement contributed less to productivity than the increase in machinery and other physical capital
   c. deteriorated, since examination scores have been falling
   d. deteriorated, since there are more young people working now than there were 25 years ago
   e. deteriorated, at least during the 1970s, since labour productivity deteriorated during that decade

4. When the number of labour hours increases very rapidly, the most likely effect is
   a. a slow increase in productivity
   b. a very rapid increase in productivity
   c. a very slow increase in total output
   d. no change in output, since workers have less capital
   e. a decline in output, since workers have less capital

5. Consider an economy in which output *per capita* grows at 2% per year, while population grows at 1.5% per year. Then, growth in real GDP is approximately what percent per year?
   a. $2/1.5 = 1.33$
   b. 1.5
   c. 2
   d. $1.5 \times 2 = 3$
   e. $1.5 + 2 = 3.5$

6. For a country in the process of development, a high saving rate is generally
   a. helpful, because it makes resources available for investment
   b. helpful, because it causes a rapid growth of aggregate demand and thus makes it easier to capture economies of scale
   c. harmful, because it causes a stagnation of aggregate demand
   d. harmful, because it promotes imports of consumer goods
   e. unimportant; there is no observable relationship (either positive or negative) between saving and growth

7. A country is overpopulated whenever
   a. the rate of population is increasing by more than 1% per year
   b. real per capita GDP is falling
   c. there is an average of more than 100 people per square mile
   d. any of a., b., or c. exists
   e. we can't conclude that any of the above necessarily means a country is overpopulated

8. The four rapidly growing economies of Asia, known as the "four tigers," have all had
   a. export-oriented policies
   b. laissez-faire economies
   c. very large and rapidly growing government sectors
   d. very large corporations that dominate the economy
   e. all of the above

9. Some developing countries, such as India, have tended to follow exchange rate policies that have resulted in their currencies being overvalued in international markets. The problem of an overvalued currency
   a. exists primarily in countries with hyperinflation
   b. results from overly restrictive monetary policy
   c. is especially likely to exist in countries that issue too much currency and not enough bank deposits
   d. makes it difficult for domestic producers to sell in foreign markets

e. makes it difficult for importers to compete with domestic producers

10. Which of the following is *not* a typical characteristic of the world's poorest countries, compared to richer countries?
    a. slow growth of population and the labour force
    b. slow growth of labour productivity and output
    c. a low level of technology in production
    d. a low level of savings
    e. a low level of consumption

11. According to Thomas Malthus, the wage rate would be depressed to the subsistence level because of
    a. the power of monopolies
    b. the desire of capitalists to exploit the working class

c. the natural tendency of population to grow more rapidly than the production of food
d. the long-run downward trend in investment
e. pestilence, war, and famine

12. Proponents of an industrial policy suggest that the government
    a. encourage investment in "winning industries," thus promoting growth
    b. discourage investment in "losing industries," such as steel, since there is no future in such industries
    c. encourage investment in grain farming, in order to restore North America's ability to feed the world
    d. avoid "lemon socialism" by discouraging investment in the citrus industry
    e. all of the above

EXERCISES

1. Fill in the blanks.
   a. Kendrick found that, during the period from 1960 to 1973, the increase in labour productivity in Canada could be attributed to the following five sources (in addition to the unexplained residual, due partly to technological improvement):
   i. _____
   ii. _____
   iii. _____
   iv. _____
   v. _____

b. The factors considered by Kendrick explain less than half of the slowdown in 1973-78. An important factor not considered may have been _____.

2. A more rapid rate of increase in population leads to a (more, less) rapid rate of growth of output. It generally acts as a (stimulus to, drag on) productivity, because the average worker has less _____ to work with. However, this effect may be offset, or more than offset, by _____, which act to (increase, decrease) productivity as the size of the economy grows.

ESSAY QUESTIONS

1. Since 1960, labour hours (L) increased at a much faster rate than earlier (Figure 17-1 in the textbook). How do you explain this rapid increase? Would you expect a rapid increase in the next decade? What do you think explains the *inverse* relationship between the growth in labour input and the increase in labour productivity? On the basis of these answers, do you have any predictions about what will happen to labour productivity in the next decade? How about the rate of growth of output? Are you confident regarding your last two answers? Why or why not?

2. Recall the "measure of economic welfare" (MEW) introduced in Chapter 6. If this, rather than GDP, were used to measure economic growth and productivity, how

would the the historical record in Figure 17-1 in the textbook be affected? How would the costs of economic growth be affected? How do your answers depend on how leisure is treated in MEW?

3. Suppose that a new industrial policy agency is set up by the Canadian government, to assist selected industries. Suppose you are chosen to run this agency. Would you favour assisting new, high-tech industries, or declining industries, or both? Or perhaps neither of these, but some other group of industries? (If so, explain how you would choose your favoured industries.) Explain what problems you might encounter in picking industries for assistance, and the problems which might result from your policies.

ANSWERS

Important Terms: 1d, 2j, 3h, 4b, 5k, 6a, 7i, 8f, 9l, 10c, 11e, 12g
True-False: 1T, 2F, 3T, 4F, 5T, 6T, 7T, 8T
Multiple Choice: 1c, 2a, 3b, 4a, 5e, 6a, 7e, 8a, 9d, 10a, 11c, 12a
Exercises: **1a.** improved quality of labour force, increase in physical capital, improved allocation of resources, economies of scale, change in capacity utilization **1b.** higher oil prices
2. more, drag on, capital, economies of scale, increase

ANSWERS TO SELECTED REVIEW QUESTIONS FROM THE TEXT

17-1. The more rapidly population grows, the smaller will be the amount of capital, land, and raw materials per person. This acts to keep productivity down. On the other hand, more people mean a larger market. To the extent that larger markets lead to economies of scale, there will be a tendency for an increase in population to cause higher productivity.

17-2. There were two major events which acted as a drag on productivity: the Great Depression and the Second World War.

During the Great Depression, investment was low as a result of business pessimism regarding returns on investment. The low rate of capital formation slowed down the increase in productivity. [We should not think of the 1930s as a complete loss from the viewpoint of productivity, however. Major technological developments took place — for example, in farm machinery, aircraft, and automobiles. A tractor of the 1920s was very primitive compared to the tractor of 1940. By 1940, tractors embodied much of present-day technology — for example, the hydraulic system.]

During the Second World War, production soared. But there was less investment than would usually occur in a high-employment economy: The first priority was war production, not investment for future productivity. Much of the investment was directed toward the weapons industry, and only part of the resulting capital could be converted into peacetime uses.

17-6. Yes, there is one big disadvantage. Selling your goods at low prices is not necessarily the best strategy. Your income may be higher if you sell at a higher price.

There is also another disadvantage. As the price of the home currency moves down on the international exchanges, inflationary pressures are created. The prices of imports rise, and so do the prices of goods that can be exported.

17-7. An increase in energy prices may cause firms to divert labour and other resources to tasks such as converting plant and equipment to more energy-efficient operation, improving the insulation of buildings, etc. It may also cause them to abandon some less energy-efficient equipment, effectively reducing the capital stock that each worker has to work with. Each of these changes would lead to a decrease in oil use. Increased energy prices may also lead to increased production in industries that produce more energy-efficient equipment, or energy-saving devices. In the long run, this may lead to reduced oil use, but not necessarily in the short run.

The reasons just cited imply that much of the productivity decline occurred because of the resources that were used up as industry was forced to adjust to the *change* in energy prices. Although the fall in energy prices in 1985/86 certainly would have reduced costs and led to increased productivity in some industries, it may, paradoxically, also have had a negative short-run productivity effect, as industries once again used resources to adjust to the price change.

17-8. This is a controversial question, since people disagree on how to evaluate the success of various elements of government industrial strategy. For example, one may argue that preservations of jobs, or enhancing Canada's technological capabilities, are at least as important as financial profitability in assessing the outcome of government aid to specific industries.

Nevertheless, there are a number of examples of large government expenditures on aid to specific industries or firms that ended up with very little to show for them: the $4 billion to develop the Canadair Challenger; the support to Dome Petroleum; the funds spent to preserve a viable fish-processing industry in the Maritimes.

One way to reduce the danger may be to spend a larger proportion of government funds in joint ventures with the private sector, so that government would spend money on risky projects only if private investors were willing to put some of *their* money at risk as well.

Across

2. This occurs when depreciation exceeds gross investment.
9. consume
11. respectful form of address
12. yes (Spanish)
13. fluctuations in economic activity (2 words)
16. interjection
17. untruths
18. observant, perceptive, smart
20. country with rapid economic growth
21. world organization (abbrev.)
23. warning sign for the superstitious
25. should always be put *after* the horse
26. what the politician did for office
28. study of the environment
33. Q/L
34. hint; gratuity
35. Witches sometimes cast one.
37. makes it difficult to see through
38. form of capital
40. zero
41. Rudolf's nose
42. describes relation between tax rates and tax revenues (2 words)

Down

1. where bright ideas pay off
3. one group of Canadian Native peoples
4. part of the eye
5. important contributor to growth
6. get away
7. nothing
8. present, favour
10. gives vent to; tunes
13. not sharp
14. visualize
15. long period of time
19. inhabitant of Asia Minor
22. helps workers to produce
24. to keep on asking
27. pioneering student of productivity and growth
29. not part of the in-group
30. a 25-year-old upwardly mobile lawyer might be one (slang)
31. slowed in the 1970s
32. Laffer's side
35. male offspring
36. take it easy; unit of bread
38. _____ Guinness, a famous British actor
39. became very expensive in the 1970s

Part Five

Three Great Macroeconomic Controversies

Chapter 18

■■■■■■■■■■■■■■■■■■■■■■■■■■■■■■■■■■

Fine Tuning or Stable Policy Settings?

MAJOR PURPOSE

This chapter deals with the one of the major, continuing controversies in macroeconomics: Should aggregate demand policies be adjusted as conditions change, or should the Bank of Canada follow a monetary policy rule? On the one side are those in the Keynesian tradition, who argue that aggregate demand should be *actively managed* in pursuit of the goals of high employment and stable prices. On the other side are the monetarists, who generally favour a rule: The Bank of Canada should aim for a *slow, steady increase in the money stock*. No matter how well-intentioned the authorities, they do not know enough to stabilize the economy. Discretionary policies do not work in practice. So say the monetarists.

This debate has been dominated by strong advocates of rules on the one hand and strong opponents on the other. One of the major conclusions of this chapter is that the question before us is not really whether we should choose a rigid, permanent rule that would be followed without regard to "how the chips fall." There is no way that future policy makers could be bound firmly to such a rule. (Even if it were feasible to enshrine a policy rule in a country's constitution, a constitution can be amended.) There is, however, a very important policy issue which remains—even if rigid, permanent rules are discarded as a logical impossibility. The issue is: Should policies be adjusted frequently in the light of unfolding conditions? Or would we be better off to aim for a stable growth of the money stock and make adjustments only rarely, when very strong evidence for a change accumulates? Unfortunately, the experience of the past quarter-century does not provide a clear answer. Sometimes discretionary policies have worked quite well; sometimes they have not. This ambiguous lesson of history is, of course, one of the reasons the controversy continues.

LEARNING OBJECTIVES

After you have studied this chapter in the textbook and study guide, you should be able to
- Describe the various steps in the active Keynesian approach to aggregate demand management
- Explain why lags make it difficult to stabilize aggregate demand through active management
- Explain the important role of potential GDP in the active approach
- Explain how problems in estimating potential GDP were a major source of difficulty during the 1970s and early 1980s
- Explain the case for and the case against a discretionary policy

If your class covers the appendix, you should also be able to
- Explain why investment is much more volatile than consumption during the business cycle
- Explain why a moderate expansion may be more likely to last than a very rapid expansion

HIGHLIGHTS OF THE CHAPTER

Keynes and his followers argued that the government has the responsibility to maintain full employment and reasonably stable prices. Particularly in the 1950s and 1960s, Keynesians believed that an untended market economy would suffer from two major problems: Aggregate demand would often be (1) inadequate and (2) unstable. Authorities should actively intervene to bring aggregate demand up to the full employment level, and then manage it on a continuing basis to offset forces of instability.

This idea was particularly influential during the 1960s, a decade that has sometimes been called the "Age of Keynes." Figure 18-1 in the textbook illustrates the general Keynesian demand-management strategy; Figure 18-2 presents the same idea as it was applied in the early 1960s. There were several major steps in bringing aggregate demand up to the full-employment level: (1) First, the path of potential GDP was estimated. (2) Next, forecasts were made of where actual GDP would go in the absence of policy changes; in other words, the size of the prospective GDP gap was estimated. (3) Finally, fiscal and monetary policies were adjusted with the objective of closing the gap in a reasonably brief period. Until about 1966, this strategy was very successful. The estimated GDP gap closed and prices remained reasonably stable. However, by the late 1960s, inflation began to accelerate, and during the first half of the 1970s, attempts to keep the economy on target seemed to result only in even more inflation, without bringing the unemployment rate down. In the years following the 1974/75 recession, the unemployment rate remained high by earlier standards, indicating that the economy was below potential. But, at the same time, inflation also remained high. With the economy's performance giving conflicting signals, it was difficult to tell what was an appropriate policy at any given time, and even more difficult to say when there should be a policy change. The experience of the 1970s gave much less grounds for optimism regarding the possibilities of Keynesian demand management than did the experience of the 1960s.

The critics of active management make five major arguments:

1. *Lags* in the operation of policies mean that the government, like the panicky helmsman, may over-react to current events.

2. Because of lags, policies developed today must be designed to deal with problems several months in the future. But economists *are only moderately successful in their ability to forecast* either the probable course of the economy in the absence of policy changes, or the effects of policy changes themselves.

3. *Prices respond even more slowly* than real output when monetary and fiscal policies are changed. As a consequence, there may be an *inflationary bias* to discretionary policies. Decision makers may choose expansionary policies for the short-run benefits of higher output, and worry later about the inflationary consequences.

4. Activists *may overestimate potential GDP.* As a result, they may strive to achieve an unattainable goal, creating strong inflationary pressures in the process. Figure 18-4 in the textbook illustrates this argument in general terms; Figure 18-5 applies it to the 1970s.

5. The active management of aggregate demand means government meddling in the economy; rules are more consistent with economic freedom than are discretionary policies.

Advocates of rules recognize, of course, that it is important to pick the correct rule—one that is consistent with economic stability. It simply won't do to pick any old rule. Some seemingly plausible rules would be a mistake. For example, the gold standard rule made the banking system vulnerable to runs; it added to the North American banking chaos of 1931-1933. However, proponents of rules believe that if the money stock were increased at a slow, steady rate, the economy would be more stable than it has been in the past when proponents of active demand management were in charge. The proposal for a slow, steady increase in the money stock is based directly on the quantity theory of money—that is, on the view that velocity V is stable. If V, in fact, is stable, then a stable increase in M will mean a stable increase in nominal income PQ.

Opponents of a monetary rule emphasize four points:

1. The government would be foolish to adopt rigid rules that may become outdated as circumstances change in unforeseen ways. Indeed, a truly rigid rule is a *logical impossibility*. Future decision makers cannot be bound inflexibly by the present. *The real issue is one of degree*: Will policies be adjusted in the light of a moderate amount of new information, or will policy changes be postponed until the evidence becomes overwhelming? While advocates of policy rules are correct in pointing out that lags create difficulties for discretionary policies, their proposals would increase lags in a major way. The government would be so committed to a course of action that it would not change policy until conditions became very bad indeed.

2. There is no guarantee that stable monetary growth will lead to a stable increase in aggregate demand. In the period since 1975, the velocity of M1 (which was the money supply concept used by the Bank of Canada during the years 1975-81 when it was pursuing a "gradualist policy") was highly unstable. Thus, a steady growth of M1 did not lead to a stable increase in aggregate demand.

3. When strong evidence does accumulate that something is wrong, the government may then make abrupt changes in policy. In other words, the desire to follow a stable policy rule may paradoxically lead to *abrupt changes in practice*. An example was provided by the Bank of Canada's monetary policy during 1981/82. As the Bank made the switch from its earlier policy of making M1 grow within a specified target range, to a policy of defending the external value of the Canadian dollar by making sure Canadian interest rates stayed close to U.S. interest rates, it produced an extreme and sudden monetary contraction, especially in 1981. According to the critics, this policy switch was a major contributor to the depth of the 1981/82 recession.

4. The rule advocated by monetarists—a slow, steady growth in the money stock—may lead to aggregate demand that is too low to buy the increasing volume of goods and services that the economy is capable of producing. In other words, the adoption of a rule aimed at slow growth of demand and stable prices may result in high unemployment and slow growth of real output.

Note the contrast between this last point and the fourth point in the earlier list of the criticisms of fine tuning. There is a significant difference in the approach of the two groups to the problems of inflation and unemployment. Advocates of discretionary policies consider monetarists heartless in their willingness to accept unemployment; monetarists consider some Keynesians to be crude inflationists.

As noted earlier, forecasting is required for the implementation of discretionary policies. Some forecasting, either formal or informal, is also needed by businesses that are planning their investment programs. Economic forecasters often use econometric models, modified by the results from surveys and the judgement of the forecaster. The record of forecasters is fair. It is much better than would come from a very simple approach, such as projecting the trends of the previous year or so. However, forecasters have not done a very good job in anticipating recessions. In particular, they substantially underestimated the depth of the severe recessions of 1974 and 1982. This is worrisome to the advocates of active demand management. It is particularly important to anticipate recessions, in order to be able to shift to more expansive policies in a timely manner.

IMPORTANT TERMS: MATCH THE COLUMNS

Match each term in the first column with the corresponding phrase in the second column.

_____	**1.**	Potential GDP
_____	**2.**	GDP gap
_____	**3.**	V
_____	**4.**	Policy rule
_____	**5.**	Recognition lag
_____	**6.**	Action lag
_____	**7.**	Impact lag

a. From time weakness begins until time it is recognized

b. If this isn't stable, money rule won't work

c. From time policy is changed until aggregate demand responds

d. Aggregate demand policies are aimed at eliminating this

e. From time weakness is recognized until policies are changed

f. Keep money growth low and stable

g. Target path for those who manage aggregate demand

TRUE-FALSE

T   F   1. Monetarists advocate that the Bank of Canada aim for a slow, steady increase in the quantity of money.

T   F   2. Those who advocate activist Keynesian demand-management policies are led by the logic of their position to make an estimate of potential GDP.

T   F   3. The case for active, discretionary monetary and fiscal policies would be stronger if economists could forecast better.

T F   4. The "action lag" is the interval between the time when action is taken, and when the action has its effect on aggregate demand.

T F   5. The "recognition lag" is the interval between the time when a problem is recognized and the time when corrective action is taken.

T F   6. The inflation rate is a leading indicator.

T F   7. If the rate of increase in productivity unexpectedly falls, potential GDP is likely as a result to be overestimated.

T F   8. With the benefit of hindsight, it has become clear that the Economic Council of Canada overestimated potential GDP by a substantial amount in the 1970s and the early 1980s.

T F   9. If the potential GDP path is overestimated, active demand managers are likely as a consequence to follow overly stimulative demand management policies.

T F   10. Because of the errors in estimating potential GDP during the 1970s, almost all economists now believe in a monetary policy rule.

MULTIPLE CHOICE

1. An economist is most likely to favour discretionary aggregate demand policies, rather than a policy rule, if he or she is in which economic tradition?
   a. Keynesian
   b. classical
   c. monetarist
   d. marginalist
   e. libertarian

2. Economists who argue for a policy rule aimed at stabilizing aggregate demand are most likely to favour which rule?
   a. the gold standard
   b. a balanced actual budget
   c. a balanced full-employment budget
   d. a steady growth in the money stock
   e. all the above rules are equally good; the thing that matters is to have some rule

3. Milton Friedman is the most famous monetarist. He argues that
   a. monetary policy should be actively managed to stabilize aggregate demand, but the budget should be kept in balance
   b. the government's budget has no major effect on aggregate demand or on the allocation of resources
   c. both monetary and fiscal policies should be actively managed to stabilize aggregate demand
   d. active monetary and fiscal policies have both been oversold as a way of managing aggregate demand
   e. active monetary policy is the best way to keep full employment without any major risk of inflation

4. Keynes was concerned that
   a. aggregate demand would be too low, although it would generally be stable

   b. aggregate demand would be unstable, even though it would generally be high enough
   c. aggregate demand was likely to be both too low and unstable
   d. inadequate productive capacity would be the major macroeconomic disease
   e. productive capacity could be kept growing at an adequate rate only if income were redistributed toward those who already had high incomes

5. The discretionary aggregate demand policies followed during the 1960s were aimed primarily at
   a. increasing the GDP gap
   b. increasing potential GDP
   c. increasing real GDP
   d. increasing prices
   e. reducing prices

6. The discretionary policies of the 1960s involved each of the following steps, except one. Which is the exception?
   a. estimate potential GDP
   b. forecast the probable course of GDP in the absence of policy changes
   c. forecast the effects of various changes in aggregate demand policies
   d. select the policies aimed at closing the GDP gap in a reasonably brief time
   e. revise the potential GDP path upward, since an even better performance now becomes possible

7. Suppose that the Economic Council of Canada forecasts a GDP gap of $20 billion for the coming year if no change is made in policies. Then, an advocate of
   a. rules would prescribe a faster growth in the quantity of money
   b. rules would prescribe a faster growth in

government spending

c. active management would prescribe an increase in tax rates, to balance the budget

d. active management would prescribe an increase in government spending

e. active management would prescribe an increase in government spending to increase real output, plus a decrease in the money stock to reduce inflation

8. The recognition lag is the lag between the time when

a. a problem is recognized and the time when corrective action is taken

b. a problem is recognized and the time when it is corrected

c. a recession begins and the time when the authorities recognize it has begun

d. aggregate demand increases and the time when producers recognize that they can raise their prices

e. aggregate demand increases and producers recognize that they should produce more

9. The time between the beginning of a downturn and the adoption of expansive aggregate demand policies is equal to the

a. recognition lag

b. action lag

c. recognition lag + the action lag

d. impact lag

e. recognition lag + the action lag + the impact lag

10. Monetarists criticize the activist approach to aggregate demand management on the grounds that

a. lags between changes in policy and changes in demand cause policy mistakes

b. the inflationary effects of an increase in aggregate demand lag after the real output effects; as a result, aggregate demand is stimulated too much and too long in many expansions

c. aggregate demand managers tend to be too ambitious

d. all of the above

e. none of the above

11. The "helmsman's dilemma" illustrates the difficulty of making policy in the presence of

a. inflation

b. deflation

c. unemployment

d. low growth

e. lags

12. Those who advocate policy rules rather than active management argue that active managers tend to a. overestimate potential and, therefore, follow inflationary policies

b. underestimate potential and, therefore, follow deflationary policies

c. underestimate growth and, therefore, follow inflationary policies

d. underestimate the effects of government spending and, therefore, rely too much on monetary policy

e. underestimate the effects of tax changes and, therefore, rely too much on monetary policy

13. Sometimes, "everything seems to be going wrong"—that is, output is falling, unemployment rising, and the rate of inflation rising. This is most likely to occur

a. early in an expansion

b. late in an expansion, about 3 or 4 months before the peak

c. early in a recession

d. late in a recession, about 3 or 4 months before the trough

e. at the trough of a recession

14. Potential GDP is most likely to be overestimated when

a. productivity is improving at an unexpectedly rapid rate

b. productivity is improving at an unexpectedly slow rate

c. population is growing

d. population is stable

e. population is declining

15. The monetarist case is based on each of the following propositions, except one. Which is the exception?

a. the desirable path of aggregate demand is one of steady, moderate growth

b. the desirable trend of prices is a gradual upward movement, by about 4% per year

c. the best way to get a steady, moderate increase in aggregate demand is by a steady, moderate increase in the money stock

d. following a monetary rule increases economic freedom and, probably, political freedom, too

16. Opponents of a monetary rule argue that, in fact, there cannot be a rigid rule because

a. it would be unconstitutional

b. the Bank of Canada, in fact, has almost no control over the money stock

c. money does not affect aggregate demand

d. money does not affect interest rates

e. future governments cannot be committed to a rule regardless of the consequences

17. Activists criticize "policy rules" on the grounds that

a. most advocates of policy rules would settle for a rate of growth of aggregate demand

that is too low, and a rate of unemployment that is too high
   b. most advocates of policy rules concentrate on fiscal policy, and ignore monetary policy
   c. most advocates of rules concentrate on changes in government spending, and ignore the effects of changes in tax rates
   d. all of the above
   e. none of the above
18. In the face of a large and predictable decrease in V, the best policy for the Bank of Canada is to
   a. increase M
   b. decrease M
   c. increase Q
   d. decrease Q
   e. increase P
19. Suppose that $C = 0.5$ GDP; $I^*_g = 100$; $G = 140$; $X = 60$; and imports are 10% of GDP. Then,

equilibrium GDP equals
   a. 500
   b. 600
   c. 750
   d. 790
   e. 1040
20. Which of the following is the best leading indicator?
   a. increases in the rate of inflation during expansions
   b. decreases in the rate of inflation during recessions
   c. any increases in the rate of inflation during a recession, because this signals a coming expansion
   d. new orders for durable goods
   e. deliveries of durable goods

EXERCISE

1. There are three lags before monetary and fiscal policies affect aggregate demand. First is the _____ lag, next, the _____ lag, and then the _____ lag. In addition, there is another lag that occurs after aggregate demand changes. Specifically, the effect of demand on (output, prices) generally lags behind its effect on (output, prices). Critics of active demand management argue that the first set of lags means that policies may destabilize the economy. The second set means that discretionary policies can have an (inflationary, deflationary) bias.

Lags are, however, not the only problem facing the managers of aggregate demand. They also have the difficult task of estimating (the path of potential GDP, the effects of monetary policy on demand, the effects of fiscal policy on demand, all of these). Suppose they overestimate the potential path. This means that, starting from a recession, they are likely to (keep expansive policies too long, abandon expansive policies too soon). The reason is that (the economy will remain below the estimated potential path, they will soon give up trying). As a result, the problem of (inflation, low growth) may become worse.

ESSAY QUESTIONS

1. Suppose that a 4% monetary rule were adopted. Then suppose that the introduction of an electronic transfer system for making payments caused a large increase in the velocity of money. What would happen to the price level? Could this have been avoided if the rule hadn't been adopted? Can you think of a rule that would allow for such contingencies?

2. Governments have objectives in addition to their economic goals—for example, national defence and getting re-elected. How do these other goals strengthen or weaken the case for discretionary policies, rather than a monetary rule?

3. A passage in the chapter highlights section reads as follows: "Advocates of discretionary policies consider monetarists heartless in their willingness to accept unemployment; monetarists consider some Keynesians to be crude inflationists."

Explain why these criticisms are made. In the first case, what defence might a monetarist have? (Hint: does it depend on the aggregate supply function?) In the second case, what defence might a Keynesian have? (Hint: does it depend on the relative social costs of unemployment and inflation?)

ANSWERS

Important Terms: 1g, 2d, 3b, 4f, 5a, 6e, 7c
True-False: 1T, 2T, 3T, 4F, 5F, 6F, 7T, 8T, 9T, 10F
Multiple Choice: 1a, 2d, 3d, 4c, 5c, 6e, 7d, 8c, 9c, 10d, 11e, 12a, 13c, 14b, 15b, 16e, 17a, 18a, 19a, 20d
Exercise: **1.** recognition, action, impact, prices, output, inflationary, all of these, keep expansive policies too long, the economy will remain below the estimated potential path, inflation

ANSWERS TO SELECTED REVIEW QUESTIONS FROM THE TEXT

18-2. If potential GDP is overestimated, expansive policies will be pursued too strongly and too long. Policy makers will mistakenly believe that the expanding aggregate demand will show up primarily in terms of an increase in real output and employment. But, as the economy approaches its unexpectedly low capacity, a rapid expansion will cause strong upward pressures on prices. Then, when the inflation becomes obvious, there may be a strong shift in policy toward restraint, contributing to a recession.

In the 1970s and early 1980s, policy makers overestimated potential GDP. The economy would probably have been more stable had the policy makers had a lower estimate of potential GDP, and followed less expansive policies.

18-3. First, there is no such thing as an absolutely rigid rule; presumably no one would want to adhere to a rule if it could be demonstrated that the rule causes instability. Thus, rules are at most "rules-of-thumb" — not rigid guides to policy. It is not clear whether the economy would be more stable with a monetary rule; the empirical work on the relationship between money and aggregate demand remains controversial. Many Keynesians fear that the particular rules advocated by monetarists would result in a trend in demand which would be too low, resulting in persistently high unemployment rates.

18-4. 1981 and 1982 were exceptionally difficult years: Inflation was about 12% in 1981, and remained as high as 10% on the average during 1982 (though it fell rapidly toward the end of the year); at the same time, unemployment shot up as high as 12% in the deep recession in 1982.

Those who argue that the Bank of Canada made things worse by reducing the monetary growth rate below its target range contend that this action contributed substantially to the depth of the recession. On the other hand, those who think that the Bank did the right thing argue that if it had allowed Canadian interest rates to fall substantially below U.S. rates, there would have been a large capital outflow and a rapid depreciation of the Canadian dollar that would have contributed to even higher inflation rates in 1981/82.

18-8.

Year	(1) Yearly sales of autos	(2) Desired number of machines	(3) Net investment	(4) Gross investment
1	100,000	100		
2	100,000	100	0	10
3	90,000	90	− 10	0
4	80,000	80	− 10	0
5	80,000	80	0	10
6	80,000	80	0	20
7	90,000	90	10	20
8	100,000	100	10	20
9	100,000	100	0	10

18-9.

Year	(1) Yearly sales of autos	(2) Desired number of machines	(3) Net investment	(4) Gross investment
1	100,000			
2	100,000	100		
3	90,000	95	− 5	5
4	80,000	85	− 10	0
5	80,000	80	− 5	5
6	80,000	80	0	10
7	90,000	85	5	15
8	100,000	95	10	20
9	100,000	100	5	15

It makes investment demand more stable. Note how columns 3 and 4 change more gradually in this table than in the answer to problem 18-8.

18-10. One of the most important considerations is whether you think that the increase in sales represents simply a spurt or a permanent increase. If it is permanent, then the case is strengthened for adding new plant and equipment. (If it is simply a spurt, then adding new capacity would be a mistake; there would be excess capacity in the coming downturn in sales.)

Other important considerations are the costs of overtime and the costs of hiring a new crew of workers for a new shift. The costs of new plant and equipment, including interest, should also be taken into account. Finally, the costs of turning away customers depend in part on whether the product is one where consumer loyalty is important. For products whose market is built up over years through advertising and other means of developing product loyalty, the costs of leaving demand unsatisfied are high.

Across

1. someone to whom money is owed
7. holiday season
9. type of lag
12. a chemical element (abbrev.)
13. on Swiss car licence plate
14. This is watched by forecasters. (2 words)
18. society of Canadian economists (abbrev.)
19. _____ of money is the key, say proponents of rules.
21. proceed
22. A healthy economy will do this.
25. Policy makers want to keep this high.
29. sound of disapproval
30. first person plural
33. Should we use this, or follow rules?
36. old
39. This level of GNP is sometimes used as a target.
40. Classical macroeconomics is built on the _____ of exchange.

Down

1. The business _____ is a major macroeconomic problem.
2. alternative to active management
3. Keynesian aggregate supply schedule reverses this.
4. our condition in the long run, noted Keynes
5, 27. peak or trough
6. sound repeated faintly
8, 34. what monetarists want
10. famous mouse
11. type of lag
15. here (French)
16. fraction of a week
17. type of lag
20. hard work
22. Eliminating this may be a policy objective. (2 "words")
23. spider's home
24. encounter (verb)
26. stylish (slang)
28. pair
31. French word, used in English to denote boredom
32. group; in tennis, lasts several games
35. Researchers get paid for this, even if not every one is good.
37. His Muslim name is Allah.
38. bear's home

Chapter 19

■ ■

How Do We Deal with the Unemployment-Inflation Dilemma?

MAJOR PURPOSE

The previous chapter explained how unemployment and inflation could coexist. This chapter explains the policy issues raised by the desire to achieve low unemployment and low inflation simultaneously. One approach is to try to reduce the equilibrium or natural rate of unemployment by steps aimed at improving the flexibility and efficiency of the labour market. (Even though the long-run Phillips curve is vertical, it is not set in concrete. The equilibrium rate of unemployment can change if labour market institutions change.) The chapter reviews efforts

to keep the inflation rate down by *incomes policies*—that is, by direct restraints on wages and prices.

This chapter also elaborates one of the conclusions of Chapter 15—that the short-run Phillips curve can shift when people's expectations change. If people try to anticipate the effects of policies, the wage-price spiral may be greatly speeded up, thus weakening the power of aggregate demand policies to bring down the unemployment rate, even in the short run.

LEARNING OBJECTIVES

After you have studied this chapter in the textbook and study guide, you should be able to
- Explain why the natural rate of unemployment can change
- List the policies that have been suggested to reduce the natural rate of unemployment
- Explain the major purposes of incomes policies
- Describe Canada's experience with wage and price controls during the 1970s, and explain the pros and cons of using such controls or other incomes policies
- Explain why the indexation of wages may permit the authorities to reduce the rate of inflation without causing a long period of high unemployment
- Explain why the indexation of wages, nevertheless, may make the inflation problem worse
- Explain how profit sharing might make the economy more flexible, and reduce the severity of unemployment during recessions
- Explain what can happen if people anticipate the effects of policies; specifically, why (1) the wage-price spiral might be speeded up and (2) why the adjustment to a lower rate of inflation might be speeded up and made less painful
- Explain why it is important for the Bank of Canada to maintain credibility
- Explain the difference between adaptive expectations and rational expectations
- Explain why aggregate demand policies might become ineffective if people's expectations are rational
- Criticize the conclusions of rational expectations theorists
- Describe briefly how European experience with unemployment has differed from Canadian and American experience over the past three decades

HIGHLIGHTS OF THE CHAPTER

This chapter explains some of the policy issues raised by the short-run and long-run Phillips curves. The chapter covers four main topics:

1. Policies to *reduce the natural rate* of unemployment
2. Incomes policies to *control inflation* without creating high unemployment
3. Other policies to *ease the transition* to lower inflation
4. The ways in which *expectations* may be formed, and how the inflation-unemployment trade-off depends on expectations.

Policies to Reduce the Natural Rate of Unemployment

The natural rate of unemployment need not be constant; it rose between the 1960s and the early 1980s; in the second half of the 1980s, it appears to have declined again. A number of proposals have been made to reduce the natural rate.

1. *Abolish the minimum wage*? Critics of the minimum wage point out that it raises the cost of hiring unskilled workers and, therefore, reduces the number of jobs offered to them.

The proposal to abolish the minimum wage is most often heard in the United States, where there is a single minimum wage covering the whole country. In Canada, where there is a separate minimum wage law in each province, as well as one for employees that are covered by federal labour law, there is little political support for doing away with minimum wages altogether. However, the fear that high minimum wages may raise the natural rate of unemployment plays a role in decisions about what the *level* of the minimum wage should be.

2. *A two-tiered minimum wage*? A two-tiered minimum wage represents one way to reduce the negative effect on employment: Employers could be allowed to pay less while newly employed workers are learning their jobs.

Many new workers are young people entering the labour force for the first time, and some Canadian provinces do have minimum wage laws that allow employers to pay teenagers a lower minimum wage.

3. *Training programs* that help the unskilled prepare for jobs.

4. The government as the *employer of last resort*? This proposal would mean a major change in the way the labour market works: The government would offer a job to anyone who could not get one in the private sector of the economy. This proposal is very controversial; it could be quite expensive and could cause a less efficient economy.

Incomes Policies

Incomes policies have often been used in both Europe and North America in efforts to break inflationary spirals without having to go through extended periods of high unemployment. In Canada, the most serious attempt at using incomes policies was the wage and price control program administered by the Anti-Inflation Board during the years 1975-78. This program specified maximum percentage increases in wages and salaries, and set targets for the maximum rate of price inflation as well.

Incomes policies are controversial. Proponents say that they are the only compassionate way to deal with the inflationary problem—the only alternative is to use the unemployed as draftees in the war against inflation. Opponents say that incomes policies may do more harm than good. For example, by suppressing inflationary pressures temporarily, they may provide the illusion of success, with the authorities unwittingly continuing expansive policies as underlying inflationary pressures build up. The result can be an explosion of inflation, and a worse situation than would be faced if the inflation had not been temporarily suppressed. The Canadian experience with the 1975-78 anti-inflation program was not encouraging. Even though the rate of price inflation came down somewhat following 1975, there was no subsequent reduction in unemployment, and by 1979/80, just after the program had ended, both unemployment and inflation were again as high as they had been in 1975 at the beginning of the program.

Critics also point out that, by interfering with the price system, incomes policies can reduce the efficiency of the economy. Proponents agree that incomes policies may create some problems, but these problems are minor compared to the unemployment caused if inflation is fought solely by restraints on aggregate demand.

Other Policies to Ease the Transition to Lower Inflation

During the 1970s, some economists suggested that the economy could move to a lower rate of inflation without high and persistent unemployment if wages were *indexed*. If wages are indexed, they are adjusted for changes in the cost of living. Wage indexation became much more common during the 1970s, when inflation was becoming both higher and more erratic.

Indexation may make it easier to unwind inflation without long periods of unemployment; money wages are more flexible, and respond more quickly to restrictive aggregate demand policies. But indexation is a two-edged sword. It can speed up a wage-price spiral. Indexation—

which represents a way in which labour tries to protect itself from erratic inflation—tends to make inflation even more erratic.

Indexation is aimed at adjusting nominal wages in order to stabilize real wages. In contrast, *profit sharing* introduces flexibility into real wages. If workers receive a significant share of their income in the form of bonuses tied to profits, labour costs move with the business cycle. During recessions, profits and bonuses—and, therefore, labour costs—fall, encouraging businesses to cut prices in order to maintain sales and output.

Expectations

To explain the basics of the acceleration theory, the last chapter used a very simple assumption—people expect the inflation of today to continue into the future. But expectations can be more complicated.

If people not only respond to current inflation, but also *anticipate* the effects of policies, a wage-price spiral can be greatly speeded up. In negotiating their contracts, people do not simply compensate for past inflation; they compensate for expected future inflation, which can exceed the present rate. The result can be a very rapid upward shift in the short-run Phillips curve (Figure 19-1 in the text).

During a period of restraint, the short-run Phillips curve can also shift very rapidly, but now in a downward direction. People take into account not only the reduction in inflation that has already occurred, but the reduction expected for the future. The rapid downward shift of the short-run Phillips curve can cause a much quicker transition to low inflation, thus reducing the overall cost in terms of unemployment.

Therefore, *credibility* is important in macroeconomic policy. When tight policies are being followed, people will adjust relatively quickly if they believe that the policies will be firmly pursued. Paradoxically, the way to stop inflation without long periods of high unemployment is to convince the public that the Bank of Canada will firmly pursue a policy of restraint, even if it does cause unemployment.

If expectations are *rational*, people make the best forecasts possible with available information on what the authorities are doing and how the economy works. Available information is, however, *not* perfect; people still make mistakes. But they do not keep making the same mistake. Their mistakes are random numbers. (In contrast, people did keep making the same mistake in the simple acceleration theory presented back in Figure 15-7 in the text.)

Some rational expectations theorists argue that demand management policies are useless as a way of reducing cyclical unemployment because, if followed consistently, they will be anticipated by the public. The only way the Bank of Canada can affect real output is by creating a surprise—that is, by trickery. But surprises mean that the Bank is behaving in an unpredictable (erratic?) way. As a result, the public is less able to figure out what is going on, and fluctuations in unemployment become larger. It is important for the Bank of Canada to *minimize* uncertainty. This, say many rational expectations theorists, can be done if the Bank follows a monetary rule, with a steady, moderate growth in the money stock.

The theory of rational expectations has provided important perceptions regarding some of the limits of policy. However, the conclusions of the rational expectations theorists are subject to two major criticisms (others are given in the text):

1. The facts don't fit the theory. According to the main body of rational expectations theory, deviations from the natural rate of unemployment should be random, relatively brief occurrences. But this was not true during the deep recession of 1981/82. And it most decidedly was not the case during the Great Depression of the 1930s.

2. A monetary rule does not necessarily lead to the most predictable outcome. *If* the Bank of Canada can identify and offset fluctuations in the economy, it can make the economy more predictable. Therefore, rational expectations theory has left the old question (which was considered in some detail in Chapter 18): Can the Bank of Canada best stabilize the economy by a rule, or by active management?

IMPORTANT TERMS: MATCH THE COLUMNS

Match each term in the first column with the corresponding phrase in the second column.

_____	**1.** Wage-price controls	**a.** Way to provide flexibility in real wages
_____	**2.** Anti-Inflation Board	**b.** An alternative to aggregate demand management as a method for controlling inflation
_____	**3.** TIP	
_____	**4.** Escalator clause	**c.** These mean that people do not make systematic mistakes
_____	**5.** Supply shock	
_____	**6.** Profit-sharing	**d.** Failure to go back to the original condition

_____ 7. Adaptive expectations
_____ 8. Rational expectations
_____ 9. Ineffective policies
_____ 10. Credibility
_____ 11. Hysteresis
_____ 12. Import price increases

e. The Bank of Canada should guard this
f. Incomes policy backed with tax incentives
g. These are based on the inflation actually observed
h. Cause difficulties for Canadian price control policies
i. Government agency charged with overseeing wage-price controls
j. Way to stabilize real wages in the face of inflation
k. With indexed wages, this can be a big problem
l. Possible result of rational expectations

TRUE-FALSE

T F 1. Between the 1960s and the early 1980s, the natural rate of unemployment fell substantially.
T F 2. Suppose that money wages were constant through time. Then, it would be possible to have a continuous downward trend in prices, if productivity rises.
T F 3. During the period in the 1970s when Canada had wage-price controls, there were specific upper limits on price increases but not on wages.
T F 4. TIP programs are supposed to work by stimulating aggregate demand.
T F 5. Wage indexation reduces uncertainty about real wage rates, but increases uncertainty about nominal wage rates.
T F 6. A COLA clause in an indexed wage contract usually provides a fixed amount to cover an increase in the cost of living, no matter what the rate of inflation.
T F 7. Wage indexation speeds up the response of inflation to an increase in aggregate demand.
T F 8. Profit-sharing has become more common in recent years, especially in some segments of U.S. business, such as the automobile and steel industries.
T F 9. If expectations of inflation are _adaptive,_ they are correct.
T F 10. According to the theory of rational expectations, people can make mistakes, but their mistakes are random.

MULTIPLE CHOICE

1. Which of the following is likely to reduce the natural rate of unemployment?
   a. a fall in the proportion of teenagers in the labour force
   b. more emphasis on fiscal policy, and less on monetary policy
   c. more generous unemployment insurance benefits
   d. a rise in the minimum wage
   e. all of the above

2. Some people have proposed introducing two "tiers" into the minimum wage, with a lower wage for those who are newly hired. Proponents argue that, if their proposal were adopted, the result would be
   a. less teenage unemployment
   b. less unemployment by older workers who might be replaced by teenagers

   c. a rightward shift of the long-run Phillips curve
   d. higher profits
   e. lower profits

3. If the government acted as the _employer of last resort_, it would
   a. hire people when they completed college
   b. hire people over 60 years of age who were unable to find jobs
   c. offer a job to anyone who could not find a job elsewhere
   d. require businesses to hire at least 10% more workers whenever the economy was in a recession
   e. all of the above

4. A U.S. proposal in the 1970s suggested that government should provide workers with "real wage

insurance.'' Taxes of workers would be cut if prices increased by more than 7%, provided the workers had agreed to limit their wage increases to 7%. One possible criticism of this proposal is that it would tend to
- a. make the income tax system less progressive
- b. cause a recession by introducing unexpected changes in fiscal policy
- c. cancel or offset the automatic stabilizing function of taxes by cutting taxes when inflation became more severe
- d. cause undue reliance on fiscal policy, rather than a reasonable combination of fiscal and monetary policies
- e. cause undue reliance on monetary policy, rather than a reasonable combination of fiscal and monetary policies

5. Which of the following policies is most likely to cause black markets?
- a. a tax-based incomes policy
- b. a two-tiered minimum wage
- c. wage-price guidelines
- d. a price freeze accompanied by restrictive monetary policies
- e. a price freeze accompanied by expansive monetary policies

6. Price controls sometimes create shortages. Shortages are most likely in the markets for
- a. luxuries, since their prices are likely to be controlled most tightly
- b. necessities, since their prices are likely to be controlled most tightly
- c. luxuries, since producers will realize that they're not very important socially, and cut back on their production
- d. necessities, since there is a tendency for the demand for necessities to increase at the most rapid rate
- e. services, since their prices are harder to control than goods

7. The major case for wage-price guidelines or controls is that
- a. they are the only way to stop inflation
- b. they are the only way to keep profits from falling when labour unions bargain aggressively for higher wages
- c. they are essential if income is to be distributed in a more equitable way
- d. they help to shift the long-run Phillips curve to the right
- e. if we avoid guidelines or controls and rely solely on tight aggregate demand policies to restrain inflation, there will be a high cost in terms of unemployment

8. Wage indexation reduces
- a. the variability of inflation
- b. the response of inflation to a change in aggregate demand
- c. uncertainty about nominal wage rates
- d. uncertainty about real wage rates
- e. both **c.** and **d.**

9. The principal argument in favour of the indexation of wages is that it
- a. protects the real incomes of workers when energy prices rise
- b. generally leads to a more stable, predictable rate of inflation
- c. keeps the unemployment rate below the natural rate
- d. keeps the inflation rate below the natural rate
- e. makes possible a quicker, less painful reduction in the rate of inflation

10. Which of the following is the strongest argument against the indexation of wages? Wage indexation
- a. makes the real wage rate more volatile
- b. makes the rate of inflation more volatile
- c. causes the rich to become richer and the poor poorer
- d. increases the costs, in terms of unemployment, of an anti-inflationary policy
- e. keeps the unemployment rate permanently above the natural rate

11. The term ''profit-sharing'' usually applies to which of the following ideas?
- a. the granting of bonuses to workers when profits are high or rising
- b. charitable giving by corporations
- c. the taxation of profits of rich corporations, combined with grants to corporations suffering losses
- d. a proportional profits tax, which takes twice as much from corporations when their profits are twice as high
- e. a progressive income tax, which redistributes profits across the economy

12. Proponents of profit sharing support it on the grounds that it would
- a. make the real incomes of labour more flexible and thus reduce the rate of unemployment during recessions
- b. make the real incomes of labour more flexible and, thus, reduce the average rate of unemployment over long periods of time
- c. increase incentives to be more efficient and, thus, reduce the rate of inflation during periods of prosperity
- d. increase incentives to be more efficient and, thus, reduce the average rate of inflation over

long periods of time
e. all of the above

13. If people anticipate the inflationary or anti-inflationary effects of changes in aggregate demand policies (rather than simply responding to past inflation), the likely result will be
  a. a more unstable inflation rate
  b. a more rapid acceleration of inflation when expansive policies are followed
  c. a more rapid deceleration of inflation when restrictive policies are followed
  d. all of the above
  e. none of the above; anticipations will change the natural rate of unemployment, not the inflation rate

14. If people anticipate the inflationary or anti-inflationary effects of changes in aggregate demand policies (rather than simply responding to past inflation), then
  a. a policy aimed at keeping the unemployment rate above the natural rate will quickly lead to an explosive wage-price spiral
  b. a policy aimed at keeping the unemployment rate below the natural rate will quickly lead to an explosive wage-price spiral
  c. an expansive aggregate demand policy will lead to a permanent reduction in the natural rate of unemployment
  d. an expansive aggregate demand policy will lead to a permanent increase in the natural rate of unemployment
  e. the economy will have a natural rate of inflation, as well as a natural rate of unemployment, because people will have a better idea of what is going on

15. Some economists argue that *credibility* of a restrictive monetary policy is the key to a quick unwinding of inflation. This conclusion is based on the idea that credibility will cause
  a. the long-run Phillips curve to shift leftward
  b. the long-run Phillips curve to slope upward to the right
  c. the long-run Phillips curve to slope downward to the right, like a short-run Phillips curve
  d. the short-run Phillips curve to shift downward more quickly when restrictive policies are followed
  e. the short-run Phillips curve to become flatter

16. If expectations of inflation are *rational,* people may make mistakes, but
  a. they make mistakes only about the rate of inflation, not about the unemployment rate
  b. they make mistakes only about the actual rate of unemployment, not about the inflation rate

  c. they make mistakes only about the natural rate of unemployment
  d. their mistakes are solely the result of uncertainty about how the economy works, not the result of uncertainty about what the Bank of Canada will do
  e. their mistakes are random

17. According to the theory of rational expectations, if a policy of expanding aggregate demand is foreseen and understood by the public, it will affect
  a. real GDP extremely strongly, since businesses will have time to prepare new investment projects
  b. prices, but not real GDP
  c. real GDP, but not prices
  d. both prices and real GDP
  e. neither prices nor real GDP, since the Bank of Canada can affect output and prices only by trickery

18. According to some proponents of the theory of rational expectations, aggregate demand policies are worthless as a way of
  a. lowering the unemployment rate
  b. lowering the rate of inflation
  c. changing people's expectations of inflation
  d. all of the above

19. According to rational expectations theorists, periods when the unemployment rate exceeds the natural rate
  a. cannot exist, because the economy is always on the long-run Phillips curve
  b. cannot exist, because the economy is always on a short-run Phillips curve
  c. will be brief
  d. will be very long, if the Bank of Canada follows a restrictive policy that the public understands
  e. will be associated with an inflation rate that is higher than expected

20. According to some rational expectations theorists, the Bank of Canada can temporarily reduce unemployment below the natural rate by trickery. However, the Bank of Canada should not do so. The main reason is that a policy of trickery
  a. is dishonest
  b. will increase uncertainty over future policies and, therefore, increase future fluctuations in unemployment
  c. will paradoxically decrease uncertainty over future policies and, therefore, increase future fluctuations in unemployment
  d. will cause the long-run Phillips curve to shift sharply to the right
  e. will cause the long-run Phillips curve to shift sharply to the left

EXERCISES

1. Suppose labour productivity in an economy increases by 3% per year; the average worker produces 3% more than in the previous year. Assume also that the labour force and population both grow by 1% per year. The nominal wage [can rise by 3% per year without causing inflation, can rise by 4% per year without causing inflation, cannot rise without causing inflation]. If the inflation rate is zero, nominal GDP will rise by an average of _____% per year over the long run, and real GDP will rise by an average of _____% per year.

2a. In Figure 19.1, an economy in equilibrium with zero inflation is at point _____. After some time at this point, suppose that aggregate demand unexpectedly increases. In the short run, the economy will move to point _____. This is on short-run Phillips curve _____, which reflects expectations of inflation of _____ per year. Now, suppose that people expect the current rate of inflation of _____ per year to continue. Contracts will be renegotiated, causing the short-run Phillips curve to shift (upward, downward) to _____. If the authorities now expand demand in an effort to keep the unemployment rate at U_T, the economy will move in the short run to point _____. If people continue to expect the current rate of inflation—whatever it might be—to continue, then a demand management policy aimed at keeping the unemployment rate at U_T, will cause the economy to move to point _____ and then to point _____.

2b. Suppose that, once the economy has reached point J by the process described in part **a**, people no longer expect the current rate of inflation to continue, but rather anticipate an acceleration of inflation to 6%. When new contracts are negotiated, the short-run Phillips curve will shift upward from its present position at _____ to _____. Now, policy makers can choose among points _____, _____, and _____,

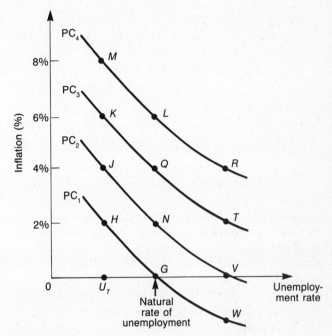

Figure 19.1

depending on the aggregate demand policies they pursue.

2c. Finally, let us go back to starting point G. Suppose now that people have rational expectations. After an extended policy debate, the Bank of Canada decides that it would like to move the economy to point H by an expansive policy. As it pursues an expansive policy aimed at point H, the economy does not move there. Instead, it may move in the short run to a point such as _____—provided that people's expectations are not only rational but correct. If, however, people make errors in forecasting the effects of the Bank of Canada's policy, they may instead move to point _____ or point _____.

ESSAY QUESTIONS

1. Critics argue that the use of wage-price controls is like trying to cure a sick person by using a thermometer that won't register higher than 98.6°. Why? How can wage-price controls lead to a "sicker" economic patient? How would the defenders of wage-price controls respond?

2. List the major criticisms of incomes policies. Now explain whether these criticisms apply more strongly to wage-price guideposts or to a wage-price freeze.

3. Do you believe that profit-sharing is desirable? Explain why or why not.

ANSWERS

Important Terms: **1**b, **2**i, **3**f, **4**j, **5**k, **6**a, **7**g, **8**c, **9**l, **10**e, **11**d, **12**h
True-False: **1**F, **2**T, **3**F, **4**F, **5**T, **6**F, **7**T, **8**T, **9**F, **10**T
Multiple Choice: **1**a, **2**a, **3**c, **4**c, **5**e, **6**b, **7**e, **8**d, **9**e, **10**b, **11**a, **12**e, **13**d, **14**b, **15**d, **16**e, **17**b, **18**a, **19**c, **20**b
Exercises: **1.** can rise by 3% per year without causing inflation, 4%, 4% **2a.** *G, H,* PC$_1$, 0%, 2%, upward, PC$_2$, *J, K, M* **2b.** PC$_2$, PC$_4$, *M, L, R* **2c.** *Q* (note: *Q*, not *N*, because the aggregate demand which is sufficient to move to *H* is more than sufficient for point *N*; the high demand causes a move to *Q* rather than *N*), *K, T*

ANSWERS TO SELECTED REVIEW QUESTIONS FROM THE TEXT

19-1. Part of the reason may be the minimum wage. Because teenagers are recent entrants to the labour force, they have little in the way of proven experience and skills, so that employers will offer them jobs only if they can pay them relatively low wages to begin with. If minimum wage legislation prevents them from doing this, the teenagers may end up unemployed.

On the other hand, even without minimum wage laws, teenagers would probably have relatively high rates of unemployment. Teenagers are more likely than older workers to quit their jobs voluntarily, as they search for better-paying jobs, or jobs that fit their particular talents and personalities.

19-3. Labour leaders have objected to wage-price guideposts because they believe that they are applied unfairly; they become primarily wage guidelines aimed at restraining wage increases, with little done on the price front. The most important reason is that a wage guidepost or wage controls can be relatively simple and straightforward: Keep wage increases to no more than *x*% per year.

No such simple price guidepost is possible—except, perhaps, for very short periods. Because of different productivity developments in different industries, some prices will and should rise rapidly (in industries of low productivity growth), while prices will and should fall rapidly in other industries (those using high technology). Thus, price guideposts or controls must by their very nature be complicated, taking into account productivity differentials, and this means that they are unlikely to be enforced as firmly as wage guideposts. In other words, labour leaders have sometimes argued that they are not against a general incomes policy—covering all incomes—but they are against an incomes policy whose specific objective is to keep down wages.

Many business executives oppose wage-price guidelines or controls because of the resulting constraints on their freedom to make business decisions. Many doubt that wage-price restraints are in the national interest because they are skeptical of the ability of government to make orderly, coherent wage and price decisions without reducing the efficiency of the economy. They also fear harassment by the government and an additional bureaucracy that would require yet more time to fill out reports for the government.

Not all labour leaders or all business executives are opposed to guideposts, however. Some believe that such guideposts hold out the best hope for a deceleration of inflation without gong through a recession.

19-4. Inflationary pressures probably increased as businesses raised their prices before the election, while they were still allowed to. For the same reason, when controls were put on in 1975, businesses were willing to comply with the limits on price increases, since they had already increased prices in 1974.

19-5. With increased exports of Canadian-produced goods and services to foreign countries, the aggregate supply of goods and services to the Canadian market will be reduced. This will tend to strengthen inflationary pressures in Canada.

19-6. (a) If wages are increased to compensate for the increased cost of oil (and energy in general), the aggregate demand for Canadian goods and services will rise, adding to the inflationary pressure from the oil price increase itself.

(b) With a favourable supply shock, wage indexation will help. With indexation, a favourable supply shock will reduce the rate of wage increases, which will moderate the growth rate of aggregate demand for goods and services and reduce inflationary pressures.

Chapter 20

■ ■

How Should We Organize the International Monetary System?

MAJOR PURPOSE

The major purpose of this chapter is to explain some of the problems that have arisen in the *international monetary system*, both during periods of fixed or pegged exchange rates, and during the decade-and-a-half since the mid-1970s when exchange rates between major currencies have been floating. It extends the discussion in Chapter 14 where we explained the interrelationship between international payments and domestic economic conditions from the vantage point of domestic policy makers; in this chapter, we look at some of these problems from a world perspective.

During the historical periods when countries have tried to maintain a system of fixed exchange rates, two problems have come to the fore: The problem of *adjustment* to changing international circumstances; and the *constraints* that the obligation to stabilize exchange rates puts on domestic policy makers.

Under the old *gold standard*, inflows and outflows of gold were a major reason for changes in the money stock, aggregate demand, prices, and unemployment. Changes in aggregate demand which resulted from gold flows were not necessarily what were needed for the domestic economy. A deficit country might go through a painful deflationary process, with high unemployment.

Under the International Monetary Fund (IMF) system, exchange rates were *pegged*, but a deficit country could escape the need for a painful deflation by devaluing its currency. However, the possibility of intermittent devaluations created another problem: How to deal with the *speculative capital flows* that often occurred when it looked as if a country might be on the verge of devaluing its currency.

The present system of *flexible exchange rates* provides countries with a *greater degree of independence* to follow the aggregate demand policies they think best for their domestic economies. However, one disadvantage with this is that it has allowed some countries to pursue highly inflationary policies. Another problem has been that exchange rates among currencies have been quite *unstable* since the mid-1970s. Moreover, the experience in the United States during the Reagan years shows that problems can still be created by the relationship between domestic policies and international transactions. Large U.S. government deficits, combined with monetary restraint, led to high interest rates in the early 1980s, to a rise in the dollar on the international exchanges, and to severe competitive problems for a number of basic industries such as autos and steel.

Finally, the *LDC debt crisis* has been a destabilizing element in the international monetary system in the 1980s. How to deal with this crisis remains a major international challenge for the 1990s.

LEARNING OBJECTIVES

After you have studied this chapter in the textbook and study guide, you should be able to
- Describe the relationship between the gold stock and the money stock under the gold standard
- Describe the mechanism of adjustment under the gold standard, and explain why it is "automatic"
- Explain the two major shortcomings of the gold standard
- Describe how the "adjustable peg" worked
- Explain how problems can arise under the adjustable peg system if people doubt that the present pegged rate will be maintained

- Explain the special role of the United States as the nth country and the U.S. dollar as the reserve currency under the adjustable peg system
- Explain the problems of adjustment, liquidity, and confidence and how they are interrelated
- State when the adjustable peg system finally broke down and explain the major reasons why it did
- Explain the principle of purchasing power parity and what it implies for the relationship between inflation rates and exchange rate changes
- Explain the concept of real exchange rates and its relation to purchasing power parity
- Describe the wide swings in exchange rates among the U.S. and Canadian dollars and other major currencies during the 1980s and suggest some reasons for these swings
- Describe the origins of the debt crisis afflicting a number of LDCs in the 1980s, and some policies that have been suggested to overcome the crisis

HIGHLIGHTS OF THE CHAPTER

This chapter deals with the problem of how the international payments system (the international monetary system) should be organized, and some problems that have arisen under the alternative systems that have been tried at various times. The topic is developed by looking at three historical exchange rate arrangements: the gold standard of the nineteenth and early twentieth centuries; the pegged-but-adjustable exchange rate system of 1945-71; and the recent system of flexible or floating exchange rates.

The Gold Standard

The gold standard is an example of a fixed exchange rate system—that is, a system which fixes the exchange rates within narrow limits. It does this indirectly, as a consequence of the fact that each country agrees to maintain the value of its currency in terms of gold. If, for example, the pound is worth 4.86 times as much, in terms of gold, as the dollar, then nobody will pay much more than $4.86 for a pound, or sell it for much less.

Under the gold standard, there was an *automatic adjustment mechanism* ensuring that there would not be large, persistent international imbalances, with one country ending up with all the gold and the others having none. Specifically, a country losing gold had an automatic decrease in its money stock for two reasons: (1) Gold itself was one form of money; when gold coins left the country, the money was directly reduced. (2) Gold was also a bank reserve. When banks had smaller gold reserves, their ability to make loans was restricted. As we saw in Chapter 11, the ability of banks to make loans helps to determine the money stock.

The decline in the money stock was the first step in the adjustment process. The remaining steps were as follows: As the money supply fell, aggregate demand, incomes, and prices fell in the deficit countries. This made the country's goods more competitive on world markets, and its trade balance therefore improved. This process was aided by an automatic increase in money and inflation in the surplus countries. With prices rising in the surplus countries, it was even easier for the deficit countries to compete. This process—involving changes in the relative prices of the goods of the deficit and surplus countries—tended to continue until balance of payments deficits and surpluses were eliminated and gold flows stopped.

Observe that the gold standard system worked through changes in domestic demand—that is, the third of the four options for dealing with an imbalance in a country's international transactions described in Chapter 14. (Note, though, that the monetary policy worked *automatically* in the case of the gold standard.) However, even though the gold standard worked to eliminate surpluses and deficits, it had two major defects:

1. The automatic mechanism could be very costly for a country with a payments deficit because the monetary contraction could cause large-scale unemployment. On the other side, inflationary pressures could be generated in the surplus countries. That is, there could be a *conflict* between the policies needed for a stable domestic prosperity and the monetary changes needed to bring about balance-of-payments adjustment.

2. The gold standard could lead to *very unstable* conditions, particularly if there was a run on the gold reserves of banks. This point was explained in greater detail in Chapter 12.

The Adjustable Peg, 1945-1971

Under the adjustable peg system:

1. Countries intervened in their foreign exchange markets as necessary, to keep the exchange rate within 1% of an official "par value."

2. Countries with temporary balance-of-payments deficits kept their exchange rates stable by selling reserves on the foreign exchange markets. Countries with temporary balance-of-payments surpluses kept their exchange rates stable by buying foreign currencies, thus increasing their foreign exchange reserves.

3. Countries facing a long-term, fundamental disequilibrium were allowed to change their official par values. The change in exchange rates would affect the prices of their goods on international markets, and help to eliminate international deficits or surpluses.

There were several major problems with the adjustable peg system:

1. It was not clear how to distinguish a "fundamental" disequilibrium from a "temporary" disequilibrium.

2. If a government tried to hold its exchange rate close to the official par when *speculators* believed that there was a fundamental disequilibrium, speculators often made large profits at the government's expense. For example, when a country had a large balance-of-payments deficit, speculators would sell its currency in large quantities. The government would have to use its reserves of foreign exchange to buy up the excess supply of its currency, in order to maintain the peg. As reserves dwindled, this strategy became less and less tenable, and the government was forced to devalue. Speculators were able to benefit by selling high before the devaluation, and buying low after the devaluation. The government, however, lost: It bought high and sold low.

3. "Surplus" countries were reluctant to revalue or to take expansionary measures that might cause inflation. As a consequence, "deficit" countries believed that they had to bear an unfair share of the adjustment burden.

An additional problem with the adjustable peg system had to do with the special position of the U.S. dollar. Under the rules of the adjustable peg system, all countries were supposed to specify the exchange value of their currencies in terms of U.S. dollars. Once they had done so, all exchange rates were determined. The United States, as the nth country, could not adjust the exchange rate of its currency against any other one. The position of the United States was further complicated by the fact that most of the foreign exchange reserves of other countries were held in the form of U.S. dollars. If the United States maintained a strong payments position (with a surplus or a small deficit), then other countries found it difficult to acquire foreign exchange reserves. But if the United States ran large deficits (thereby providing other countries with dollars), the holders of U.S. dollars might fear that it would be unable to maintain the convertibility of dollars into gold, as it was pledged to do under the adjustable peg system. This could induce them to sell their dollars for gold, which would deplete U.S. gold reserves, making it even more difficult for the United States to maintain the dollar's convertibility. Thus, a "run" on U.S. gold reserves could start, similar in nature to the banking panics of the nineteenth and early twentieth centuries.

When signs of such a run did develop in 1971, the United States decided to suspend convertibility of the U.S. dollar into gold. Despite some attempts to patch up the system during the next two years, more and more countries opted for flexible exchange rates and, by 1974, the adjustable peg system had essentially disappeared.

Flexible Exchange Rates

Since the mid-1970s, most industrialized nations have been on flexible exchange rates, with the prices of their currencies being allowed to change in response to changes in the demand and supply for them in the exchange markets. There are two principal arguments in favour of flexible exchange rates:

1. When pegged exchange rates break down, flexible rates may be the only feasible option. The lack of a good alternative may be the strongest argument for flexible exchange rates.

2. They permit fiscal and monetary policies to be directed primarily toward the important goal of stabilizing the domestic economy, rather than toward maintaining the exchange rate.

At the time exchange rates were allowed to float, the hope was that in practice, exchange rates would remain fairly stable. However, in reality, there has been considerable instability.

One reason has been that countries have had very different domestic inflation rates. According to the principle of *purchasing power parity*, when two countries have different inflation rates, the exchange rate between their currencies would be expected to change in such a way as to reflect the changes in their purchasing power (that is, the "real exchange" rate between them would remain constant). For example, if country A had an inflation rate of 10% per year—that is, country A's currency was losing 10% of its purchasing power per year—and country B had a 3% inflation rate, then the purchasing power parity theory predicts that A's currency will depreciate by 7% per year (10% − 3% = 7%) against B's currency.

In practice, relative inflation rates can only explain *some* of the changes in the exchange rates among major currencies that have taken place since the mid-1970s.

Another reason has been divergent macroeconomic policies. In particular, many economists believe that the large federal budget deficits and high interest rates in the United States during most of the Reagan administration were a major reason for the rapid appreciation of the U.S. dollar and the resulting large U.S. trade deficits.

Because of the problems that the flexible rate system has had in the 1980s, there have been suggestions that some form of compromise between pegged and flexible rates (such as systems of "target zones" or "crawling pegs") should be tried. To avoid some of the disadvantages of fluctuating exchange rates, some of the Western European nations set up the *European Monetary System*, which provides for pegged rates among their currencies. However, there is more flexibility in this system than in the earlier systems of pegged rates. For example, rates do not have to be kept so close to the official value.

Finally, this chapter explains the origins of the debt crisis that has caused difficulties for a number of LDCs, and also for many financial institutions in the industrialized countries. This crisis arose in the late 1970s, as many countries borrowed heavily in the international capital market when world oil prices sky-rocketed. Rising interest rates in the early 1980s made it increasingly difficult for these countries to meet their debt service obligations, and several of them have gone through a process of *debt rescheduling* or renegotiation. Although a number of ways have been tried to resolve the crisis, it will be a long time before it is fully overcome.

IMPORTANT TERMS: MATCH THE COLUMNS

Match each term in the first column with the corresponding phrase in the second column.

_____	**1.** Adjustable pegs	**a.** Reduction in the par value of a currency
_____	**2.** Gold standard	**b.** Predicts that exchange rate changes will reflect inflation rates
_____	**3.** Par value	**c.** Exchange rates that have been adjusted for inflation
_____	**4.** Fundamental disequilibrium	**d.** Allows country to postpone paying
_____	**5.** Purchasing power parity principle	**e.** Pegged in principle but frequently adjusted
_____	**6.** Devaluation	**f.** Only changed when there is fundamental disequilibrium
_____	**7.** Real exchange rate	**g.** Provided both exchange rate stability and adjustment mechanism
_____	**8.** Speculate	**h.** Works to eliminate surpluses or deficits
_____	**9.** Debt rescheduling	**i.** Reason for devaluation
_____	**10.** Adjustment mechanism	**j.** Officially chosen exchange rate
_____	**11.** Crawling peg	**k.** Buy something in anticipation of a price rise

TRUE-FALSE

T   F   **1.** Under the gold standard, the adjustment mechanism worked primarily through changes in aggregate demand, not through changes in exchange rates.

T   F   **2.** Under the gold standard, a country was expected to change its par value in the event of a fundamental disequilibrium.

T   F   **3.** With a pegged exchange rate, sales of reserves are a good way to deal with international deficits, in both the short run and the long.

T   F   **4.** Under the pegged-rate system of the IMF, a country was expected to change its par value in the event of a fundamental disequilibrium.

T   F   **5.** The gold standard was automatic; it would work without government intervention. This means that it was an example of a clean float.

T   F   **6.** Under a pegged exchange rate system, when foreign exchange speculators make profits, governments generally lose.

T   F   **7.** By "self-fulfilling expectations," economists mean any speculation undertaken at the recommendation of government authorities.

T   F   **8.** According to the purchasing power parity principle, whenever a country has a positive rate of price inflation, its currency will depreciate against other currencies in world exchange markets.

T   F   **9.** If country A and country B have different rates of inflation, then the real exchange rate between their currencies must change.

T   F   **10.** If two countries have different rates of price inflation and the real exchange rate between their currencies stays unchanged, then the nominal exchange rate between their currencies must be changing.

T   F   **11.** The LDC debt crisis in the 1980s affected both oil-importing and oil-exporting countries.

MULTIPLE CHOICE

1. Under the old gold standard, an inflow of gold into Britain worked to:
a. automatically increase the British money stock
b. increase the British money stock, but only if the central bank engaged in open market purchases of government securities
c. automatically decrease the British money stock
d. decrease the British money stock, but only if the central bank sold government securities on the open market at the same time
e. automatically increase the British government's deficit

2. Under the old gold standard system, an inflow of gold into Britain caused what sequence of events?
a. an increase in the British money stock, an increase in the British price level, and an increase in British exports
b. an increase in the British money stock, an increase in the British price level, and an increase in British imports
c. an increase in the British money stock, an increase in the British price level, and an increase in spending by foreign visitors to Britain
d. an increase in the British money stock, an increase in the British price level, and a decrease in spending by British visitors to foreign countries
e. an increase in the British money stock, an increase in the budget deficits of the British government, and an increase in British exports of goods

3. Under the old gold standard, a country faced a conflict between the policies needed for domestic stability and those needed for international adjustment when:
a. it was losing gold and was in a recession
b. it was gaining gold and was in a recession
c. its prices were rising and its tariffs were also rising
d. its unemployment rate was high

e. its inflation rate was high

4. Which of the following is *not* a common criticism of a system of fixed or pegged exchange rates?
a. it may make a country lose control of its monetary policy
b. it tempts governments to follow more inflationary policies than its neighbours
c. it may lead to a great deal of uncertainty if speculators begin to anticipate a devaluation
d. it tends to make a small country (such as Canada) highly sensitive to business fluctuations in larger countries (such as the United States)
e. it may force a country with high unemployment to follow contractionary policies

5. Under the original IMF system (prior to 1971), the par value of a currency was:
a. the value of the currency whenever central banks kept bond prices stable
b. the value of the currency whenever central banks followed a monetary rule
c. the official price of the currency, usually specified in terms of the U.S. dollar
d. the value of the currency when policies were up to par, and inflation was low
e. the value of the currency when policies were up to par, and both inflation and unemployment were low

6. From time to time, speculation was a major problem under the adjustable peg system of the early IMF. The major cause of severe speculation was:
a. the wildly fluctuating price of government securities
b. the wildly fluctuating price of gold
c. the wild upward and downward movements in the price of oil
d. speculators would win if the par value were changed, but would not lose much if the par value were held
e. speculators would win if the IMF made loans to a country to help it maintain the par value of its currency

7. Under the IMF system of adjustable pegs, one problem was that of "self-fulfilling expectations." This meant that:
   a. when countries expected to have surpluses, they, in fact, had them
   b. when countries expected to have deficits, they, in fact, had them
   c. when officials expected to avoid a devaluation, they usually succeeded, because of the power of positive thinking
   d. when speculators thought that a currency might be devalued, they sold it, increasing the probability that it, in fact, would have to be devalued
   e. when speculators thought that a currency might be devalued, they bought it, increasing the probability that it, in fact, would have to be devalued

8. Under the IMF system of adjustable pegs, some countries followed "stop-go" aggregate demand policies. A major reason for this was:
   a. the short-run Phillips curve sloped upward to the right with a pegged exchange rate; this meant that authorities had to switch policies often
   b. the short-run Phillips curve sloped upward to the right with a pegged exchange rate; this meant that authorities had to follow a monetary rule. Changes in velocity then caused instability
   c. the short-run Phillips curve sloped upward to the right with a pegged exchange rate; this meant that authorities had to rely on monetary policy rather than fiscal policy
   d. the short-run Phillips curve sloped upward to the right with a pegged exchange rate; this meant that authorities had to rely on fiscal policy rather than monetary policy
   e. a country might restrict aggregate demand when it was losing foreign exchange reserves, and switch to expansive ("go") policies when the balance of payments improved

9. Between 1981 and 1985, when the U.S. dollar was rising strongly on the international exchanges:
   a. foreigners were acquiring U.S. assets, and the U.S. was running a trade surplus
   b. Americans were acquiring foreign assets, and the United States was running a trade surplus
   c. foreigners were acquiring United States assets, and the United States was running a trade deficit
   d. Americans were acquiring foreign assets, and the United States was running a trade deficit
   e. changes in exchange rates encouraged more foreigners to visit the United States

10. U.S. macroeconomic policies contributed to the sharp rise in the exchange value of the U.S. dollar between 1980 and 1984. Specifically:
   a. expansive monetary and fiscal policies made U.S. inflation higher, and this strengthened the dollar
   b. the combination of government deficits and monetary restraint resulted in high interest rates, which encouraged foreigners to buy U.S. assets
   c. the combination of government surpluses and monetary restraint resulted in high interest rates, which encouraged foreigners to buy U.S. assets
   d. the combination of government surpluses and monetary restraint resulted in low interest rates, which encouraged investment in the United States
   e. the combination of government deficits and monetary restraint resulted in low interest rates, which encouraged investment in the United States

11. Suppose that an exchange rate between the United States and Britain is initially in equilibrium, at £1 = \$2.00. Now, suppose that domestic prices in the United States double while domestic prices in Britain remain constant. Then, according to the purchasing power parity theory, the new equilibrium exchange rate will be:
   a. £1 = \$1.00
   b. between £1 = \$1.00 and £1 = \$2.00, but we can't say exactly where
   c. still at £1 = \$2.00
   d. between £1 = \$2.00 and £1 = \$4.00, but we can't say exactly where
   e. £1 = \$4.00

12. With fixed exchange rates, an increase in the U.S. inflation rate tends to increase Canada's inflation rate because:
   a. it increases the demand for Canadian exports
   b. it tends to raise the price of goods imported into Canada
   c. it tends to cause an increase in the stock of money in Canada
   d. it tends to increase aggregate demand in Canada
   e. all of the above

13. Suppose that in 1996, the inflation rate in Canada is 5%, whereas in Britain it is 10%. Suppose also that at the beginning of the year, the exchange rate between the Canadian dollar and the British pound is \$2 = £1. If the real exchange rate remains constant, then at the end of the year the nominal exchange rate would be about:
   a. \$2.15 = £1

b. $2.05 = £0.90
c. $2.10 = £1.05
d. $1.90 = £1
e. $1.70 = £1

14. Suppose that in 1996, the inflation rate in Britain is 20% whereas in Canada it is 10%, and that at the beginning of the year the exchange rate between the Canadian dollar and the British pound is $1 = £0.50. Suppose that at the end of the year the exchange rate is $1 = £0.52. Then, during that year, the changes in the nominal and real exchange rates between the dollar and the pound have been such that:
  a. the dollar has depreciated in real terms but has appreciated in nominal terms
  b. the dollar has appreciated in both nominal and real terms
  c. the dollar has appreciated in real terms but depreciated in nominal terms
  d. the dollar has depreciated in both nominal and real terms
  e. in nominal terms the dollar has depreciated and the pound has appreciated

15. In the European Monetary System (EMS), exchange rates among the Western European currencies are:
  a. permanently fixed, because the gold standard was restored for transactions within Europe
  b. permanently fixed by a new international bank that coordinates monetary policies among the European member nations
  c. pegged-but-adjustable, with wider bands than under the old IMF system
  d. pegged-but-adjustable, with narrower bands than under the old IMF system
  e. freely flexible

16. In the mid-1980s, Canada's GDP was some $500 billion in Canadian dollars. At about that time, the foreign debts of either Brazil or Mexico, in American dollars, was approximately:
  a. $100 million
  b. $10 million
  c. $10 trillion (10,000 billion)
  d. $1 billion
  e. $100 billion

17. The LDC debt crisis of the 1980s:
  a. affected only nations that were net oil importers
  b. was aggravated by high world interest rates in the early part of the decade
  c. was due in part to the bankruptcy of the World Bank in 1982
  d. has affected mostly countries in Africa and Asia
  e. all of the above

18. According to World Bank estimates, the net flow of resources (new loans less payments of interest and principal on old loans) into the developing countries in 1986 was:
  a. about $50 billion per year
  b. about $25 billion per year
  c. 1/2 of 1% of the GDP of industrialized nations, on average
  d. about zero
  e. none of the above; there was a substantial net *outflow* of resources *from* the developing countries

19. Suppose that in 1980, the exchange rate between the Ghanaian Cedi and the Nigerian Naira was 10 Cedis per Naira. Suppose further that in 1985 prices in Ghana were 3 times higher than in 1980, while in Nigeria they rose by 100% between 1980 and 1985. According to the theory of purchasing power parity, we would expect the exchange rate in 1985 to be:
  a. 6 2/3 Cedis per Naira
  b. 1.5 Cedis per Naira
  c. 15 Cedis per Naira
  d. 20 Cedis per Naira
  e. 300 Cedis per Naira

The next question is mainly for those who have studied Box 20-2 in the text.

20. Suppose that, on the foreign exchanges, $1 = 3 DM, while $1 = 12 francs. The exchange rate between the DM and the francs will then be:
  a. 1 DM = 36 francs
  b. 1 DM = 4 francs
  c. 1 DM = 1 franc
  d. 1 franc = 4 DM
  e. 1 franc = 36 DM

EXERCISE

Suppose two countries, A and B, trade with each other. The currency of country A is called the AA and the currency of B is called the BB. Suppose initially that the exchange rate is AA 1 = BB 1. Now suppose that during the course of a year, prices in A rise by 10% while prices in B rise by 20%. If the real exchange rate between the AA and the BB is to remain unchanged, the nominal exchange rate at the end of the year must be approximately AA 1 = BB _____ .

Suppose the nominal exchange rate at the end of the year is AA 1 = BB 1.15. Then, in terms of real exchange rates, the BB has (appreciated, depreciated) against the AA. As a result, net exports from B to A would be expected to (increase, decrease).

Suppose now that interest rates in both A and B during that year were 22% per year. Then the real interest rate in A was _____% and in B _____%.

If interest rates, inflation rates, and nominal exchange rate changes had been known at the beginning of the year, one would have expected capital to flow from (A to B, B to A). An investor in A buying bonds in B at the beginning of the year and then selling the bonds (with accrued interest) and converting the proceeds back to AAs at the end of the year would have realized a return of about _____%, while an investor in B who invested in assets denominated in AAs and then converted the funds back to BBs at the end of the year would have had a return of about _____%.

In order for the real rates of interest in A to be the same as in B (where the nominal rate of interest was 22%), the nominal rate of interest in A would have had to be _____%. If the real rate of interest in A and B had been the same, and the real exchange rate had been constant, the rate of return to an A investor who invested in B bonds during the year would have been (higher than, about the same as, lower than) that to an A investor who invested in A bonds.

ESSAY QUESTIONS

1. Suppose that, under the adjustable peg, the British government announced that it was going to devalue the pound by 10% in one week. How would this affect the demand and/or supply of pounds today? What would happen to the British government's holdings of dollar reserves? Would there be much risk in speculating today in the market for pounds? Why or why not? Would the government, in fact, be able to wait for a week before devaluing? Why or why not?

2. In early 1969, there was a public controversy between the German central bank (which wanted to raise the par value of the DM) and the German government (which didn't). What effect do you think this had on exchange markets? Why do you think the central bank took the position that it did? Why do you think the government took the position that it did?

3. Many people believe that there is a relationship between the two large U.S. deficits of the early 1980s—the budget deficit of the U.S. federal government, and the deficit in the current account of the U.S. balance of payments. How might one cause the other?

ANSWERS

Important Terms: **1**f, **2**g, **3**j, **4**i, **5**b, **6**a, **7**c, **8**k, **9**d, **10**h, **11**e
True-False: **1**T, **2**F, **3**F, **4**T, **5**F, **6**T, **7**F, **8**F, **9**F, **10**T, **11**T
Multiple Choice: **1**a, **2**b, **3**a, **4**b, **5**c, **6**d, **7**d, **8**e, **9**c, **10**b, **11**e, **12**e, **13**d, **14**a, **15**c, **16**e, **17**b, **18**e, **19**c, **20**b
Exercise: **1.** 10, depreciated, increase, 12%, 2%, B to A, 7%, 40%, 12%, about the same as

ANSWERS TO SELECTED REVIEW QUESTIONS FROM THE TEXT

20-1. Under the old gold standard, a country's money supply was tied to its gold stock. The reduction in the money supply in countries that were losing gold would ultimately lead to lower prices of these countries' goods in world markets. Thus, their exports would increase and their imports decrease; but this improvement in their balance of payments would stop the loss of international reserves — that is, it would stop the gold outflow.

20-4. If a country admitted that it was considering a revaluation, speculators in other nations would immediately begin to buy up that country's currency, hoping to resell it later at a higher price in terms of their own currencies. If the country's central bank were to try to "hold the line" by selling its currency to the speculators, it would expose itself to the risk of large losses (see the answer to the next question).

20-5. Before the Deutschmark rose in value, the speculators were able to buy D-marks at relatively low prices from Germany's central bank in exchange for foreign currencies. After the D-mark had been allowed to rise in value, the speculators sold their marks back to the central bank for a higher price than that at which they were bought. The speculators profited, since they were able to buy low and sell high. The central bank did the opposite, and lost.

20-6. If the funds that a country borrows are invested

in projects that raise its capacity to produce and export, a steady build-up of debt need not lead to a crisis: The increased production and exports may be more than enough to cover the interest and principal repayments on the foreign debt, and still leave something over to raise the living standards of the country's own citizens.

20-7. (a) Assuming flexible exchange rates, the capital inflow would lead to a short-run appreciation of the country's currency. Once the appreciation had gone far enough so that investors came to expect that the currency would depreciate *in the future*, the capital inflow would come to an end: The country's high interest rate would be offset by the expectation of a future depreciation of its currency.

(b) If today's exchange rate were Skr 1 = Nkr 1.10, Norwegians investing in Sweden would earn a return of 11% (the 6% interest rate in Sweden, plus the expected increase of 5% in the value of the Swedish krona); that is, less than the 13% they could earn by keeping their funds in Norway.

If today's exchange rate were Skr 1 = Nkr 1.05, investing in Swedish assets would earn a Norwegian 16%.

Today's exchange rate would be about Skr 1 = Nkr 1.08, since this would yield the same return on an investment in Sweden as the 13% prevailing in Norway.

20-8. (a) Looking at the real exchange rate, the lira has appreciated by 5%.

(b) 1.10 lira.

(c) With inflation in Italy being higher, you would expect nominal interest rates there to be higher as well, though you cannot tell by precisely how much, since it is *expected*, not actual, inflation rates that influence interest rates. Since the lira appreciated in real terms, there was probably a capital inflow into Italy.

Answers to Crossword Puzzles

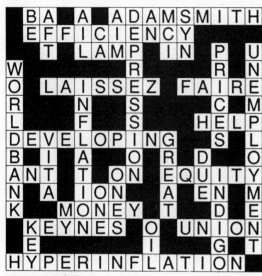

CHAPTER 1

CHAPTER 8

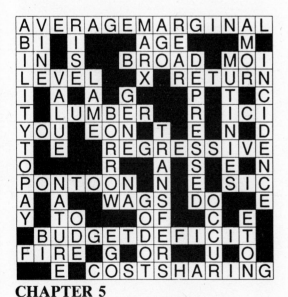

CHAPTER 5

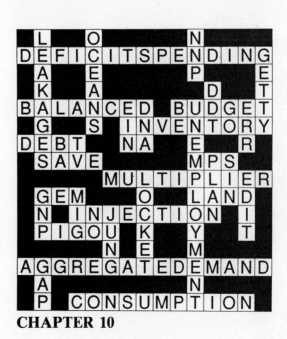

CHAPTER 10

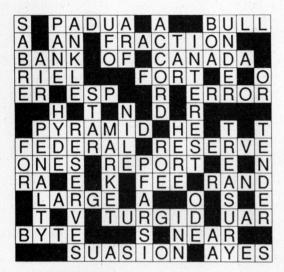

CHAPTER 12

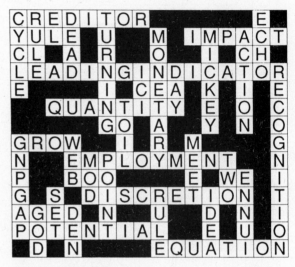

CHAPTER 18

CHAPTER 17

■ ■

STUDENT REPLY CARD

In order to improve future editions, we are seeking your comments on **STUDY GUIDE,
Third Canadian Edition, by Blomqvist, Wonnacott, and Wonnacott, to accompany
AN INTRODUCTION TO MACROECONOMICS**.

After you have read this text, please answer the following questions and return this form via
Business Reply Mail. *Thanks in advance for your feedback!*

1. Name of your college or university: _____

_____

2. Major program of study: _____

3. Are there any sections of this text which were not assigned as course reading? _____

If so, please specify those chapters or portions. _____

_____

_____

_____

4. What did you like *best* about this book? _____

_____

_____

5. What did you like *least*? _____

_____

_____

6. How can we improve future editions? _____

_____

_____

_____

_____

If you would like to say more, we'd love to hear from you. Please write to us at the address
shown on the reverse of this card.

- - - - - - - - - - - - - - - - - - - *CUT HERE* -

CUT HERE

- - - - - - - - - - - - - - - - - - - *FOLD HERE* - - - - - - - - - - - - - - - - - -